Reining in the Competition for Capital

Reining in the Competition for Capital

Ann Markusen
Editor

2007

W.E. Upjohn Institute for Employment Research
Kalamazoo, Michigan

Library of Congress Cataloging-in-Publication Data

Reining in the competition for capital / Ann Markusen, editor.
  p. cm.
  Includes bibliographical references and index.
  ISBN-13: 978-0-88099-295-4 (pbk. : alk. paper)
  ISBN-10: 0-88099-295-6 (pbk. : alk. paper)
  ISBN-13: 978-0-88099-296-1 (hardcover : alk. paper)
  ISBN-10: 0-88099-296-4 (hardcover : alk. paper)
  1. Capital movements. 2. Capital market. 3. Fiscal policy. 4. Competition, International. I. Markusen, Ann R.
    HG3891.R449 2007
    332'.041—dc22

2006103084

© 2007
W.E. Upjohn Institute for Employment Research
300 S. Westnedge Avenue
Kalamazoo, Michigan 49007-4686

The facts presented in this study and the observations and viewpoints expressed are the sole responsibility of the authors. They do not necessarily represent positions of the W.E. Upjohn Institute for Employment Research.

Cover design by Alcorn Publication Design.
Index prepared by Diane Worden.
Printed in the United States of America.
Printed on recycled paper.

Contents

Preface vii

1 Institutional and Political Determinants of Incentive Competition 1
Ann Markusen and Katherine Nesse

2 The Sources and Processes of Tax and Subsidy Competition 43
Kenneth P. Thomas

3 The Fiscal Consequences of Competition for Capital 57
Peter Fisher

4 How the EU Manages Subsidy Competition 87
Adinda Sinnaeve

5 Solving the Problems of Economic Development Incentives 103
Timothy J. Bartik

6 Negotiating the Ideal Deal: Which Local Governments Have the Most Bargaining Leverage? 141
Rachel Weber

7 Do Better Job Creation Subsidies Hold Real Promise for Business Incentive Reformers? 161
William Schweke

8 Nine Concrete Ways to Curtail the Economic War among the States 183
Greg LeRoy

The Authors 199

Index 201

About the Institute 215

Preface

Across the globe, communities and their civic and business leaders find themselves increasingly preoccupied with the mobility of capital, most tangibly in the pressures to produce large incentives packages to attract and retain private sector employers. Each individual expression, interest, or demand for concessions sets off flurries of energy, negotiations, and press furor. Entire communities are plunged into considerable anxiety, often in a cloud of uncertainty about what is being offered or threatened, their options, and the outcomes. Information is imperfect, and the "market for jobs" imbalanced. Cities and regions may lose their bids and wonder if they offered too little or whether the outcome had been decided long before the bidding. Or, they may win and find that the promised jobs do not materialize, or are short-lived, or go to newcomers who drive up the local cost of living. Worse, they may find that the opportunity cost of subsidies is stiff. Investments in infrastructure, human capital, or entrepreneurship that would do more for diversified local development are foregone, while state and local government have a hard time meeting operating costs because of tax giveaways over the long term.

This book explores the causes, character, and potential remedies for the growing spatial competition for capital. The authors, from the United States and Europe, are economists, political scientists, lawyers, and nonprofit public policy leaders. Each was invited to give a paper at a spring 2004 conference, *Reining in the Competition for Capital,* hosted by the University of Minnesota's Humphrey Institute of Public Affairs. Each author was chosen for his or her unique expertise and proven track record in path-breaking intellectual contributions and workable policy solutions on the subject of incentive competition. Before the conference, each submitted a draft for public Web-based distribution. At the conference, each paper was presented and responded to by a panel of three commentators from diverse walks of life, followed by a 20-minute debate by the larger audience. We strived to ensure that every point of view was represented in the debate, from site consultants, mayors, and subsidy critics to Federal Reserve Bank vice presidents and members of Congress, as the acknowledgements below demonstrate. At the close of formal sessions, all participants were invited to a two-hour discussion, where new directions for action and research were debated. All these lively intellectual encounters were incorporated into the authors' final drafts and our overview.

Five conclusions emerge from this project. First, the phenomenon of interregional competition for capital is increasing in intensity and becoming a pressing problem for many governments, regions, and communities. It is spreading across the globe, especially in larger countries with decentralized fiscal responsibility for economic development planning. The book tracks the proliferation of this competition from the United States, where it is almost completely uncontrolled, and Europe, where it is severely regulated, to countries like Brazil and India, where large multinational corporations seeking to locate branch plants are effectively using techniques developed in the United States to extract large concessions from inexperienced state governments.

Second, the spread of incentive competition has been facilitated by institutional innovations in the market for jobs and tax base, especially the rise of site consultants, many working for large multinational accounting firms. These spatial job brokers extract the potential rents inherent in plant location deals from communities and sell them to companies "supplying" jobs. The absence of regulation of site consultants—the fact that they are not prohibited from working both sides of the market simultaneously and work on a commission basis—worsens the quality of information open to the "buying" community in an incentive market where firms have a monopolistic position to begin with.

Third, ideas and politics weigh heavily in the game of incentive competition. Three distinctive views of the problem vie for attention. Some economists argue that all subnational incentives for individual firms should simply be outlawed (or taxed away by national governments) because they distort competition. Other economists, building on the famous Tiebout "voting with their feet" celebration of independent local governments in metropolitan areas, argue that incentive competition is healthy and efficient. Yet other economists believe that well-structured incentives can produce beneficial regional economic development. For this group, the challenge is how to structure them to achieve local and interregional welfare in an imperfect market. We unpack these three views, each grounded in economic reasoning, and show how they are variously espoused by protagonists and brokers in the market for jobs. We also explore the insights of political scientists who contribute an understanding of political imperatives and motivations to the mix. As a group, with some nuanced disagreement, the authors espouse the third, middle-ground position.

Fourth, opportunity costs are given very short shrift in the drama of incentive competition. All energies, in the exciting and often very rapid (and sometimes secretive) bidding to attract or retain a plant or office, are focused on the particular terms. Media, political, and policy discussions rarely weigh the particular incentive, its cost over the long term and hypothetical benefits, against alternative uses of the same resources for the community. Tax expenditures in particular seem costless, since they are not included in budgets explicitly and are only paid out over the long term. Several of the papers argue for unified and long-term economic development budgets that clarify for decision makers and citizens the true costs of each package offered and the foregone opportunities to allocate the resources involved to other private sector developments such as incubators and venture capital funds for local start-ups, to education and job training investments in the existing workforce, or to infrastructure and amenities that would make the region more attractive to both firms and workers as a place to do business and live.

Fifth, reforms that rein in the competition for capital and ensure that it serves legitimate job-creating ends are possible, have been pioneered in a number of nations, regions, and localities, and are espoused by a growing movement of diverse constituents. The European system, which prohibits company subsidies except under very strict conditions and then only if permitted by the European Commissions' regulatory agency, effectively limits subsidy competition by discouraging most offers from ever being made. It requires a fairly large regulatory apparatus. However, American experts and admirers largely agree that a similar national regulatory system for the United States is politically very unlikely in the near future. Instead, pioneering innovations at the state and local levels are more likely to be successfully built into modifications to current law at all levels in the federal system.

The authors in this volume present a broad set of such workable reforms, including regulation of site consultants; mandated transparency in negotiations, bids, and deals; better structured deals (e.g., shorter-term incentives, pay-as-you-go arrangements); performance requirements and clawbacks for subsidized firms; and adoption of unified economic development budgets. In these carefully structured and hard-fought reforms, the authors conclude, lie the solutions to the excesses of subsidy competition. Successful reform will preserve subnational governments' abilities to tailor and pursue economic development goals to maximize benefits for their communities while eliminating the uneven playing field that results in disappointing employment or tax base outcomes or impoverishment of the local treasury.

We thank the Humphrey Institute of Public Affairs and its Dean, J. Brian Atwood, for the resources to hold the conference as part of the Institute's Signature Studies initiative, and to Professor Robert Kudrle and Jill Buckley for shepherding it through the process. Thanks to my Humphrey Institute colleagues for their feedback from a seminar on this topic, especially Joe Ritter. The Project on Regional and Industrial Economics' two extraordinary assistants, Michael Leary and Katherine Murphy, handled all the arrangements for the conference and guided the book manuscript through its preproduction stages. Research assistants Christina Connelly and Katherine Nesse did prodigious amounts of literature review and contacted numerous worldwide experts. Our thanks to Kevin Hollenbeck, the publications director at the Upjohn Institute, for his efficient handing of the book preparation and production process, and to Allison Hewitt Colosky and Richard Wyrwa for copyediting and marketing work.

We are grateful to the session chairs and official commentators on papers at the conference, some of whom also helped us update the papers. For the session on Kenneth Thomas's paper: George Latimer, former mayor of St. Paul, Minnesota; William Testa, vice president, Federal Reserve Bank of Chicago; Roderick Meicklejohn, head of competition policy section, directorate-general for economic and financial affairs, European Union; Stephen Quick, Inter-American Development Bank. For the session on Peter Fisher's paper: Matt Kane, Northeast-Midwest Institute; Art Rolnick, vice president, Federal Reserve Bank of Minneapolis; Frank Mauro, executive director, Fiscal Policy Institute, Albany, NY; and Senator John Hottinger, Minnesota State Senate. For the session on Adinda Sinnaeve's keynote: Chris Farrell, Minnesota Public Radio; and Roy Malmrose, U.S. Trade Representative's Office, Washington, DC. For the session on Timothy Bartik's paper: Rebecca Yanisch, Chandler Group Executive Search, Inc.; Laura Kalambokidis, professor of applied economics, University of Minnesota; Robert Isaacson, research director, Minnesota Department of Employment and Economic Development; and Steve Mercil, Minnesota Investment Network Corporation. For the session on Rachel Weber's paper: Sean Kershaw, president, Minnesota Citizen's League; John Chell, executive director, Arrowhead Regional Development Commission; Tracy Gray-Barkan, research/policy analyst, Los Angeles Alliance for a New Economy; and Bruce Maus, president, Corporate Real Estate, Inc., Eagan, Minnesota. For the session on the paper by Udo Prestchker of the Organization for Economic Cooperation and Development, Paris (not included in this volume; accessible at www.hhh.umn.edu/projects/prie/c4c_papers.html): Curtis Johnson, CitiStates Group, St. Paul, Minnesota; Virginia Carlson, professor of urban and regional planning, University of Wisconsin at Milwaukee and the Brookings Institution; Mark Ritchie, president, Institute for Agricultural and Trade Policy, Minneapolis; and Enrique Dussel Peters, professor, graduate school of economics, Universidad Nacional Autónoma de México, Mexico City. For the session on William Schweke's paper: Joel Kramer, executive director, growth and justice, Minneapolis; Robert Lynch, professor of economics, Washington College and the Economic Policy Institute; Nancy Straw, president, West Central Initiative, Minnesota; Kris Jacobs, executive director, JOBS NOW Coalition, St. Paul; and Dr. Joel Yudken, economist, AFL-CIO, Washington DC. For the session on Greg LeRoy's paper: Dave Hage, editorial board, Minneapolis Star-Tribune; Andrew Isserman, professor of economics and urban planning, University of Illinois, Urbana–Champaign; David Minge, Circuit Court, former U.S. Congressman, Minnesota; and Lee Munnich, director, state and local policy program, Humphrey Institute of Public Affairs.

Many others made contributions to this project through their participation in the conference and willingness to speak with us at various stages and share their insights and their written work: Melvin Burstein, former vice president and general counsel, Federal Reserve Bank of Minneapolis; Joe Cortright, director, Impresa Consulting, Portland, Oregon; Paul Cheshire, professor, London School of Economics; Robert Chirinko, professor, Emory University; Clelio Campolina Diniz, professor, Universidade Federal de Minas Gerais; Kevin Fletcher, economist, International Monetary Fund; Michael Luger, professor, University of North Carolina at Chapel Hill, Kenan-Flagler Business School; Elizabeth Lynn, assistant director, McCune Foundation; Ted Moran, assistant professor, Georgetown University; Clarisse Morgan, counsellor, rules division, World Trade Organization; Phedon Nicolaides, professor, European Institute of Public Administration in Maastricht (Netherlands); Alan Peters, professor, University of Iowa; Michael Schuman, former director, Green Policy Institute; Beth Siegel, president, Mt. Auburn Associates, Somerville, Massachusetts; Tom Stinson, state economist, Minnesota Department of Finance; Robert Stumberg, professor, Georgetown University, Harrison Institute for Public Law; Robert Tannenwald, vice president, Federal Reserve Bank of Boston; Bill Waren, adjunct professor, Georgetown University, Harrison Institute for Public Law; Al Watkins, science and technology program coordinator, World Bank; Daniel Wilson, economist, Federal Reserve Bank of San Francisco; and Fiona Wishlade, director, European Policies Research Centre.

Above all, my thanks to the authors of the papers in this volume for the quality of their work, the original ideas they contributed, the time they spent on this project, and the feedback they gave for our overview. I hope that the volume as a whole makes a substantial contribution to an understanding of the historical trends and institutional and behavioral context for incentive competition, and that the ideas and experience shared herein will help to encourage active, efficient, equitable, and environmentally sustainable local economic development practices while conserving public resources and avoiding the waste in beggar-thy-neighbor competitions.

Ann Markusen

1
Institutional and Political Determinants of Incentive Competition

Ann Markusen
University of Minnesota

Katherine Nesse
University of Illinois at Urbana-Champaign

Incentive competition is on the rise. It is costly, generally inefficient, and often ineffective even for the winning regions. Yet some regions do very well by attracting large, new facilities that create sustained jobs, bolster the tax base, and have multiplier effects. The nation states of Europe have developed an effective regulatory system that curtails abuse, but the United States, Canada, and Australia have grappled with forms of cooperation and regulation less successfully. Incentive competition is spreading to developing countries, especially as responsibility for and fiscal capacity to support economic development have devolved to subnational levels of government. Local governments also compete for mobile capital, export-oriented as well as retail. Incentive competition for capital is an increasingly important public policy issue, because it consumes considerable resources, alters the spatial distribution of economic activity, and entails large opportunity costs for citizens and businesses.

In this chapter, we argue that incentive competition cannot be adequately approached in a game theoretic, microeconomic fashion. The phenomenon deserves a historical explanation that probes national and global institutional and political changes shaping the rise and character of bidding wars. Our treatment is thus interdisciplinary, incorporating insights from economics, economic history, geography and regional science, political science, political sociology, and urban and regional planning. This chapter is both an original interpretation of the origins and analytics of the "regional market for jobs and tax capacity" and an introduction to and framing of the contributions in the volume.

We first show that incentive competition is proliferating, not just in the United States and other OECD countries, but also in large, developing countries with federal power sharing, such as Brazil, India, and China. Many more state and local governments have been thrust into such competition worldwide, and the total amount spent on incentive competition has been rising rapidly. Incentive competition is also waxing among nations, and we explore briefly how the policy and institutional environment differs in these cases.

In an effort to analyze the source of this trend, we offer an institutional and political interpretation of the rise of incentive competition. To economic and geographic causes such as falling transportation and communication costs, vertical disintegration of firms, and a greater spatial division of labor within firms, we stress three additional developments: the rise of site consultants who broker deals between firms and governments; the spread of devolution across the globe, with its delegation of responsibility for economic development to subnational governments; and the significance of politics and political calculus on the part of participating governments.

We then contrast three different approaches to incentive competition, each with its own economic logic and cast of characters. First, we review the relatively benign view that incentive competition is a healthy way for communities to compete for mobile firms with optimal packages of public services at tax prices and that the outcome is efficient. We review the prisoner's dilemma approach, which views incentive competition in game-analytic terms and concludes that it has at best a zero sum and at worst a negative efficiency outcome. We offer our own model, what we call the "market for jobs and fiscal capacity" approach, in which information asymmetries not only disadvantage government competitors for jobs but are created and maintained as rent-producing devices through the intermediation of the site consulting industry. For each of the three competing theories, we identify the conceptualization of the market in which incentives are negotiated, the actors and their assumed behavior, market outcomes, normative underpinnings, and strengths and weaknesses from both analytical and policy points of view.

Our model, with its explicit institutional and political dimensions, favors the retention of local government's ability to allocate resources to and regulate economic development activity but advocates reforms that will improve the performance of the market for jobs. This position, in contrast to the "leave it alone, it is good" or the "tax or regulate it away" recommendations of the other approaches, is compatible with most of the findings and recommendations of other authors in this volume.

We then ask what is known about the outcomes of incentive competition, referring to various contributions in this volume and others' work. We find it quite mixed. In some cases, incentives can and do create jobs and enhance the tax base in ways that are efficient, equitable, and environmentally benign. But microeconomic theoretic approaches limit the assessment of outcomes too narrowly, and the political drama of incentive competition tends to crowd out other economic development paths. We challenge the implicit premise that external investments of plants or facilities are the only route to regional economic development, reviewing the evolution of export base theory. Endogenous entrepreneurial activity, investments in human capital and amenities, and even reshaping local consumption patterns can yield significant long-term job growth. Bidding wars divert decision-makers' attention from a broader portfolio of economic development tools and options. Incentive packages thus incur large opportunity costs. We argue for a unified economic development budget as a policy innovation for evaluating and improving incentive offers. We support many of the reforms spelled out by the other authors in this volume.

IS THE GEOGRAPHIC COMPETITION FOR CAPITAL INCREASING?

Many writers and economy watchers contend that the spatial competition for capital is increasing and more intense than ever. In this volume, both Kenneth Thomas and Timothy Bartik make this statement, echoing notable book-length treatments by Bluestone and Harrison (1982); Noponen, Graham, and Markusen (1993); and more recently Friedman (2006). Little hard evidence is offered for this view beyond the surge in transnational capital flows and internationally traded commodities, concentrated deindustrialization, and an appeal to our common experience. Thomas's argument is that greater fluidity of capital across regional and national borders increases the number of sites that are possible for any particular investment and thus makes the problem less manageable for competing governments.

Yet worldwide, regional and local communities with responsibility for their own economic development perceive that the competition for mobile capital, linked to the expectation of extraregional exports, is increasing. Many communities are directly affected when companies show an interest in sites and ask what can be done to help them; those that have not been so lucky are interested in becoming candidates. Does a review of national and subnational government behavior around the world suggest that competition for mobile physical capital has increased? Have governments increased their involvement in bidding wars, and has the size of packages offered increased? Our answer is a cautious "yes."

In the United States, the evidence is fairly strong that incentive competition has increased since the 1960s. "Bidding wars" for specific plants or facilities have become widespread, with incentive packages escalating in total worth. In addition, firms already operating in jurisdictions are now asking for comparable concessions just to remain open and retain jobs. LeRoy (2005) has done a masterful job of documenting hundreds of individual cases of successful and failed incentive competitions in the United States over the past 20 years.

Hard evidence of an increase in numbers of governments involved and size of incentives is harder to come by, because of the complexity of modeling and testing for change over time. However, two recent studies suggest that incentive competition in the United States has increased over the past few decades. Using state-level data on manufacturing income, capital and labor and their tax-adjusted prices, Chirinko and Wilson (2006) show that investment tax incentives have become increasingly common and increasingly large over the period 1963–2004. Peter Fisher, in Chapter 3, cites data showing that in the 1990s, the average incentive package available to new business investment in 20 U.S. states increased from 10 percent to 30 percent of gross business taxes.

The competition for mobile capital in the United States is not solely a late twentieth century phenomenon. In the nineteenth and twentieth centuries, communities across the United States competed for agricultural capital, railroad lines, grain mills, meatpacking plants, and steel mills, as well as farmers and workers (Sbragia 1996). Fascinating histories have been written about the competition for mobile facilities, public and private, in certain sectors and in entire regions. For example, Lotchin (1984) reveals how California cities competed for large military bases in the late nineteenth and early twentieth centuries, and Markusen et al. (1991) show how Colorado Springs out-competed other U.S. cities for the army air bases, the Air Force Academy, and the Space Command from the 1930s to the 1980s. Cobb (1993) reveals how southern states crusaded for industrial development by attempting to lure branch plants in the period from 1936 to 1990. But the character of this competition has changed. In the following section, we address the postwar emergence of an organized U.S. "market" for mobile plants and the jobs and tax base that they bring, the product of institutional innovations that are now spreading to other continents.

Other countries with federal systems have long experienced similar subnational competition for large capital investments, but the stakes have ballooned in recent decades. Australia has a long history of competition for capital among states, led by its major East Coast cities (Berry 1984). Lagging regions such as South Australia used subsidies to lure major East Coast suppliers—in the auto industry, for instance—in the post-World War II era (Wanna 1980). In 2003, following Rupert Murdoch's News Corporation's extraction of A$100 million in concessions to build the $430 million Fox Studios development in Sydney, all but one of Australia's state governments, Queensland, signed an agreement to end investment bidding wars, pledging to exchange information on projects where companies attempt to play one state against the other (State of Victoria 2003). Queensland, the fastest-growing region, refused to participate because at the time it was successfully bidding corporate headquarters and facilities away from Victoria and New South Wales with undisclosed deals. In 2006, five states signed a five-year renewal, agreeing to cooperate against multinational efforts to pit them against each other, to provide each other with an annual report on attraction activities, and to construct a mechanism where concerns about breaches can be raised. Queensland again refused to join, and thus the agreement does not include efforts by states to use tax cuts or other incentives to lure business from interstate rivals (Hughes 2006).

Regional competition for capital may be waxing in Europe as well. The European states, as Adinda Sinnaeve describes in Chapter 4, made a historic decision to rein in the competition for capital among member states and locations within them. In the 1957 Treaty of Rome that formed the European Union, they agree to ban most subsidies to business for plant locations except under certain circumstances. Underdeveloped regions are permitted to attract businesses with incentives, and certain types of inducements—for job training and R&D, for instance—are permitted. The regulatory system is highly effective, especially at deterring incentives from being offered. Modest reforms are contemplated (Wishlade 2004), but by and large, the regime is robust.

Nevertheless, as European countries devolve economic development responsibility to lower levels of government, a response to the demand for autonomy on the part of regions (e.g., Spain) and central government fiscal fatigue, the phenomenon of incentive competition may reemerge. The European Union regulatory scheme does not extend to local governments' use of their own resources or taxing powers to attract new plants or facilities, unless national governments compensate them for such incentives, and court cases are now pressing regions' rights in this regard (Nicolaides 2005, 2006). Yet to date, such subnational discretionary powers are quite limited, and the conditions set by the courts on their use are quite restrictive.

Since the early 1990s, the American-style regional competition for capital is proliferating in developing countries, especially within large countries with federal systems of governance such as Brazil and India, and in China. Nowhere has it been fiercer than among Brazilian states in their competition for 22 new assembly plants planned and built by foreign auto companies since 1995. Despite Brazilian laws forbidding the reduction of state taxes to attract business, fiscal competition has been rampant and has resulted in excessively large incentives packages that radically relocated the industry away from Sao Paulo to four neighboring states (Rodriguez-Pose and Arbix 2001; Varsano, Ferriera, and Afonso 2002). The cost per job created appears to be much higher (on the order of $54,000 to $340,000 per job) than in the United States (Oman 2000), and incentives have induced 40 percent more automaking capacity in Brazil than would otherwise have been built (Farrell, Remes, and Schulz 2003). India, where economic development responsibilities and fiscal tools have been devolving to the states, is hosting greater fiscal competition and larger tax incentives packages (Venkatesan 2000; Schneider 2004).

In China, recent fiscal reforms give cities and regions greater responsibility for local economic development. Cities can now launch large development projects and retain the resulting income (rents, taxes), and they can customize their investment to the specifications of individual foreign investors. Although they cannot engage in bonding, they can form partnerships with banks and foreign investors, and have done so to finance huge infrastructure projects. Concomitantly, a fierce battle for competitive status has broken out, with cities ranked nationally on their success in attracting capital. Xu and Yeh (2005) describe the proliferation of this competition and its dangers, in that Chinese cities (and banks) face only soft budget constraints; if returns do not materialize, the nation state is required to bail them out. This creates conditions, they argue, for excessive and inefficient investments. In reality, enormous differences in natural resources, accessibility and physical infrastructure dominate the locational calculus of mobile firms in China (Yeung 2003).

Incentive competition occurs between nations as well as within them. Smaller countries increasingly believe that they must compete for mobile capital with each other. They have been protagonists in high-profile bidding wars, as in the famous shopping expedition of John DeLorean to Puerto Rico, Ireland, and Northern Ireland to site his auto plant. The winning total incentive package can add up to as much as 75 percent of the total investment cost of a project (Guisinger 1995). In the 1990s, newly independent and democratic Eastern European countries competed for European, Japanese, and American plants, often with little assurance that such incentives deals might be effective (Helinska-Hughes and Hughes 2003). Following the fall of the Berlin wall, Eastern European countries such as Poland and Bulgaria offered special location incentive packages with very mixed results. Critics argue that these countries would have been better off investing in the overall business environment and infrastructure and that their use has eroded the tax base without significantly attracting investment (Sorsa 2003). As these countries join the EU, they must bring their practices in line with the EU's regulatory framework.

A small but important literature documents and addresses growing incentive competition among Canada, the United States, and Mexico both before and after the North American Free Trade Agreement (NAFTA) (DeMont 1994; Jenkins 1987; Leyton-Brown 1979–1980). An increase in the size of subsidies to the auto industry in the United States and Canada is documented by Thomas (1997), who attributes it to fiercer competition for auto plants. Several policy researchers have made the case for a European-type commission in NAFTA to regulate incentive competition among the three countries (Graham and Warner 1994; Pastor 2001).

Although we do not address incentive competition between nations in this volume, some policy initiatives at multilateral and bilateral levels have begun to address it. East Asia is a focal point for strategy and experimentation. A study of Cambodia, Lao PDR, and Vietnam found that incentives are expensive and not very effective (Fletcher 2002). Another policy analyst concluded that competition among countries in Southeast Asia for inward investment may be unavoidable, but that national incentive offers should be streamlined and designed to limit the drain on budgets and the potential for corruption (Tseng 2002). Another considers the Asian-Pacific region ripe for an investment code that would put limits on incentive levels, simplify incentive instruments, create greater transparency, and evaluate the results of incentives (Guisinger 1995).

Investment competition between nation-states is distinguished from the subnational focus of our study in that the former is governed by international organizations such as the World Trade Organization (WTO), the International Monetary Fund (IMF), and the World Bank. Each of these organizations has an interest in reining in the use of subnational tax incentives and subsidies to minimize trade distortions. The WTO has opposed export or local content performance requirements in return for incentives and allows other countries to apply countervailing duties against export subsidies, while the IMF and World Bank encourage borrowers to reduce subsidies (Guisinger 1995). In a carefully reasoned paper, Schweke and Stumberg (1999) anticipate that subnational economic development could become illegal in the new global policy environment. However, a recent WTO World Trade Annual Report focused on the issue of subsidies acknowledges that some subsidies can benefit society and offset the negative externalities of economic activity and that both national and subnational governments have legitimate objectives in using them, including for economic development. The WTO remains concerned that such subsidies may be trade-distorting. The report notes that few governments fully meet their notification obligations under the WTO, contributing to a serious lack of information and transparency on the use and effect of subsidies, a situation aggravated by lack of common definitions of subsidy practices (WTO 2006).

There undoubtedly will be future tussles over WTO policies toward subsidies at all levels of government. If EU-type reasoning is followed, a case might be made for allowing developing but not developed nations to use incentives, analogous to the permissiveness the EU rules show to underdeveloped regions in Europe. Currently, the WTO estimates that 21 developed countries spend almost $250 billion on subsidies of all types, almost 85 percent of all countries' subsidies. The average ratio of subsidies to GDP is lower in developing countries than developed, though there are large variations within each country group (WTO 2006, pp. 112–114). Developed countries, which have the largest stake in preserving subsidies, appear to have successfully argued within the WTO that many subsidies are not primarily trade-motivated but are designed to build infrastructure, foster new industries, promote research and develop new knowledge, protect the environment, redistribute income, and help poor consumers (WTO 2006, p. xxii).

To summarize, then, incentive competition is on the rise, as demonstrated in the energies devoted to it by subnational governments and the size of incentive packages. It is most common in nations with federal structures that share taxing and economic development powers with state and local governments. Although analogous competition occurs among nation states, it is better regulated and subject to international organizational scrutiny. Technological change has obliterated many former barriers to interglobal location, enabling such competition. But incentive competition is also very much shaped by important institutional and political changes, to which we now turn.

INSTITUTIONAL AND POLITICAL SOURCES OF INCENTIVE COMPETITION

In regional bidding wars, the principal actors are state or local governments and private sector employers. Incentive packages are put together by the governmental unit, in response to an expression of interest, and sometimes demands, by the potential employer, who may state that he/she also has other potential sites in mind. Each set of actors operates in a historically evolved institutional context that conditions their options and responses (Markusen 2003). In this section, we argue that two important institutional changes have altered this environment: the rise of site consultants as a third party in the process, and increasing devolution of economic development responsibilities from central to subnational governments. In addition, the motivations of regional political leaders exacerbate the intensity of bidding wars, with negative social and economic results.

American regional scientists and public finance economists were long puzzled by a seemingly paradoxical phenomenon: despite dozens of surveys of the determinants of firm plant location that placed geographical tax differentials very far down on the list of factors that matter, state and local governments continue to feel that they must offer incentives and lower tax burdens. Firms surveyed from the 1950s well into the 1980s dismissed the importance of taxes as an interregional siting factor—instead, transportation costs, raw material access, labor costs, land costs, infrastructure, and access to markets dominated their locational calculus. But in the past decade or so, firms are now more likely to claim that taxes matter, and empirical estimates suggest that they do matter in terms of differential job creation (Bartik 2007; Wasylenko 1997). Why this shift?

Falling transportation and communications costs are one contributor, as noted by Bartik in Chapter 5. These ease the friction of distance and make other determinants—land costs, labor costs, and infrastructure more important. Yet these costs have been falling for at least two centuries as sequential transportation breakthroughs (steam ship, railroad, trucking, containerization) and communications breakthroughs (telegraph, telephone, radio, and radar) without triggering much incentive competition until recently. Corporate vertical disintegration and greater geographical separation of sequential stages in the production process also have contributed, creating a spatial division of labor in which routine manufacturing or final assembly can be located in far-flung sites for either cost or market access reasons, while management, research and development, advance manufacturing, and other functions are placed elsewhere (Fröbel, Heinrichs, and Kreye 1979; Markusen 1985).

Our view is that these explanations contribute to but are inadequate for fully accounting for the spread of subsidy competition and the size of recent incentive packages. Two recent institutional forces are central to this process. First, an entrepreneurial innovation in the site selection process has altered the institutional environment: the rise of the site location consultant. Even though firms did not consider tax differentials important, they were in a position to extract concessions or "rents" from regions in the negotiating process. Research on defense industry location over the decades demonstrates that company leaders were often completely oblivious to the potential profit they could make by relocating their facilities elsewhere and selling existing sites, often adjacent to major airports, for tremendous returns—engineers dominated management circles, and to them, real estate was just an unimportant happenstance (Markusen et al. 1991). We hypothesize that this attitude toward local government and its tax/service offerings prevailed for U.S. firms until the emergence of site consultants.

The rise of site consultants as brokers in the location process is a fascinating story. The Fantus Corporation pioneered this line of work in the 1930s and dominated the field until the late 1970s, by which time they had relocated 4,000 plants, mostly to low wage, antiunion, low business tax and nonurban sites in the south. Fantus, named after its industrial real estate founder, specialized in comparative analysis of potential sites for companies looking to locate new branch plants or offices, When son-in-law Leonard Yaseen took over the business, he began to charge for the analysis. In the 1950s, when fears of strategic bombing were strong, the U.S. government began promoting the dispersal of military manufacturing plants, amplifying the market for site relocation services. In the same era, Fantus began to help large corporations investigate overseas locations. Yaseen then suggested that companies play one location against the other, demonstrating that the tax and subsidy savings generated could cover his fee. Working the trade media and corporate networking channels, Fantus became a major opinionmaker in the market for sites. For instance, Yaseen dismissed New York City as a place to do business, a function of personal animosity despite his location there. In 1975, Fantus authored the first state "business climate" rankings, setting off state bidding wars. Eventually, Fantus was sold to the accounting firm Deloitte & Touche, and other firms entered the site selection business (Cobb 1993; LeRoy 2005).

Over time the industry has become more fragmented, split between independent consulting firms, large international accounting firms, and law firms, but is still quite oligopolistic in character, especially in the large plant location business. Its success has been linked to other developments in corporate governance: the rise of institutional investors and their pressuring of management for higher short-term returns, the ascendancy of professional managers, and the growth of real estate as a corporate asset class.[1]

This site brokering business has become institutionalized in ways that enhanced the rate of return for site consultants and their clients. The emergence of a brokering function diminishes competition among suppliers of jobs and tax base by standardizing the way large corporations approach subnational governments (Thomas 2000, p. 31). Site consultants began to hold specialist conferences and create organizations like the World Association of Investment Promotion Agencies (Raines 2003). Trade magazines such as *Corporate Location* and *Site Selection*, supported by advertising dollars from site location firms, encouraged negotiating firms to choose several states/cities to approach and play off against each other, even if they already had decided on an optimal location. They list deal winners and losers in every issue.

Site consultants began working for the other side, too, marketing their services to cities and regions on the grounds that they have knowledge about firm priorities that government officials do not have. When hired, consultants gain access to knowledge of cities and states' fiscal circumstances and economic development strategies that they can then use in service of their corporate clients (LeRoy 2005). However, site consultants' loyalties almost always lie with the interests of the job-selling corporation, especially, as is common, when they earn their fees on a commission basis. The higher the tax break and subsidy package extracted, the higher their fees. In real estate sales, where this lopsided relationship is also pervasive, many states have banned such dual agency. In Chapter 8, Greg LeRoy argues that site location consultants have come "to occupy a space where they defy norms about professional ethics and the proper representation of opposing parties," noting that commissions can run up to 30 percent of the value of acquired subsidies.

Our argument, then, is that a concerted institution-building process has introduced a new set of players, site consultants, into the spatial competition for jobs. As we argue in the next section, their success can be attributed to economic rents that can be extracted from job-hungry governments, especially when information asymmetries can be exploited and even created.

A second institutional change contributes significantly to the ferocity of subsidy competition among subnational governments. Over the past 20 years, national governments have engaged in a process of devolution, abandoning the practice of regional policies aimed at balancing uneven development and relegating responsibility for economic development to subnational governments. More and more countries, large and small, are creating federal systems of shared powers, following the apparently successful models of the United States and Germany, where multipolar urban systems (Markusen and Gwiasda 1993) ameliorate private city-centric rural to urban migration and create competition among subnational governments. In the United States, the federal system has long dampened enthusiasm for the type of national regional policies practiced in Europe—the territorially based Congress (in contrast to a party-based Parliament) acts as an informal resource distribution system instead (Markusen 1994).

Devolution has complex sources of political support. Many state and local governors and politicians welcome greater control over public and private investments decisions, especially if their regions have suffered from neglect from a former political regime, as in such diverse settings as Cataluña, Wales, Chile, Nicaragua, and South Korea. In some cases, devolution is tied to powerful political movements for greater autonomy, including the assertion of cultural identity. Economists preoccupied with efficiency in location government spending and taxation, à la Tiebout (1956b), argue that public services can be better tailored to regional and local preferences under decentralized structures. Devolution has been favored and strongly incentivized by international organizations such as the IMF and the World Bank as a means of fiscal discipline for national governments in developing countries where regional policy often provided fertile ground for corruption and wasteful spending. National leaders often see devolution as offering relief from expensive (and sometimes inefficient) regional programs and a budget-saving windfall. Concern for uneven development, for the cumulative causation process so elegantly analyzed by Myrdal (1957) and Kaldor (1970), and for the distributional consequences of mobile investment, including the inefficient underutilization of local infrastructure in declining regions (Markusen 1979), is much less often articulated in national economic policymaking in the early twenty-first century.

However, devolution is neither a simple nor universally successful way of deploying public responsibility for economic development. In the United States, the implicit role model, state governments have had powerful tools for raising revenues and engaging in public infrastructure provision since the Constitution was drafted in 1787. In general, they have in turn delegated revenue-raising and bonding powers to local governments. As a result, subnational governments have considerable but uneven resources to bring to bear on economic development. In many contemporary instances of devolution, central governments give their states and localities economic development responsibility but do not complement them with adequate resources or revenue-raising powers (Llanes 1998). Furthermore, most subnational governments have little expertise or experience with economic development, exposing them to greater information asymmetries in bargaining with multinational corporations and their site consultants. As a result, devolution may quicken incentive competition among states and localities while exacerbating disparities in economic outcomes, as shown by Markusen and Diniz (2005) for Latin America, and Schneider (2004) for India, where the wealthiest states usually win such competition.

Politics are also important. Scholars have long contended that economic development practice cannot be understood without an appreciation for political structure and interest group politics. Molotch (1976) made the seminal and durable case that localities develop "growth machines" comprised of groups who own local assets or make their living selling or maintaining them and who do not have options for expanding or relocating elsewhere. In general, Molotch argued, these groups will develop inordinate influence in local politics and push for policies that induce aggregate population growth. In a survey of European cities, Gordon and Jayet (1991) document the rise of recognizable urban growth machines in Europe, and Cheshire and Gordon (1996) offer a pessimistic view of the ability of territorial agreements to rein in such competition. More recently, Lovering (2003) offers a theory of the regional service class as a group with high stakes in the attraction of outside capital. These political economy theories predict that subnational governments will overinvest in incentives that help owners of local-specific assets at a net cost to local residents.[2]

A number of policy analysts have offered behavioral explanations for why state and local politicians will espouse and energetically pursue large incentive packages even when they are risky, unnecessary, damaging to the fiscal future of the locality, displacing, or place extraordinary burdens on constituents to fund future services. For one, politicians are motivated by the desire to be reelected, which relies on name recognition and on contributions from individuals and businesses. These often lead to high-profile, large commitments to and ribbon-cutting ceremonies for new plants and facilities, often in the richest, fastest-growing areas, even when economic development programs passed by legislatures contain explicit language that favors smaller firms and poorer regions (Dewar 1998; Luger and Bae 2005; Wolman and Spitzley 1996). For another, local officials may want to be seen as proactive in economic development matters and fear that nay-saying will provide fodder for opponents in future elections or saddle the region with a bad reputation among the site consultants who they see as gatekeepers to job-creating investment (Reid and Gatrell 2003; Wolman 1988). Brazilian state governments are subject to similar political distortions, affecting incentive competition and leading to bankruptcy (Rodriques-Pose and Arbix 2001).

These institutional features caution against treating the spatial market for jobs as a conventional market. On neither side of this market are the participants operating from simple microeconomic demand and supply positions. Politicans, as demanders of jobs, are motivated by features of the political process as well as the collective welfare of their constituents. Companies, as suppliers of jobs, rely on site consultants to massage the market in their interests; they act as surrogates for firm managers. In the following section, we review the various models that others have used to conceptualize subsidy competition and offer a third, institutionally grounded view.

ANALYTICAL APPROACHES TO INCENTIVE COMPETITION

Schematically, analyses of and policy implications toward spatial incentive competition can be divided into three camps. One argues that incentive competition is an efficient way of allocating public resources to economic development because it sets up a competition among units of government for mobile capital. This approach approves of the status quo and is opposed to any attempt to regulate or eliminate such competition. A second camp argues that incentive competition is inefficient because it distorts the location of productive capacity from what it would have been in the absence of subsidies, and recommends that it be outlawed or taxed away at higher levels of government. A third camp argues that subnational governments should and do have responsibility for economic development but that contemporary excesses are associated with asymmetries in the market for jobs that should be regulated. Next, we lay out the logic of each of these positions, comparing how each conceptualizes the market for subsidies, how policy posture follows from these, and which economic and political agents are aligned with each.

Tiebout-Type Models of Spatial Competition for Firms

The "let it be" camp conceives (often implicitly) of the siting process and subsidy bargaining between units of government and firms as taking place in a spatially differentiated market for public services, in which firms seek a set of public services, inputs into their production process, at the lowest possible tax price. Each competing government offers a supply of such services at a tax price. The market is thus structured as a straightforward competition between site and service-offering governments and site-searching firms. Since there are many demanders and suppliers on both sides of the market, the resulting allocation of firm investments will optimize the use of scarce public sector resources and maximize overall local welfare, as firms with different public service needs will be drawn to the specific communities that offer these at the lowest cost.

This model is an analog of the famous Tiebout (1956b) argument in favor of fragmented local governments. In Tiebout's model, households searched across metropolitan local governments for the utility-maximizing mix of public services (schools, public safety, and so on) at the lowest tax price. The Tiebout argument has been used as a post facto rationale for the efficiency of competing local governments in U.S. metropolitan areas, a form of state-level devolution that dates back to the late nineteenth century. Although it has been hotly contested, especially on equity grounds (Markusen 1974), the theory has proven to be as robust as the proliferation of local jurisdictions. In the United States, the National Governors' Association, although it has many times debated the issue, has repeatedly rejected any attempts to curtail subsidy competition (Kayne and Shonka 1994). Similarly, in Europe, Tiebout-type arguments that tax competition can be welfare-improving have been used to oppose tax harmonization among EU states (Varsano, Ferriera, and Afonso 2002).

The Tiebout-like approach has several virtues. One is its acknowledgement of the linkage between taxes and services received by firms. In various other approaches, and in practice, this link is broken, and the notion that firms' taxes pay for services rendered disappears. The procompetition approach is also appealing because it offers a way of disciplining public officials whose behavior may otherwise not be in the interests of taxpayers.

On the other hand, this approach is highly simplistic. It assumes that the market for public services is transparent and that all parties have access to full information. It ignores the fact that, in reality, bargaining takes place as a time-constrained drama between a single firm and (or so communities believe) multiple bidding jurisdictions. It cannot easily cope with the fact that from a community's point of view, firms aren't just public service consumers and taxpayers, but are also suppliers of jobs. Finally, it operates from a single, selective optimality criterion—efficiency. Many citizens and practitioners of economic development care as much about equity, and in some cases, environmental impacts, as they do about efficient resource allocation.

Prisoner's Dilemma Approaches

The second position, the "suppress it" view, argues that subsidy competition is inefficient because it wastes resources by luring firms away from sites they would otherwise favor. In addition, some economists also argue that as a result of shortfalls in revenue associated with tax giveaways, public goods such as education, parks, and public infrastructure will be undersupplied (Burstein and Rolnick 1995; Zodrow and Mieszkowski 1986). Burstein and Rolnick make both these arguments in their call for Congress to tax away state and local business-specific tax and subsidies. Others reason that the mix of public services will be skewed by incentive competition to favor business interests at residents' expense—too many business centers and airports but not enough parks or libraries (Keen and Marchand 1997).

Economists making these arguments conclude that incentive competition is at best a zero-sum proposition, because little or no net new investment is created across regions, but more likely to be negative, because of public goods under-provision. Following such competition to its logical end, one economist notes, could mean that if every government copies the bids of every other government, the firm will end up where it would have gone anyway, no net new investment will be created, and all governments will have reduced taxes so that public spending is suboptimal (Graham, 2003, pp. 69–71).

That is a general equilibrium approach, but theorists working on this problem often conceptualize it as a "prisoner's dilemma," a single event, or game, in which a government (a prisoner) is bidding against other governments (other prisoners) for a single plant or facility. They would all be better off if they offered nothing, or the same package, the logic goes, but since they do not know each others' bids, a "race to the bottom" is likely (Oates 1972).

The use of the prisoner's dilemma game to characterize spatial competition for capital has a long history (Thomas 2000). Cooper (1972) first used it to characterize subsidy competition between countries, followed by Guisinger (1985). Quite sophisticated formulations have recently been offered, including Wohlgemuth and Kilkenny's (1998) modeling of state governments' optimal response to a firm's threat to relocate, taking into account both asymmetrical information and the fact that other firms in the state may, if the relocation buy-off succeeds, demand similar tax and subsidy relief.

The prisoner's dilemma model and its predicted outcomes are useful in demonstrating that firms can extract rents in return for their decision to locate new facilities or even to retain current employment. Indeed, the increasing exploitation of such rents may itself have exacerbated the mobility of capital, lowering the cost of relocation for firms. It is also useful in highlighting the information asymmetry that encumbers most bargaining, and it raises the interesting question why governments do not collude by sharing intelligence on bids to avoid rent extraction. It underscores the plausibility of overall welfare loss from incentive competition. It also captures how many governments perceive the situation, although such perceptions may themselves be a product of the popularization of the model by journalists and site consultants.

But there are problems with the prisoner's dilemma framework. It is a highly stylized, simplistic formulation. It is an event-based model, which makes it difficult to evaluate strings of repeat games, especially since the cast of characters may change (Wood 2003). Rachel Weber, in Chapter 6, makes the point that certain jurisdictions may accumulate skill through repeat games that improve their prospects and bargaining power. (Firms that employ site consultants pay them to accumulate such skills on their behalf.) Repeat games may also help competing governments learn the virtues of collaborating, as game theory predicts more generally (Dixit and Skeath 2004, Chapter 11) and as demonstrated in the European and Australian cases we discuss above. A central theme of Thomas's (2000) seminal book, *Competing for Capital*, is that iteration makes it possible for governments to cooperate to regulate investment competition, Ironically, some national governments (e.g., Australia) have recently adopted competition policies that consider such collaboration potentially "anticompetitive."

The prisoner's dilemma model cannot easily encompass institutional changes in interests, power, and actors, including the rise and behavior of site consultants. It does not permit information asymmetries to be constructed. In its more simplistic formulations, it allows bidders only to give or not give firm-specific subsidies. Yet, the model's assumptions can be modified to permit such intermediate positions (Buchholtz 1998; Thomas 2000). Harder to build into this model are the other paths governments might follow to attract firms: lowering the overall tax rate, improving infrastructure, investing in schools or research and development, worker retraining, and provision of amenities.

Some versions of the prisoner's dilemma model predict that winning governments will actually be worse off (e.g., Graham 2003). But others show analytically that use of a prisoner's dilemma model does not necessarily produce a "winner's curse" (Thomas 2000, Appendix). Bartik, in Chapter 5, argues that the jobs and tax base created can more than cover the costs of incentives if offers are carefully crafted. He also argues that losing bidders may be better off not being saddled with excess debt and shrinking tax revenues. When modelers begin relaxing assumptions, the welfare losses and gains from incentive competition become less clear, with some winning and some losing (Varsano, Ferriera, and Afonso 2002).

The remedy indicated by the simplistic application of this model—taxing away subsidies and tax breaks nationally—is a relatively conservative notion. It is driven by a focus on interregional efficiency rather than the welfare of individual regions. As Bartik notes, some economists making this argument (Burstein and Rolnick 1995) have no complaint with across-the-board tax reductions for all business, even though these could be highly inefficient from the point of view of the public sector and would create particularly difficult circumstances for economically distressed local areas.

Finally, the prisoner's dilemma model has difficulty comprehending the complexity of the market for investment. In actuality, government decision makers have multiple constituencies with competing claims, and their motivations are more complex than the model suggests. An ingenious corrective for this deficit is offered by Basinger and Hallerberg (2004), two political scientists who note that the empirical evidence for the race to the bottom is actually quite weak. They argue that political institutions and organizations mitigate the predicted downward spiral. Modifying the prisoner's dilemma model by allowing domestic politics to modify governments' behavior, they argue that governments may be resistant to requests for tax breaks. For instance, ruling parties may have strong commitments to social programs or be ideologically opposed to tax cuts. Both Thomas and LeRoy in this volume make the case that mobilized citizens can make a difference in politicians' willingness to engage in incentive competition or in the type of deals struck.

The Market for Jobs and Tax Capacity Approach

A less elegant but more complex view is that regional governments are preoccupied with creating jobs and amplifying tax capacity. While the two approaches reviewed above are rooted in public finance and microeconomics, this view is more attentive to institutional structure and behavior and common among economists, geographers, planners, and other researchers working on economic development. The market in which governments face firms seeking sites can thus be considered a market for jobs and tax base, rather than for public services or for capital investments. State and local governments offer incentives in return for promised jobs, revealed in both the rhetoric accompanying announcements of sitings and in efforts to hold firms to their job-creating commitments with clawback provisions or penalties for nonperformance, though the latter are often weak. In a similar analysis of the "market for economic development," Weber (2002a) uses an institutionalist transactions cost framework to conceptualize this process.

Jobs thus generated are socially valuable, in that they lower local unemployment, raise local labor force participation, enable skill acquisition, and have progressive effects on the local income distribution (Bartik 2001, 2004; Courant 1994). The jobs created also generate higher incomes for residents, who in turn spend the additional income on local goods and services that generate yet other jobs and are invested in housing that generates real estate taxes. Jobs and expanded tax capacity are valued by residents, by politicians for their announcement value, as we argued above, and by the local growth machine as well. Competing governments can be characterized as competing for jobs and tax base, and firms looking for sites as supplying them. The firms pursue incentives as a rent-seeking activity (Weber 2002a; Wolkoff 1992). In what follows, we focus on job creation and less on tax capacity, because it applies more generically to international as well as domestic cases, and because the institutional setting for incentive competition at the submetropolitan level is more particularistic, involving the retail sector and the growing role of planners and local government officials in real estate development (Weber 2002b).

Evidence for the pivotal role of jobs in such bargains comes from a remarkable study by Gabe and Kraybill (2002), who argue that firms have an incentive to overannounce the numbers of jobs they will create to increase the size of incentives offered. In a study of 366 Ohio establishments' expansions between 1993 and 1995, they found that those that received incentives overannounced employment targets but created no new jobs (and actually led to a reduction in the overall number of jobs), while those that did not receive incentives accurately forecast their job expansion and did create new jobs. Gabe and Kraybill, citing Krueger (1974), suggest that the puzzling job decline in establishments winning incentives might be explained by firm reallocation of resources away from internal efficiencies in production and toward rent-seeking.

We view incentive competition as taking place in a spatial "market for jobs" that is an institutional innovation of site consultants who work to maintain information asymmetries that permit rent-taking. As Weber argues in Chapter 6 of this book and elsewhere (2002a), the power balance in the market for jobs is uneven, in part because local governments "are embedded in space and not footloose like businesses." She notes that businesses are better able to control the flow of information during incentive negotiations and that the size of the incentive package they need "to make a project feasible may be much smaller than what they would have the public sector believe." Local governments are not privy to actual cost structures and hurdle rates.

Institutional economists have long understood the importance of opportunistic behavior and the role of information asymmetries in facilitating it (Williamson 1975). Close observers of incentive competition note that government officials rarely possess accurate information regarding an investor's true intentions (Bachelor 1997; Thomas 2007; Weber 2007). Reid and Gatrell (2003, pp. 112–113) argue that companies that least need incentives have the resources to most effectively engage in opportunistic behavior. They cite documented cases where, after large incentives packages had been granted on the presumption of competition, corporate executives admitted that other sites were never seriously considered.

LeRoy (2005) details how site consultants encourage candidate communities to think of themselves as in competition with other communities, sometimes creating high-profile bidding, as in the Chicago/Denver/Dallas competition for Boeing's relocating headquarters, but often not revealing the identity of competitors. Governments are counseled to keep their bids top secret, the implied sanction being permanent black-balling by the site brokering consultants. Thus, collusion among localities is suppressed, while the site consulting brokerages can be seen as practicing a sort of informal collusion on behalf of firms to maximize the rents that can be extracted. This is why site-seeking firms themselves do not invest in site selection but purchase such services from a supplier sector.

The way that the site consultant sector organizes and mediates incentive competition reveals the extent to which information asymmetries are created and maintained as a condition of rent extraction. Gabe and Kraybill (2002, p. 707) document how the state of Ohio interacts with the site selection industry. Every year, the state submits to *Site Selection* magazine its list of firm attractions or expansions in the state with announced creation of 50 or more jobs. The magazine then uses this data to compare business growth in states across the nation. By creating this competition and a data base that solicits state announced job expansions, the site selection industry has created an incentive for states to list (and thus to subsidize) as many projects as possible to improve the state's ranking relative to other states. Site consultants, especially when acting as dual agents, can horde information that they have on firms' intentions and on the larger field of competition, including the willingness and ability of other communities and states to offer incentives.

The "market for jobs" approach generally accepts the necessity for governments to compete for capital and to use tools at hand in pursuit of jobs and community well-being. The policy implications, then, focus on how to curtail rent-taking, improve transparency in location decisions, understand why some tools are better than others, and help governments understand the complicated current and long-term trade-offs associated with developing an incentive offer.

Among the virtues of the market for jobs approach is this focus on institutional factors—on the messy, complicated way that subsidy competition unfolds in reality and how an expanded set of actors (including politicians, growth machines, and site consultants) behave under such circumstances. It acknowledges the centrality of the desire for jobs as a motivation for competing governments. Yet in doing so, it has the disadvantage of obscuring the role of taxes as a price for public services and neglects the negative long-term consequences of associated tax erosion.

Most of the authors in this book work from a market for jobs and tax capacity point of view, although Bartik's strong defense of state and local governments' legitimate economic development role and rejection of higher level prohibitions shares elements of the Tiebout-based approach. Thomas, using a prisoner's dilemma approach, concludes that subsidy competition has efficiency, equity, and environmental drawbacks and should be regulated, but does not believe subsidies are always bad policy. Fisher's chapter summarizes the evidence on long-term corporate tax erosion and is in that sense compatible with the prisoner's dilemma implications. All three call for reforms and make specific detailed recommendations for reform.

Normative Issues

In evaluating the power and usefulness of those three approaches, it is useful to acknowledge differences in underlying normative posture. In general, economists using Tiebout-type or prisoner's dilemma models work from an explicit assumption that economic efficiency is the sole concern of economic analysis and rationale for policy intervention. However, in economic development practice, a strong case is often made by economists and planners for equity and environmental quality norms co-equal with efficiency (Fitzgerald and Leigh 2002). Much of economic development practice is framed by an overarching concern for jobs, and not just any jobs, but quality jobs and jobs for the hardest to employ. Bartik, in Chapter 5, states that more local employment is a social good and points out that if all local governments competed in a smart way, it is not obvious that their optimal economic development subsidies would impose a net efficiency cost on other jurisdictions.

In this volume, distributional concerns receive careful attention. Bartik, Schweke, Weber, and LeRoy all address the creation of quality jobs. Bartik (1993) evaluates incentives for their ability to produce jobs for existing residents rather than newcomers and finds that in the long run, about 80 percent of new jobs in local economies are reflected in more population rather than higher employment rates. However, Bartik (1991) also finds that spurts of local growth benefit locals at the back of the labor queue and less-skilled and African American workers especially. Schweke specifically addresses the targeting of incentives to those regions and individuals most in need of work.

Others—Thomas, for instance—are sensitive to the regressive distributional impact of subsidies that favor owners of capital at the expense of residents of the community and worsen the income distribution. Fisher, in Chapter 3, gives hard estimates for the degree of regressivity that has accompanied the erosion of state and local business taxes overall. Thomas addresses harmful environmental consequences, as when subsidies induce building in a floodplain or when negative externalities are imposed on neighboring communities.

In his chapter, Fisher cautions against attributing all observed negative fiscal trends in recent years to incentive competition. He offers three other plausible hypotheses. For one, conservative ideological opposition to the size of the public sector per se may be contributing. For those who believe government is too large, the strategy is to "starve the beast," first by cutting taxes and then by claiming fiscal responsibility and the necessity to cut services. For another, there is the durable though minority "supply side" theory that contends that growth is only possible by lightening the tax burden on business. Third, some conservatives forthrightly attack progressive income taxes, a form of class warfare rationalized by the tenuous idea that cutting capital gains taxes for individuals will stimulate new business activity in the same state. These are important normative and ideological contributors to conflict over subnational taxation. In legislatures and city councils where the Republican party has dominated (including the national Congress for the last decade), business tax base erosion and tax regressivity have been on the rise.

Inequities are also possible between firms and among regions. Subsidies to particular firms can also be inequitable between owners of capital and their employed workers, when some firms are unfairly subsidized at the expense of their competitors, an argument recently made in important U.S. court cases and pressed by nonrecipient firms in their bid for similar concessions. Indeed, important cases are currently working their way through the courts using the Interstate Commerce Clause that prohibits restraints on trade as a rationale for striking down incentive packages targeted at interstate firm moves.

In general, too, richer states and localities walk away with the prizes, as Varsano, Ferriera, and Afonso (2002) find in Brazil; Schneider (2004) in India; and Luger and Bae (2005) in North Carolina. In Chapter 6, Weber describes how this happens at the local level in the United States: the more assets a place possesses, the more leverage, expertise, and decisional independence it will have and the better negotiating position it will establish. In contrast, poorer jurisdictions will have to offer more to succeed and are much more likely to give away the store to lure a plant, often without demanding performance.

DOES INCENTIVE COMPETITION YIELD ECONOMIC DEVELOPMENT FOR WINNERS?

A paradox in debate over incentive competition is that there is little agreement about whether engaging in it results in benefits for bid-winning states and localities. The evidence, most of it on the U.S. case, is mixed. For an initial assessment of the international case, see Guisinger (1986).

Some researchers argue that incentives are too small to matter to firms in their choice of location. Their evidence is based on surveys in which firms respond to questions about which spatially differentiated factors of product matter most to them in siting plant and facilities (Guisinger 1992; Enrich 1996; Farrell, Remes, and Schulz 2003). Greenstone and Moretti (2003) find that cities winning high-profile plants in the United States did better than their losing competitors, but as Fisher argues in Chapter 3, the researchers assumed that the incentives were decisive rather than bargained for after the fact.

Up through the late 1980s, the consensus was that economic development incentives had at best an ambiguous impact on growth and probably little to no impact at all (Eisinger 1988; Peters and Fisher 2002). Since then, a number of empirical studies have shown that tax incentives and other subsidies do make a difference in regional growth rates (Bartik 2007; Hines 1995; Newman and Sullivan 1988; Phillips and Goss 1995; Wasylenko 1997). The evidence appears stronger for job creation than net positive tax effects (Peters and Fisher 2002). Bartik (1994) argues that it is highly likely that incentives are always revenue negative. The causality is so complex, however, that at least one researcher, reviewing the U.S. case, has concluded that no one really knows what the effectiveness or welfare implications of incentive competition are (Graham 2003, p. 71).

Even if governments that engage in successful incentive offers subsequently generate more output, jobs, and tax revenues, it does not necessarily constitute economic development. For one thing, it may not be positive for the state or country as a whole, if other jurisdictions lose jobs and tax base as a result. And there are the distributional consequences as well, where tax burdens are shifted to residents and the quality of public services declines. Fisher's chapter shows the long-term erosion in business tax shares of state revenues, from a high of nearly 10 percent in 1980 to just under 5 percent by 2002. Peters and Fisher (2002), in a study of state enterprise zones, show that during just eight years in the 1990s, the effective state tax rate on new investment fell by 30 percent. LeRoy's (2005) book cites many cases of local governments unable to pay for operating expenses and other services following risky underwriting of competed projects, including long-term responsibility for paying off bonds used to build infrastructure that is subsequently unused. Citizens of these jurisdictions are thus now shouldering a higher share of the tax burden for public services (without any clear increase in the share devoted to them) and are going without services they might otherwise have enjoyed.

Furthermore, even for bid-winning localities whose jobs and tax base expand, economic development outcomes might have been more positive had those resources been used differently. Each subsidy and tax expenditure involves opportunity costs for governments and their citizens. Even better jobs and greater tax capacity might have resulted from alternative allocations of economic development resources. To this final question we now turn.

IS ATTRACTION OF EXTERNAL EXPORT-PRODUCING PHYSICAL CAPITAL THE ONLY ROUTE TO JOBS?

So far, we have not tied incentive competition to an important, hallowed theory in economic development—that a region's overall growth is tied to its ability to export to other regions goods and services that in return permit it to import the goods and services that it cannot competitively produce. The prominence of export base theory as a conception of macro growth at the subnational level has not been seriously questioned in the half century since it was formulated, though at the national level, some national governments have engaged in an alternative import substitution strategy, an approach much discredited in recent years. In our view, incentive competition is embraced by state and local governments because leaders believe that only export-oriented activity will generate net new jobs. (Intrametropolitan bidding wars for retail jobs simply decides who gets the jobs without altering the total created.)

In this section we review the history of export base theory, sometimes called economic base theory, and evaluate the evidence on its power to explain aggregate regional growth.

Historically, the world economy has experienced large swings in openness, followed by significant slowdowns and retrenchments. Economic integration is not a unilateral progression over time, nor are exports reliably the leading source of regional economic growth. In the first half of the nineteenth century, economist Douglass North (1966) elegantly demonstrated that slave-cultivated southern cotton drove the aggregate U.S. capital accumulation and the growth rate. After the Civil War, the United States retreated behind high tariff barriers to nurture its own manufacturing economy, growing robustly from an internal elaboration of the division of labor, especially the synergy between increasingly capital-intensive agriculture and producer goods manufacturing (Hobsbawm 1975). Thus, in successive eras, regional and national economic growth has been variously oriented externally or internally. Shifts from one to the other are linked to developments in technology, especially in transportation and communications, but also to political and institutional changes.

We currently live in an era that is preoccupied with trade. Most economists argue that regions must specialize and export more than ever before, because the penetration of inexpensive and often high-quality imports is eroding whole segments of local and regional economies (Howes and Markusen 1993). Ever since North's (1955) elegant statement of it, indebted to Innis's (1930) staples theory, the export base argument goes more or less as follows. In a trade-integrated world, regions outside of one's own are superior producers of many goods and services locally consumed, and in order to be able to pay for these imports, the region must specialize in certain exportable goods and services. In the mid-twentieth century world, with its sophisticated globe-transcending transportation systems that reached far into little hamlets everywhere, the power of this theory was manifest. Economists codified the theory into the economic base model, ubiquitously used even today in multiplier analysis.

Nevertheless, from the beginning, the theory had its critics. In his famous debate with North, Tiebout (1956a) pointed out an obvious logical flaw in the theory: the world economy as a whole does not export. In addition, a regional economy's ability to provide for itself increases as its income from exports grows, resulting in import substitution. Tiebout also argued that people have different consumption patterns in different regions, complicating the model's application. But more importantly, Tiebout argued for an endogenous theory. Harkening back to Adam Smith, he posited that an elaborating internal division of labor could spur regional growth without export growth. His theory was brilliantly applied by Lindstrom (1978) in her renowned book on the early Philadelphia region, where she showed that a relatively autarchic region grew robustly from growing synergies between diversified farming and more urban manufacturing industries. Bartik (2004) makes the modern case for non-export-oriented sources of job and tax base growth by noting that cases where a new local-serving activity absorbs underutilized land or labor, or where it increases overall productivity.

Subsequently, practitioners of economic development vigorously debated and experimented with import substitution and export-based strategies for regional and national development, especially in the developing world. Many industrialized countries, among them the United States and Japan, nurtured their early industrial economies behind large tariff barriers and succeeded in import substitution on a massive scale. In the 1970s and 1980s, Latin American countries in particular tried to follow this path, but the strategy's apparent failure brought an emphasis on export base strategies back into fashion.

Yet the evidence on the relationship between overall growth and export growth is far from established. In recent decades, economists working in international development have begun to question the lead role of exports in explaining GDP growth for both developing and developed countries. As early as the 1960s, Ball (1962) argued that export expansion could retard domestic development by siphoning off investment. Others have argued that exports may be a consequence rather than a cause of economic growth. In a number of carefully constructed empirical tests, scholars find mixed evidence on both the existence of a relationship and the direction of causality. Jung and Marshall (1985) found that for 37 developing countries, evidence on the period 1950–1981 supports the export promotion thesis in only four cases; five countries reduced exports with growth, while four countries experienced export growth with output reduction. Ghartey (1993) concluded that export-driven development appears to explain growth in Taiwan but not Japan or the United States. In a five-country study, Sharma, Norris, and Wai-Wah-Cheung (1991) found that Japan and Germany experienced export-led growth from 1960 to 1987 but in the United States and the United Kingdom, output growth appears to have induced export growth.

Thus, at the national level there is no clear evidence that exports drive overall growth. There is equally strong evidence that endogenous developments—new product creation first aimed at local markets and process innovations that increase productivity—may drive growth and prompt export expansion. What about regional growth? Why might locally oriented economic activity drive overall regional growth in an increasingly competitive world?

Several hypotheses have been advanced. For one, an innovation aimed at a local market might turn out to have much broader applicability and become an exported product or service (Cortright 2002). Boeing's original seaplanes, designed for Seattle use, are an example. For another, people are also mobile and may choose locations to live and work based on amenities, creating more local-serving activities paid for with asset income or entitlements (like Social Security) earned elsewhere (Nelson and Beyers 1998). Many midsized American metropolitan areas have grown principally from retiree in-migration, and many larger cities have grown through immigration not tied to specific jobs. Third, secular changes in consumption patterns, linked to demographic characteristics such as aging or labor force participation decisions such as two-parent households, may result in disproportionate demand for local-serving industries. Markusen and Schrock (2006) find that over the period 1980–2000, the local-serving occupations in the 30 largest U.S. metros outpaced job growth in export base occupations by four to one. For a more general treatment of the potential for local-serving economic development strategies to produce growth, see Markusen (2007).

The evidence is thus not compelling that exogenous growth, linked to export demand and the attraction of mobile capital, is more powerful than endogenous growth from human capital investments, innovation, an elaborating local division of labor, amenities-led population growth, or consumption shifts. Exports do matter, but they are not everything. If this is the case, decisions about firm subsidies should be embedded in a portfolio approach to economic development, in which the short- and long-term opportunity costs of particular incentives are weighed against alternative investments that might be superior from a normative point of view for the community involved. LeRoy's chapter includes a call for unified development budgets as one way to implement just such a portfolio approach. Schweke, St. George, and Rist (1998) did the original conceptual work on unified development budgets. To date, the best application of the concept is the study published by Mountain Association for Community Economic Development (2005) for the state of Kentucky.

CONCLUSION AND SUMMARY OF THE CONTRIBUTIONS

With the authors in this volume, we conclude that state and local governments should, and in many countries do, have the responsibility for shepherding economic development in their communities. As Weber states, taxes and expenditures are among the few tools they have to pursue good jobs and long term stability for their constituents, along with certain regulatory strategies. The policy challenge is not to embrace incentive competition or fully suppress it, but to reform it in ways that encourage the benefits to exceed the costs and to achieve normative goals on efficiency, equity, and environmental fronts. Even the European Union, as Sinnaeve articulates, distinguishes between good subsidies and bad.

The chapters in this book are rich in policy recommendations aimed at local, state, and national governments, based on careful reasoning and empirical evidence. Political scientist Thomas makes the case for the excesses of contemporary subsidy competition and tells a sordid tale of information asymmetry and political machinations at the local level in a particular subsidy case. Although he favors eliminating incentive competition with a European Union–type regulatory system, he believes this is unrealistic for the United States. Sinnaeve acknowledges the downside of the EU system—it requires a heavy administrative burden, struggles with the right balance between rule-making and flexibility, and does not fully suppress illegal aid. Other nations, however, might be well-advised to adopt an EU-type regulatory regime because it has achieved impressive gains in deterring subsidy offers and eliminating distorted competition.

Bartik reviews the conditions under which incentives are reasonable, advising the use of cost/benefit analysis for governments engaging in negotiations and competitions. He cautions against looking only at jobs and tax revenues and suggests including the costs and benefits of public services and the prospects for local versus nonlocal hiring.

Schweke critiques an existing incentive program in North Carolina, the William S. Lee Act, that was designed to favor poorer counties but has not, and proposes two targeted state tax incentive programs in its place. One would kick in during cyclical downturns, creating jobs by giving firms tax credits for wages of newly hired workers, spurring a substitution of labor for capital. The other would target the highest unemployment counties in the state by giving employers wage and benefits subsidies to hire unemployed, local workers. These programs would induce job creation in regions and among workers who most need work, in contrast to the Lee Act, which has subsidized mainly large firms to locate in wealthy suburban areas around the largest cities, bringing many of their workers with them. Schweke's proposals demonstrate the careful tailoring that must be undertaken to ensure that the reforms, rather than prohibitions, will be able to address the inefficiencies and inequities of incentive competition.

Bartik, Weber, and LeRoy offer detailed reforms to improve the operation of the jobs market. These include transparency, performance requirements, community benefits agreements, pay-as-you-go deals, school board say on TIF and tax abatements (to prevent erosion of public funds for schools), unified development budgets, and multijurisdictional tax regime reforms, such as closing corporate reporting loopholes and repealing the single sales factor formulation at the state level. Weber focuses her recommendations on local public officials and how they might improve their bargaining position in deal-making. LeRoy, appreciating the virtues of simple and straightforward remedies, offers fewer, simpler laws and stronger enforcement. His set of nine reforms includes three innovative ideas: disclosure of state-by-state taxes paid to corporate shareholders (which would raise the visibility of exploitation of differentials in state tax systems), using federal spending as a carrot (and a stick) against job piracy; and defining site location consultants as lobbyists and regulating them accordingly.

Although many state and local government and interest group leaders have been seeking incentive competition reform in the United States and elsewhere for some time, there has been a quickening of interest and a coalescing of ideas and organizational energy in the last decade. As the excesses worsen and governments feel greater pressure to spend time and resources in business recruitment, many observers think that the time is ripe for significant reform along the lines of the proposals offered in this book. A great deal of credit goes to LeRoy and his organization, Good Jobs First, which has served as an important clearinghouse for information on subsidy competition and applied research shop for evaluating outcomes of past deals.

As the market for jobs goes global and devolution deepens, the site consulting industry is entering new territory, especially in developing countries. A great challenge for economists, economic development practitioners, and activists working on these issues is to cope with this internationalization of subsidy competition. State and local governments in more developed nations may find themselves pitted not so much against each other but against competitors yet farther afield with whom it is even more difficult to communicate and compare notes. Economic development officials, politicians, and the public in developing countries where incentive competition is spreading need ideas, help and cooperation from experts and organizations that are already successfully regulating such competition, as in the European Union, or who are slowly winning battles in transparency requirements, deal negotiations, court cases, and broader views of economic development strategy and tools. We hope that this volume contributes substantially to this effort.

Notes

1. Rachel Weber, personal communication with the author, 2006.
2. Timothy J. Bartik, personal communication with the author, 2006.

References

Bachelor, Lynn. 1997. "Business Participation in Economic Development Programs: Lessons from Six Ohio Cities." *Urban Affairs Review* 32(5): 704–722.

Ball, Roy. 1962. "Capital Imports and Economic Development: Paradoxy or Orthodoxy?" *Kyklos* XV: 610–623.

Bartik, Timothy J. 1991. *Who Benefits from State and Local Economic Development Policy?* Kalamazoo, MI: W.E. Upjohn Institute for Employment Research.

———. 1993. "Who Benefits from Local Job Growth: Migration or the Original Residents?" *Regional Studies* 27(4): 297–312.

———. 1994. "Jobs, Productivity, and Local Economic Development: What Implications Does Economic Research Have for the Role of Government?" *National Tax Journal* 47(4): 847–862.

———. 2001. *Jobs for the Poor: Can Labor Demand Policies Help?* New York: Russell Sage Foundation.

———. 2004. "Local Economic Development Policies." In *Management Politics in Local Government Finance.* 5th ed. J. Richard Aronson and Eli Schwartz, eds. Washington, DC: International City/County Management Association, pp. 355–390.

———. 2007. "Solving the Problems of Economic Development Incentives." In *Reining in the Competition for Capital,* Ann Markusen, ed. Kalamazoo, MI: W.E. Upjohn Institute for Employment Research, pp. 101–137.

Basinger, Scott, and Mark Hallerberg. 2004. "Remodeling the Competition for Capital: How Domestic Politics Erases the Race to the Bottom." *American Political Science Review* 98(2): 261–276.

Berry, Michael. 1984. "The Political Economy of Australian Urbanisation." *Progress in Planning* 22(Part 1): 1–83.

Bluestone, Barry, and Bennett Harrison. 1982. *The Deindustrialization of America: Plant Closings, Community Abandonment, and the Dismantling of Basic Industry.* New York: Basic Books.

Buchholtz, David E. 1998. "Competition and Corporate Incentives: Dilemmas in Economic Development." PhD dissertation, Durham, NC: Duke University.

Burstein, Melvin L., and Arthur J. Rolnick. 1995. "Congress Should End the Economic War Among the States." In *Annual Report 1994.* Minneapolis, MN: Federal Reserve Bank of Minneapolis.

Cheshire, Paul, and Ian R. Gordon. 1996. "Territorial Competition and the Predictability of Collective (In)Action." *International Journal of Urban and Regional Research* 20(3): 383–399.

Chirinko, Robert, and Daniel J. Wilson. 2006. "State Investment Tax Incentives: A Zero-Sum Game?" Paper prepared for the 2006 NTA Annual Meetings, Boston, November 16–18.

Cobb, James C. 1993. *The Selling of the South: The Southern Crusade for Industrial Development, 1936–1990.* 2nd ed. Urbana, IL: University of Illinois Press.

Cooper, Richard N. 1972. "Economic Interdependence in the 1970s." *World Politics* 24(2): 159–181.

Cortright, Joseph. 2002. "The Economic Importance of Being Different: Regional Variations in Tastes, Increasing Returns, and the Dynamics of Development." *Economic Development Quarterly* 16(1): 3–16.

Courant, Paul N. 1994. "How Would You Know a Good Economic Development Policy If You Tripped over One? Hint: Don't Just Count Jobs." *National Tax Journal* 47(4): 863–881.

DeMont, John. 1994. "Fast Frank: How New Brunswick's Premier Turned His Province into Canada's Social Laboratory." *Maclean's* 107(15): 22–28.

Dewar, Margaret. 1998. "Why State and Local Economic Development Programs Cause So Little Economic Development." *Economic Development Quarterly* 12(1): 68–87.

Dixit, Avinash, and Susan Skeath. 2004. *Games of Strategy.* 2nd ed. New York: W.W. Norton and Company.

Eisinger, Peter. 1988. *The Rise of the Entrepreneurial State.* Madison, WI: University of Wisconsin Press.

Enrich, Peter D. 1996. "Saving the States from Themselves: Commerce Clause Constraints on State Tax Incentives for Business." *Harvard Law Review* 110(December): 377–468.

Farrell, Diana, Jaana Remes, and Heiner Schulz. 2003. "New Horizons: Multinational Company Investments in Developing Countries." http://www.mckinsey.com/mgi/publications/newhorizons/index.asp (accessed October 25, 2006).

Fitzgerald, Joan, and Nancey Green Leigh. 2002. *Economic Revitalization: Cases and Strategies for City and Suburb.* Thousand Oaks, CA: Sage Publications.

Fletcher, Kevin. 2002. "Tax Incentives in Cambodia, Lao PDR, and Vietnam." Prepared for the IMF Conference on Foreign Direct Investment: Opportunities and Challenges for Cambodia, held in Lao P.D.R. and Vietnam, Hanoi, Vietnam, April 16–17.

Friedman, Thomas. 2006. *The World Is Flat: A Brief History of the Twenty-First Century.* New York: Farrar, Straus & Giroux.

Fröbel, Folker, Jürgen Heinrichs, and Otto Kreye. 1979. *The New International Division of Labour: Structural Unemployment in Industrialised Countries and Industrialisation in Developing Countries (Studies in Modern Capitalism).* New York: Cambridge University Press.

Gabe, Todd, and David Kraybill. 2002. "The Effect of State Economic Development Incentives on Employment Growth of Establishments." *Journal of Regional Science* 42(4): 703–730.

Ghartey, Edward. 1993. "Causal Relationship between Exports and Economic Growth: Some Empirical Evidence in Taiwan, Japan and the U.S." *Applied Economics* 25: 1145–1152.

Gordon, Ian, and H. Jayet. 1991. "Territorial Policies between Co-operation and Competition." Paper presented to the North American Congress of the Regional Science Association, New Orleans, November 7–11.

Graham, Edward M. 2003. "Attracting Foreign Direct Investment to the United States: the Joust Between the Federal Government and the States." In *The New Competition for Inward Investment: Companies, Institutions and Territorial Development,* Nicholas Phelps and Philip Raines, eds. Cheltenham, UK: Edward Elgar: pp. 61–78.

Graham, Edward M., and Mark A. A. Warner. 1994. "Multinationals and Competition Policy in North America." In *Multinationals in North America,* Lorraine Eden, ed. Calgary: University of Calgary Press, pp. 463–501.

Greenstone, Michael, and Enrico Moretti. 2003. "Bidding for Industrial Plants: Does Winning a 'Million Dollar Plant' Increase Welfare?" NBER working paper no. 9844. Cambridge, MA: National Bureau of Economic Research.

Guisinger, Stephen E. 1985. "A Comparative Study of Country Policies." In *Investment Incentives and Performance Requirements: Patterns of International Trade, Production, and Investment,* Stephen E. Guisinger and Associates, eds. New York: Praeger, pp. 1–55.

———. 1986. "Do Performance Requirements and Investment Incentives Work?" *World Economy* 9(1): 79–96.

———. 1992. "Rhetoric and Reality in International Business: A Note on the Effectiveness of Incentives." *Transnational Corporations* 1(2): 111–123.

———. 1995. "Harmonizing Investment Incentives in the APEC Process." *Journal of Northeast Asian Studies* 14(4): 38–50.

Helinska-Hughes, Ewa, and Michael Hughes. 2003. "Joining the Competition: Central and Eastern European Challenge to Established FDI Destinations." In *The New Competition for Inward Investment: Companies, Institutions and Territorial Development,* Nicholas Phelps and Philip Raines, eds. Cheltenham, UK: Edward Elgar, pp. 155–172.

Hines, James R. Jr. 1995. "Altered States: Taxes and the Location of Foreign Direct Investment in the United States." *American Economic Review* 86(5): 1076–1094.

Hobsbawm, Eric. 1975. *The Age of Capital: 1848–1875.* London: Weidenfeld & Nicholson.

Howes, Candace, and Ann Markusen. 1993. "Trade, Industry, and Economic Development." In *Trading Industries, Trading Regions,* Helzi Noponen, Julie Graham and Ann Markusen, eds. New York: Guilford Press, pp. 1–44.

Hughes, Duncan. 2006. "Queensland Snubs States on Poaching Agreement." *The Australian Financial Review.* August 2, 1:8.

Innis, Harold. 1930. *The Fur Trade in Canada: An Introduction to Canadian Economic History.* New Haven, CT: Yale University Press.

Jenkins, Rhys. 1987. *Transnational Corporations and the Latin American Automobile Industry.* Pittsburgh: University of Pittsburgh Press.

Jung, Woo, and Peyton Marshall. 1985. "Exports, Growth and Causality in Developing Countries." *Journal of Development Economics* 18(1): 1–12.

Kaldor, Nicholas. 1970. "The Case for Regional Policies." *Scottish Journal of Political Economy* 17(3): 337–348.

Kayne, Jay, and Molly Shonka. 1994. *Rethinking State Development Policies and Programs.* Washington, DC: National Governors' Association, Economic Development and Commerce Policy Studies, Center for Policy Research.

Keen, Michael, and Maurice Marchand. 1997. "Fiscal Competition and the Pattern of Public Spending." *Journal of Public Economics* 66(1): 33–53.

Krueger, Anne. 1974. "The Political Economy of the Rent-Seeking Society." *American Economic Review* 64(3): 291–303.

LeRoy, Greg. 2005. *The Great American Jobs Scam: Corporate Tax Dodging and the Myth of Job Creation.* San Francisco: Berrett-Koehler Publishers.

Leyton-Brown, David. 1979–1980. "The Mug's Game: Automotive Investment Incentives in Canada and the United States." *International Journal* 35(Winter) 170–184.

Lindstrom, Diane. 1978. *Economic Development in the Philadelphia Region, 1810–1850.* New York: Columbia University Press.

Llanes, Marlen. 1998. "Contrasts in Decentralization: Causes and Consequences of Success and Failure in Chile and Nicaragua." PhD dissertation, New Brunswick, NJ: Rutgers University.

Lotchin, Roger W. 1984. *The Martial Metropolis: U.S. Cities in War and Peace.* New York: Praeger.

Lovering, John. 2003. "MNCs and Wannabes—Inward Investment, Discourses of Regional Development, and the Regional Service Class." In *The New Competition for Inward Investment: Companies, Institutions and Territorial Development,* Nicholas Phelps and Philip Raines, eds. Cheltenham, UK: Edward Elgar, pp. 39–60.

Luger, Michael, and Suho Bae. 2005. "The Effectiveness of State Business Tax Incentives: The Case of North Carolina." *Economic Development Quarterly* 19(4): 327–345.

Markusen, Ann. 1974. "The Economics of Social Class and Metropolitan Local Government: A Summary." *National Tax Association, Papers and Proceedings,* May.

———. 1979. "Regional Economic Contraction and Intergovernmental Finance: A Theoretical Perspective." *National Tax Association, Papers and Proceedings,* May.

———. 1985. *Profit Cycles, Oligopoly and Regional Development.* Cambridge, MA: MIT Press.

———. 1994. "American Federalism and Regional Policy." *International Regional Science Review* 16(1, 2): 3–15.

———. 2003. "An Actor-Centered Approach to Economic Geographic Change." *Annals of the Japan Association of Economic Geographers* 49(5): 395–408.

———. 2007. "A Consumption Base Theory of Development: An Application to the Rural Cultural Economy." *Agricultural and Resource Economics Review* 36(1): 1–13.

Markusen, Ann, and Clelio Campolina Diniz. 2005. "Differential Regional Competitiveness: Opportunities and Constraints." In *Asymmetries in Regional Integration and Local Development,* Paolo Giordano, Francesco Lanzafame, and Jorg Meyer Stamer, eds. Washington, DC: Inter-American Development Bank, pp. 116–161.

Markusen, Ann, and Vickie Gwiasda. 1993. "Multi-Polarity and the Layering of Functions in World Cities: New York City's Struggle to Stay on Top." *International Journal of Urban and Regional Research* 18(2): 167–193.

Markusen, Ann, Peter Hall, Scott Campbell, and Sabina Deitrick. 1991. *The Rise of the Gunbelt: The Military Remapping of Industrial America.* New York: Oxford University Press.

Markusen, Ann, and Greg Schrock. 2006. "The Distinctive City: Divergent Patterns in American Urban Growth, Hierarchy and Specialization." *Urban Studies* 43(8): 1301–1323.

Molotch, Harvey. 1976. "The City as a Growth Machine." *The American Journal of Sociology* 82(2): 309–332.

Mountain Association for Community Economic Development. 2005. *Accounting for Impact: Economic Development Spending in Kentucky.* Berea, KY: MACED.

Myrdal, Gunnar. 1957. *Economic Theory and Underdeveloped Regions.* London: Duckworth.

Nelson, Peter B., and William B. Beyers. 1998. "Using Economic Base Models to Explain New Trends in Rural Income." *Growth and Change* 29(3): 295–318.

Newman, Robert J., and Dennis H. Sullivan. 1988. "Econometric Analysis of Business Tax Impacts on Industrial Location: What Do We Know and How Do We Know It?" *Journal of Urban Economics* 23(2): 215–234.

Nicholaides, Phedon. 2005. "State Aid and Taxation by Subnational Authorities." *European State Aid Law Quarterly* 3: 21–30.

———. 2006. "The Boundaries of Tax Autonomy." *European State Aid Law Quarterly* 1: 99–101.

Noponen, Helzi, Julie Graham, and Ann Markusen, eds. 1993. *Trading Industries, Trading Regions.* New York: Guilford Press.

North, Douglass. 1955. "Location Theory and Regional Economic Growth." *Journal of Political Economy* 63(3): 243–258.

———. 1966. *Economic Growth of the United States, 1790 to 1860.* New York: Norton.

Oates, Wallace. 1972. *Fiscal Federalism.* New York: Harcourt Brace Jovanovich.

Oman, Charles P. 2000. *Policy Competition for Foreign Direct Investment: A Study of Competition among Governments to Attract FDI.* Paris: Organisation for Economic Co-operation and Development.

Pastor, Robert A. 2001. *Toward a North American Community: Lessons from the Old World for the New.* Washington, DC: Institute for International Economics.

Peters, Alan, and Peter Fisher. 2002. *State Enterprise Zone Programs: Have They Worked?* Kalamazoo, MI: W.E. Upjohn Institute for Employment Research.

Phillips, Joseph, and Ernest Goss. 1995. "The Effect of State and Local Taxes on Economic Development: A Meta-Analysis." *Southern Economic Journal* 62(2): 197–316.

Raines, Philip. 2003. "Flows and Territories: The New Geography of Competition for Mobile Investment in Europe." In *The New Competition for Inward Investment: Companies, Institutions and Territorial Development,* Nicholas Phelps and Philip Raines, eds. Cheltenham, UK: Edward Elgar: pp. 119–136.

Reid, Neil, and Jay D. Gatrell. 2003. "Uncertainty, Incentives, and the Preservation of an Industrial Icon: The Case of Toledo Jeep." In *The New Competition for Inward Investment: Companies, Institutions and Territorial Development,* Nicholas Phelps and Philip Raines, eds. Cheltenham, UK: Edward Elgar: pp. 99–118.

Rodriguez-Pose, Andres, and Glauco Arbix. 2001. "Strategies of Waste: Bidding Wars in the Brazilian Automotive Sector." *International Journal of Urban and Regional Research* 25(1): 134–154.

Sbragia, Alberta. 1996. *Debt Wish: Entrepreneurial Cities, U.S. Federalism, and Economic Development.* Pittsburgh: University of Pittsburgh Press.

Schneider, Aaron. 2004. "Accountability and Capacity in Developing Country Federalism: Empowered States, Competitive Federalism." *Forum for Development Studies* 31(1): 33–56.

Schweke, William, Jim St. George, and Carl Rist. 1998. "Creating a 'Unified Development Budget' for North Carolina." Presentation at NEA Roundtable Discussion on Educational Finance and State Structural Deficits, October 19–20.

Schweke, William, and Robert Stumberg. 1999. "Could Economic Development Become Illegal in the New Global Policy Environment?" Working paper. New York: Corporation for Enterprise Development.

Sharma, Subhash, Mary Norris, and Daniel Wai-Wah-Cheung. 1991. "Exports and Economic Growth in Industrialized Countries." *Applied Economics* 23(4A): 697–708.

Sorsa, Piritta. 2003. "Special Investment Incentives May Come at a High Cost to the Economy." *Capital* 9: 8–14.

State of Victoria, Australia. 2003. "States Agree to End Investment Bidding Wars." Media Release, September 5. http://www.dpc.vic.gov.au/domino/Web_Notes/newmedia.nsf/955cbeae7df9460dca256c8c00152d2b/fb21eee7f27c4044ca256d9a0080fb0b!OpenDocument (accessed August 8, 2006).

Thomas, Kenneth P. 1997. *Capital Beyond Borders: States and Firms in the Auto Industry, 1960–1994.* Basingstoke, UK: Macmillan.

———. 2000. *Competing for Capital.* Washington, DC: Georgetown University Press.

———. 2007. "The Sources and Processes of Tax and Subsidy Competition." In *Reining in the Competition for Capital*, Ann Markusen, ed. Kalamazoo, MI: W.E. Upjohn Institute for Employment Research, pp. 43–55.

Tiebout, Charles. 1956a. "Exports and Regional Economic Growth." *Journal of Political Economy* 64(2): 160–169.

———. 1956b. "A Pure Theory of Local Expenditures." *Journal of Political Economy* 64(5): 416–424.

Tseng, Wanda. 2002. "FDI Conference—Concluding Remarks, August 17." Written as a result of the IMF Conference on Foreign Direct Investment: Opportunities and Challenges for Cambodia, held in Lao P.D.R. and Vietnam, Hanoi, Vietnam, April 16–17. http://www.imf.org/external/pubs/ft/seminar/2002/fdi/eng/ (accessed August 19, 2006).

Varsano, Ricardo, Sergio Guimaraes Ferreira, and Jose Roberto Afonso. 2002. "Fiscal Competition: A Bird's Eye View." Discussion paper no. 887. Rio de Janeiro, Brazil: Instituto de Pesquisa Economica Aplicada.

Venkatesan, R. 2000. *Study on Policy Competition among States in India for Attracting Direct Investment.* New Delhi, India: National Council of Applied Economic Research.

Wanna, John. 1980. "The Economic Development of South Australia: a Marxist Analysis." *Journal of Australian Political Economy* 9(November): 2–24.

Wasylenko, Michael. 1997. "Taxation and Economic Development: The State of the Economic Literature." *New England Economic Review* March/April: 37–52.

Weber, Rachel. 2002a. "Do Better Contracts Make Better Economic Development Incentives? *Journal of the American Planning Association* 68(1): 43–55.

———. 2002b. "Extracting Value from the City: Neoliberalism and Urban Redevelopment." *Antipode* 34(3): 519–540.

———. 2007. "Negotiating the Deal: Which Local Governments Have the Most Bargaining Leverage?" In *Reining in the Competition for Capital*, Ann Markusen, ed. Kalamazoo, MI: W.E. Upjohn Institute for Employment Research, pp. 141–159.

Williamson, Oliver. 1975. *Markets and Hierarchies: Analysis and Antitrust Implications A Study in the Economics of Internal Organization.* New York: The Free Press.

Wishlade, Fiona. 2004. "The Beginning of the End, or Just Another New Chapter? Recent Developments in EU Competition Policy Control of Regional State Aid." European Policy Research Papers no. 54. Glasgow: European Policies Research Centre, University of Strathclyde.

Wohlgemuth, Darin, and Maureen Kilkenny. 1998. "Firm Relocation Threats and Copy Cat Costs." *International Regional Science Review* 21(2): 139–162.

Wolkoff, Michael. 1992. "Is Economic Decision Making Rational?" *Urban Affairs Quarterly* 27: 340–355.

Wolman, Harold. 1988. "Local Economic Development Policy: What Explains the Divergence between Policy Analysis and Political Behavior?" Journal of Urban Affairs 10(1): 19–28.

Wolman, Harold, and David Spitzley. 1996. "The Politics of Local Economic Development." *Economic Development Quarterly* 10(2): 115–150.

Wood, Andrew. 2003. "The Politics of Orchestrating Inward Investment: Institutions, Policy and Practice in the Industrial Midwest." In *The New Competition for Inward Investment: Companies, Institutions and Territorial Development,* Nicholas Phelps and Philip Raines, eds. Cheltenham, UK: Edward Elgar, pp. 79–98.

World Trade Organization. 2006. *World Trade Report 2006: Exploring the Links Between Subsidies, Trade and the WTO.* http://www.wto.org/english/news_e/pres06_e/pr447_e.htm (accessed August 8, 2006).

Xu, Jiang, and Anthony Yeh. 2005. "City Repositioning and Competitiveness Building in Regional Development: New Development Strategies in Guangzhou, China." *International Journal of Urban and Regional Research* 29(2): 283–308.

Yeung, Godfrey. 2003. "Scrambling for FDI: The Experience of Guangdong Province in Southern China." In *The New Competition for Inward Investment: Companies, Institutions and Territorial Development,* Nicholas Phelps and Philip Raines, eds. Cheltenham, UK: Edward Elgar, pp. 193–212.

Zodrow, George R., and Peter Mieszkowski. 1986. "Pigou, Tiebout, Property Taxation, and the Underprovision of Local Public Goods." *Journal of Urban Economics* 19(3): 356–370.

2
The Sources and Processes of Tax and Subsidy Competition

Kenneth P. Thomas
University of Missouri–St. Louis

Tax and subsidy competition has two structural sources: the need of governments for investment, what Winters (1996) calls the "investment imperative" in his updating of Lindblom (1977); and the mobility of capital. Together, they create a dynamic in which governments must compete for investment in what, since World War II, has been an ever-widening market. Today, as virtually all governments engage in this behavior, the "market for investment" is one where the "sellers" (potential investors) have certain advantages over the "buyers" (governments).[1] First, capital mobility is increasing, making more locations feasible sites for any particular investment, thereby intensifying competition. Examples range from national and regional governments bidding on auto assembly plants, to suburbs fighting to land the sales tax revenue that comes from a retail development. Second, while uncoordinated sanctioning of adverse government policies occurs, there also exists coordination among direct investors through the operations of site location consultants. These consulting firms work to extract greater concessions in negotiations over individual projects, and in doing so create an atmosphere where governments believe it is necessary to offer incentives to be considered for an investment project at all. Finally, information asymmetries favor firms over governments. The latter have little idea of what is truly necessary to offer to land a particular investment, nor do they know when the next desirable investment opportunity will come along (particularly at the level of truly large projects, of which there are only about 200–300 annually in the United States). Coordination of government policies is the logical way to blunt the dynamic of competition for investment. Only the European Union, however, has proved successful at this; favorable basic laws (the Treaty of Rome) and a centralized monitoring and enforcement capacity have enabled the EU to exert some control over the investment-attraction activities of Member State, regional, and local governments within its territory (Thomas 2000).

This chapter begins with a discussion of why a market for investment arises in a capitalist system with multiple polities. It highlights the investment imperative and documents the growing mobility of capital. It argues that the two-sided prisoner's dilemma that comprises a market has been reduced to a single prisoner's dilemma among the buyers of investment due to inherent advantages investors possess. This result emphasizes the need for comprehensive, cooperative solutions among governments, at the state level to regulate cities' behavior, and at the federal level to regulate states.

The bulk of this chapter analyzes the use and abuse of location incentives—those subsidies, of whatever form, that are used to attract investment to a particular jurisdiction. It briefly reviews the potential efficiency, equity, and environmental drawbacks to these subsidies, and then focuses on several case studies that illustrate the main policy dilemmas that arise with the use of location incentives. Several important themes stand out: backroom deals, lack of transparency and effective citizen participation, the pernicious influence of site location consultants, and the comingling of eminent domain abuse with subsidy abuse.

The cases considered all come from the St. Louis metropolitan region. Missouri has been prominently noted as one of the country's worst abusers of tax increment financing (LeRoy 2005, p. 146), and as one of the worst abusers of eminent domain (Berliner 2003, p. 117). The St. Louis region is notably more abusive than the Kansas City region, as documented by the Brookings Institution (Luce 2003, p. 16; see also LeRoy 2005, p. 146).

The chapter concludes with a number of policy recommendations. To preview them briefly, they are the introduction of transparency and accountability legislation, as pioneered in Minnesota, guarantees of effective citizen participation in the economic development process, a national ban on relocation subsidies, and eventual establishment of rules about what is and is not an allowable subsidy, along with the means to monitor and enforce these rules.

THE MARKET FOR INVESTMENT

The market for investment consists of governments competing for investment and firms competing for investment sites. It arises as a result of two structural features of the world's political-economic system. First, as it has been for over 500 years, the global economic system is capitalist in nature. Since most economic activity is private under capitalism, the ability of government to produce the investment it needs is limited. Second, the world is a political system with multiple polities. This is the ultimate structural basis for the mobility of capital, as Chase-Dunn (1981, p. 31) argues. Thus, in a capitalist system with multiple polities, governments must compete with each other for investment, whether the competition takes place between nations or in subnational units such as U.S. states, Canadian provinces, and cities.

Governments depend on private investors for investment because without it there is neither economic activity to tax (and hence no way to attain their goals, whatever they might be) nor economic outcomes conducive to reelection. This classic formulation of Lindblom (1977) (the "privileged position" of business) has been updated by Winters (1996, p. 1–41), who extends it to nondemocratic states, and grounds it in more general theories of resource dependence. Because securing investment is a prerequisite to any goal government might have, Winters calls this the "investment imperative." However, if capital were not mobile, governments and firms would simply negotiate over the conditions of investment (perhaps only implicitly). The addition of capital mobility intensifies this dynamic by forcing governments to compete for investment with other governments in the same structural situation.

In general, capital mobility refers to the *ability* of owners of capital to place it in a variety of locations (this must be distinguished from actual capital movements). For nonfinancial capital (the focus of this chapter), we can think of it also as the ability to coordinate production over an extended geographical scale. For both financial and nonfinancial capital, these are importantly determined by the costs of transportation and communications. These costs have been falling dramatically, especially since the end of World War II. For example, the cost of international phone calls fell in real terms approximately 95 percent between 1945 and 1990, and international passenger transport costs fell by about 80 percent in the same period. We have, of course, witnessed further innovations in both of these areas, and rapidly declining costs to use them (Thomas 1997, p. 64–66).

As mentioned above, the concept of a "market for investment" suggests that there is competition among sellers (investors) as well as among buyers. In practice, there is a lot more competition for investment than competition for investment sites. First, capital mobility is increasing. This means there is an increasing number of economically feasible sites for any given investment, leading to an intensification of the bidding wars over each investment, as firms have more options open to them *and* the collective action problem faced by governments becomes less tractable (Thomas 2000, p. 27–29).

Second, governments suffer from substantial information asymmetries in their courting of investment. While a company interested in investing in a particular jurisdiction will have gathered a tremendous amount of information on that location, its political leaders, etc., the government may not even know the identity of the firm they are dealing with; they may only talk to a site location consultant shopping for incentives (at least at the early stages). Government officials will not know the firm's true decision criteria, and may not even know whether there are sites with which they are competing (Thomas 2000, p. 32). Finally, they do not know when the next desirable project will come along. Loveridge (1996, p. 152) estimated that there were only 200–300 large-scale projects annually in the United States, with 15,000 investment attraction agencies pursuing them.

The third advantage favoring firms over states is that while states must organize to achieve cooperative results, uncoordinated action by firms may lead to their taking the same action. For example, if a given state inaugurates stricter antipollution laws, the likelihood is that any firm affected by this will mark that state off its list for future investment. This need not require any cooperation or even communication by the firms involved; it simply is a logical reaction to the new incentives each faces, as Lindblom (1977) has emphasized. In addition to this uncoordinated sanctioning of adverse government policies, the widespread use of site location consultants has introduced an element of coordination into the behavior of direct investors that bond rating agencies provide for bond and stock investors. Sinclair (1994, pp. 144–145) has shown that bond ratings are affected by the rating agencies' preferences for government policies that have no necessary impact on their ability to service a loan. Similarly, site location consultants, in addition to trying to drive the very best bargain for their clients on each individual investment, also strive consciously to create a climate in which governments believe it is necessary to offer incentives in order to be considered for any investment. They do this both in private, preliminary discussions about individual projects, and through public comments in the press. In this way, location consulting firms help to coordinate the behavior of companies seeking investment sites. Moreover, they exacerbate the information asymmetry discussed earlier, and often receive a percentage of the incentive they obtain for their clients, giving them further incentive to drive up incentive packages (Buchholz 1998, Chapter 5).

Taken together, these three factors explain why the market for investment, a two-sided prisoner's dilemma in theory like any other market, in fact reduces to a single prisoner's dilemma among the buyers of investment. The usefulness of this model is demonstrated in both the United States and Canada, where voluntary "no-raiding" agreements among states or provinces have been universally unsuccessful (Thomas 2000, pp. 167–168; 177). The ultimate solution to these bidding wars lies in what game theory would call third-party enforcement, which means that states must regulate the investment attraction activities of their local governments, and the federal government must curb the bidding war among the states. We are, however, a long way from such a solution being politically viable, so the next section will consider the processes of competition for investment with a view toward illuminating the near-term reforms that may be achievable.

LOCATION INCENTIVES

Location incentives are those subsidies used to attract investment to a particular jurisdiction. They can take many forms: direct grant, tax break, free land, subsidized loan, etc. Some subsidies that started out as incentives to attract investors to a particular state have become so widely copied that it is now more reasonable to consider them what the EU calls "operating aids," that is, subsidies for ongoing production. The classic example is the sales tax exemption for new equipment. The

Council of State Governments (Chi and Leatherby 1997, p. 2) classifies these tax breaks as "incentives," but their incentive function has been completely blunted by the almost total spread of these programs throughout the country. A related form of subsidy with locational goals is the "retention incentive," a subsidy given to prevent a firm from leaving its present jurisdiction. New York City, whose companies are frequently targeted by other jurisdictions, awarded over $2 billion in retention subsidies between 1987 and 2000 (Good Jobs New York 2003).

Location subsidies are not always a bad policy. However, like all subsidies, they can have important potential drawbacks in the areas of efficiency, equity, and the environment. In terms of efficiency, subsidies can induce firms to locate to inefficient locations, to continue inefficient production, and can harm efficient unsubsidized competitors. The major equity concern is that subsidies go to the owners of capital, who receive funds from the average taxpayer. This makes the after-tax, after-subsidy distribution of income more uneven than it would have been in the absence of subsidies. Finally, for an important subset of subsidies, the aided activity has harmful environmental consequences, such as building in a floodplain. These factors should give us pause when we consider whether a subsidy is an appropriate policy in a specific situation (Thomas 2000, pp. 4–5, 169–170). This section now turns to several case studies that illustrate the main policy dilemmas that arise with the use of location incentives. Rather than discussing high-profile national searches, such as those recently conducted by Boeing, I will analyze several of the far more common smaller deals funded by municipal and/or state governments.

Cases

In 1997, Mastercard International announced its intention to consolidate several St. Louis area facilities to a single location, not necessarily in Missouri. A consolidation can lead to an intense bidding war because it means that the firm involved is threatening to disinvest from one or more locations. As psychologists and game theorists have noted, people tend to fear the loss of an existing benefit more than they fear not receiving a new benefit of the same size ("hysteresis") (Hardin 1982, pp. 82–83). The auto industry, which has suffered from overcapacity in North America for decades, has seen several major cases of head-to-head consolidation, such as GM's pitting of Arlington, Texas, and Ypsilanti, Michigan, against each other (Thomas 1997, p. 127). In the Mastercard case, the company was reported to have considered 15 cities altogether, with the final decision coming down to a faceoff between Dallas and the outer-ring St. Louis suburb of O'Fallon (*Saint Louis Post-Dispatch*, various issues). For Mastercard's anticipated investment of just over $90 million, the state of Missouri put together an incentive package worth $42 million, plus several million more in tax abatements from O'Fallon and the local Francis Howell School District.[2] This example highlights several of the points made earlier: Mastercard clearly had a better idea of what was going on with the state and local governments in Missouri than Missouri government officials knew of Mastercard's intentions and options. There were numerous feasible options for the site, so Missouri officials could not simply assume that Mastercard was bluffing about the possibility of leaving the state altogether. While press reports do not indicate whether Mastercard used a site location consultant, the company apparently used a tactic consultants recommend. Without having access to Mastercard decision makers and documentation, it is impossible to say what the lowest amount of subsidy the company was willing to accept, but it likely was considerably less than what it received.

Much of what currently passes for "economic development" in U.S. localities is the subsidization of retail facilities. While Missouri likely overpaid for Mastercard, it was at least retaining jobs (and has since added several hundred new jobs at the site) that pay on the order of $50,000 per year. Retail jobs, by contrast, contain a high proportion of low-pay, zero or low-benefit, often part-time jobs. Why economic development agencies pursue them so aggressively is difficult to explain.[3] For example, tax increment financing (TIF) is a subsidy widely used around the country for attracting retail operations (auto dealerships in California, Wal-Marts everywhere, mixed-use retail/housing developments, etc.). In many cases, TIF is close to a straight cash grant in its structure: developers receive their money as soon as they have paid for the eligible costs specified in a redevelopment plan, while the city obtains the money to pay the developer by issuing revenue bonds backed by the incremental tax revenue the project is expected to generate.[4] When state law allows a municipality to capture some of the sales tax increment, for example 50 percent in Missouri, a Wal-Mart can be shopped around to cities until it finds one willing to give it a TIF. Municipal governments have proved generally willing, but often have received stiff resistance from citizen organizations that form to fight the plan. Similarly, independent developers dangle pet projects in front of municipal governments until one bites. Numerous examples of sales tax-driven TIFs exist in the St. Louis metropolitan area, including the suburbs of Richmond Heights (Galleria), Brentwood (Brentwood Pointe, Brentwood Promenade), Maplewood (Wal-Mart), and Des Peres (West County Center), the last a case of alleged blight in a city with a median family income over $90,000 in 1990 (*St. Louis Post-Dispatch* various issues).

O'Fallon, Missouri (estimated population 65,000), is the fastest growing city in the state. St. Charles County, in which it is located, has a higher adjusted median household income than any other county in both Missouri and Illinois (*O'Fallon Journal* 2005). Located across the Missouri River from St. Louis County, O'Fallon and St. Charles County in general are experiencing rapid migration from the city of St. Louis and its inner-ring suburbs. Yet officials in the main municipalities (O'Fallon, Wentzville, St. Peters, and St. Charles) have been more than willing to subsidize retail development, as if it weren't going to follow the residents. St. Peters has used TIF to build a Costco discount supercenter. St. Charles TIF'd the redevelopment of a shopping center located just off the exit from the main thoroughfare in Missouri, Interstate Highway 70. In 2003, O'Fallon proposed to bulldoze its downtown and give the developers involved $47 million in subsidies to build a new one at a total cost of $220 million. This case (in which I was an active participant, having moved there in 2002) illustrates many of the common problems seen in competition for investment. The following account is based on my experience in the battle against this project as well as reports in the *St. Louis Post-Dispatch* and the *O'Fallon Journal.*

The project began shrouded in secrecy, even from members of the Downtown Partnership, a consultative group that had been organized by the city. When the city announced the project in March 2003, a majority of the Downtown Partnership's members resigned.

To determine if downtown redevelopment qualified for the use of tax increment financing, the city hired the consulting firm Peckham Guyton Albers and Viets (PGAV). Like its competitors in the St. Louis market, PGAV has virtually never seen a TIF project it said did not qualify, and PGAV concluded that O'Fallon's mixed-use "Downtown Plan" qualified for TIF. By contrast, in Kansas City the Economic Development Council has full-time staff to work for the TIF Commission. Of the proposed TIFs studied by the Kansas City City Auditor, 43 percent were discouraged by TIF staff, 24 percent were denied by the TIF Commission, and 33 percent were approved (Funkhouser 1998, p. 88). The small size of municipalities in the St. Louis area reduces the level of expertise available to them and increases the number of competitors for any development project. Unsurprisingly, the Brookings Institution (Luce 2003, p. 16) found that there are far more abuses of the original intent of the TIF statute (i.e., to develop economically deprived or "blighted" areas) in the St. Louis area than in the Kansas City area.

Many of the approximately 100 businesses and 50 homeowners did not want to move, and the city made it clear that it would use its power of eminent domain if necessary. As has been the case in many other instances around the country, subsidy abuse goes hand in hand with what might be called "eminent domain abuse," where rather than taking property for infrastructure or other government uses, a city will make a legislative finding that a private development project is a "public use" and replace one private business with another. U.S. Supreme Court rulings have long directed lower courts to give great weight to legislative findings, and up to now they have been virtually impossible to challenge in court, for eminent domain (most recently in the 5–4 *Kelo v. New London* case) or for tax increment financing. However, the Michigan Supreme Court ruled 9–0 in 2004 that such takings were unconstitutional, and the U.S. Supreme Court in *Kelo v. New London* held that states could give property owners greater protection against economic development projects if they so desired.[5]

In Missouri, municipalities are required to do a cost-benefit analysis of any TIF project outside Kansas City that is carried out as part of the consultant's determination of the project's eligibility for TIF. The problem here, as we see in other examples of competition for investment, is that these analyses end at the jurisdictional border. Indeed, they often end at the development area's border, ignoring the effects of subsidized competition on sales of other firms, making much of the sales tax increment "phantom increment," as I called it in testimony before the O'Fallon Board of Aldermen.

In many cases, elected officials try to thwart citizen participation. In Hazelwood, Missouri (an inner-ring suburb of St. Louis), the city refused to accept charter amendment petitions, urged people to remove their names from them, and passed the ordinances establishing a TIF at their last meeting before Christmas, leaving opponents 20 days to acquire signatures referring the ordinances to the ballot at the worst possible time of the year to do so (they did not get enough signatures in time). In O'Fallon, the city threatened to charge people a fee for putting up a "Preserve Old Town O'Fallon" yard sign (it eventually backed down), refused to allow signs in Board of Aldermen meetings, and its public relations firm set up an Astroturf "citizens' group" to fight the opposition Old Town Preservation Committee. However, in the O'Fallon case, citizen opposition was so widespread that a majority of aldermen were swayed against the project, and the mayor withdrew it in August 2003.

CONCLUSION

This chapter highlights both the structural sources of competition for investment and the concrete policy issues that arise when a city or state pursues an investment. There are several policy conclusions we should take away from this analysis. First, too much economic development activity takes place behind closed doors. In many states, there is no way to even find out how much state and local governments give in subsidies. The first recommendation, then, is to adopt transparency and accountability legislation, as pioneered in Minnesota, which requires state and local governments to report all subsidies individually and to take sanctions against firms that fail to keep their commitments. If the true extent of subsidization becomes widely known, I believe it will become a more salient issue than it has been in many states. Some states may need strengthening of their Sunshine Laws (in O'Fallon, aggressive use of Missouri's Sunshine Law yielded a great deal of valuable information). In addition, there should be a guarantee of a referendum on large projects which completely change the character of a city (something unavailable in O'Fallon's case due to its classification as a Fourth Class city). Second, Congress should enact a national ban on relocation subsidies. Since these merely move jobs from one place to another with no benefit to the country as a whole, they are the most egregious type of subsidy and one that is widely recognized as a problem. At the time of this writing, the case *Cuno v. Daimler-Chrysler* is before the U.S. Supreme Court. If the Appellate Court's decision is upheld, it would invalidate certain investment tax credits in Ohio and other states (Johnston 2006). Similarly, states should ban the use of in-state relocation subsidies, which has been a problem with TIF use in Minnesota's Twin Cities area (LeRoy and Hinkley 2000). In the long run, I would argue that we need to move closer to the European Union's model of establishing rules about what is and is not an allowable subsidy, along with the means to monitor and enforce these rules. That has been the only model of successfully controlling location and other subsidies (Thomas 2000, pp. 238–240).

Notes

The author thanks the participants in the "Reining in the Competition for Capital" conference for their feedback, along with comments from Dennis Judd, Terry Jones, Lana Stein, and Andrew Glassberg.

1. The term "market for investment" was coined by Guisinger (1985, p. 13). He considers firms to be the "buyers" of investment sites, and governments to the "sellers" of those locations. However, due to the structural imbalances described below, it is more natural to see the market as truly one for the investments rather than the investment sites, making states the "buyers" and companies the "sellers."
2. Interestingly, multiple Lexis/Nexis searches of MasterCard and Dallas, as well as contact with the business editor of the *Dallas Morning News*, turned up no references to such negotiations in Texas publications. This suggests that while the company said it had other options it was considering, it was in fact was only considering the St. Louis area. One site location consultant told me he routinely recommends this stratagem to his clients. Numerous instances of this practice are documented in LeRoy (2005). Note that I reject his contention in Chapter 2 that subsidies almost never affect location choices. This is inconsistent with his acceptance of a prisoner's dilemma model of avoiding subsidies. If subsidies do not increase the probability of landing an investment or cutting a ribbon, a prisoner's dilemma cannot arise.
3. It may have to do with the size of the municipality. Smaller governments are usually not held accountable by their voters for overall macroeconomic outcomes, so their economic development efforts are aimed more at tax revenue than job creation (Thomas 2000, p. 44n29). However, by the logic of my model, the over-

all location pattern of retail facilities is likely to be little changed if all municipalities use location subsidies than if all refrained from doing so.
4. In Missouri, many TIFs, especially smaller ones, are financed on a pay-as-you-go basis. In such cases, TIF is not equivalent to a cash grant because the stretching out of payments over time reduces the present value relative to the nominal value. See Missouri Department of Economic Development (2005).
5. See the following pages from the Institute for Justice Web site: http:/www.ij.org/private_property/michigan/index.html and http://www.ij.org/private_property/connecticut/index.html (accessed February 2005).

References

Berliner, Dana. 2003. *Public Power, Private Gain.* Washington, DC: Institute for Justice.

Buchholz, D. 1998. "Competition and Corporate Incentives: Dilemmas in Economic Development." PhD dissertation, Durham, NC: Duke University.

Chase-Dunn, C. 1981. "Interstate System and Capitalist World-Economy: One Logic or Two?" *International Studies Quarterly* 25(1): 19–42.

Chi, K.S., and D. Leatherby. 1997. *State Business Incentives: Trends and Options for the Future.* Lexington, KY: Council of State Governments.

Funkhouser, M. 1998. *Performance Audit: Tax Increment Financing.* Kansas City, MO: Office of the City Auditor.

Good Jobs New York. 2003. Online database of New York City retention subsidies. http://www.goodjobsny.org/deals.htm (accessed February 16, 2004).

Guisinger, Stephen E. 1985. "A Comparative Study of Country Policies." In *Investment Incentives and Performance Requirements,* S.E. Guisinger and Associates, ed. New York: Praeger, pp. 1–55.

Hardin, R. 1982. *Collective Action.* Baltimore: Johns Hopkins University Press for Resources for the Future.

Johnston, David Cay. 2006. "Justices to Weigh Tax Breaks." *New York Times,* March 1, C:1.

LeRoy, Greg. 2005. *The Great American Jobs Scam: Corporate Tax Dodging and the Myth of Job Creation.* San Francisco: Berrett-Koehler Publishers.

LeRoy, Greg, and Sara Hinkley. 2000. *Another Way Sprawl Happens: Economic Development Subsidies in a Twin Cities Suburb.* Washington, DC: Good Jobs First.

Lindblom, C.E. 1977. *Politics and Markets: The World's Political-Economic Systems.* New York: Basic Books.

Loveridge, S. 1996. "On the Continuing Popularity of Industrial Recruitment." *Economic Development Quarterly* 10(2): 151–158.

Luce, T. 2003. *Tax Increment Financing in the Kansas City and St. Louis Metropolitan Areas.* Washington, DC: Brookings Institution.

Missouri Department of Economic Development. 2005. *2004 Annual Report: Tax Increment Financing Projects in Missouri.* Jefferson City, MO: MDED.

O'Fallon Journal. Various issues.

Saint Louis Post-Dispatch. Various issues.

Sinclair, T.J. 1994. "Passing Judgment: Credit Rating Processes as Regulatory Mechanisms of Governance in the Emerging World Order." *Review of International Political Economy* 1(1): 133–159.

Thomas, Kenneth P. 1997. *Capital Beyond Borders: States and Firms in the Auto Industry, 1960–94.* London: Macmillan.

———. 2000. *Competing for Capital: Europe and North America in a Global Era.* Washington, DC: Georgetown University Press.

Winters, J.A. 1996. *Power in Motion: Capital Mobility and the Indonesian State.* Ithaca, NY: Cornell University Press.

3
The Fiscal Consequences of Competition for Capital

Peter Fisher
University of Iowa

To state and local officials, competition for capital has become the driving principle underlying economic development policy, and the policy tools most readily available are tax cuts and direct subsidies. Thus, this chapter is partly about the long-run revenue gains or losses from economic development incentive programs. Such programs are invariably touted as measures to expand the tax base and increase revenues, and officials generally assume that incentives in the long run more than pay for themselves. Is this really the case?

This chapter is also about the ways in which competition for capital alters tax and budget policies more broadly. Has the perception by state and local officials that they must constantly compete for investment and jobs changed the structure of state and local tax systems? Has there been a broad shift away from taxes on business? Has this increased the regressivity of state-local tax systems? Have budget priorities shifted as well?

COMPETITION FOR CAPITAL: THE POLICY TOOLS

The need for the broader view becomes clear as soon as one attempts to determine what constitutes an effort to compete for capital. Let's consider the range of possibilities, from the narrowest to the broadest.

Discretionary incentives
- One-time subsidy packages negotiated with a specific firm.

- Discretionary grant or loan programs provided out of annual appropriations, where the firm must apply for funding. The programs could subsidize capital expenditure, provide free public infrastructure improvements, or pay for job training.
- Discretionary tax abatements and tax increment financing. These programs require no explicit funding, and so have no annual limits statewide.

Entitlement incentives

- Investment tax credits, jobs tax credits, or R&D credits under the state corporate income tax. Here the firm receives the benefit automatically, provided the investment is in an eligible sector and that the size of the investment or number of new jobs exceeds some threshold. There may be geographic targeting: enterprise zones are the major example.
- Local property tax abatements, where they are largely formula driven, once eligibility criteria have been met.

Tax cuts

- Competitive tax provisions. These are features of the tax code that apply to every corporation (though not equally) and that do not require investment or job creation on the part of the business, but where there is nonetheless a competition rationale presented to justify the tax expenditure. Examples are single-factor apportionment, exemption of inventories from property taxation, and exemption of fuel and utilities from the sales tax. These tax provisions are often advertised by economic development agencies as reasons to locate in their state.
- Broad-based tax cuts, such as rate cuts, that apply across the board to any business. Again, the arguments made in their favor may differ little from the more explicit development incentives: we have to cut taxes to remain competitive. The arguments may be extended beyond taxes that clearly fall directly on business to cuts in individual income taxes, for example, or the tax on capital gains.

Before addressing the broader effects of competition on tax structure and regressivity, we will explore what we know about the fiscal effects of explicit economic development subsidies: the discretionary incentive programs and the entitlement tax incentives. We begin by attempting to define what we mean by "fiscal effects" in such cases.

MEASURING FISCAL EFFECTS

What is a fiscal benefit? A particular governmental action (such as providing a direct subsidy or cutting a tax) will have a positive fiscal effect if, in the long run, it increases business activity and the new activity adds more in tax revenues than it causes in additional public service costs. There will then be a fiscal surplus to be distributed to the rest of the taxpayers as lower taxes or better services or both. (If the fiscal surplus materializes only after some period of time, the discounted value must be positive.) Public service costs can rise in a number of ways, from direct expenditure benefiting new businesses, to increased expenditure to serve new populations induced to in-migrate, to rising labor costs for government because of upward pressure on wages and land prices.

This formulation ignores the distributional question: How is the surplus distributed among the population? As we will see, distribution is an important issue, but for now we will focus on measuring the fiscal surplus. The logical place to begin is with the direct revenue from a new business. When an incentive program is put in place, subsequent investment will produce both direct revenue gains and direct revenue losses. The investment that would not have occurred but for the incentive produces a gain; the remaining investment produces a loss, to the extent that it received the incentives (because they were entitlements or because they were awarded on the false belief that they were necessary). As we will see, we have some pretty good estimates of direct fiscal effects.

What about the direct expenditure necessitated by new business? It is of course very difficult to measure or generalize about the local investment in infrastructure, or the ongoing increases in expenditure for services such as police and fire protection, that is caused by new business activity. It is a common assumption that these expenditures are not large, and that business activity generally produces a sizable fiscal surplus. That's certainly the argument made for seeking new commercial and industrial tax base—that this will permit tax relief for residents.

Indirect effects are even more problematic. Here we must estimate the net fiscal effects of growth in the labor force or reduction in the local unemployment rate, including demands for additional services and the additional taxes produced by in-migrants or newly employed residents. These effects come about not only from the employment in the business receiving the subsidy, but new investment also may stimulate business expansion in supplying sectors, or in demanding sectors (who previously had to import inputs).

When new jobs are created in a community, those new jobs must be filled by persons in that community's labor market in one of four ways:

1) By drawing people from the ranks of the unemployed within the labor market.

2) By drawing people into the area's labor force who were not previously seeking work.

3) By inducing people to migrate into the labor market.

4) By drawing people away from existing jobs (which are then left unfilled; if these jobs are, in turn, filled in one of the other ways, such as through in-migration, then the ultimate effect of the new jobs is simply in-migration).

In other words, new jobs can have four effects: lowering the unemployment rate, increasing the labor force participation rate, inducing in-migration, or displacing existing jobs. Research on the effects of "labor demand shocks"—a sudden increase in jobs as a result of a new plant or plant expansion—indicates that for every 100 new jobs in a region, about 7 will be filled from the ranks of the unemployed, about 16 by drawing existing residents into the labor force, and the remaining 77 from in-migration (Bartik 1991, p. 95). These are the long-run effects (after several years); in the short run, there may be a more substantial reduction in unemployment, but as in-migration continues in response to the new job opportunities, the unemployment rate will creep back up again. Research also shows that such labor demand shocks will not have a significant long-run effect on wage rates for a given occupation; thus there will be little or no job displacement (Bartik 1991, Chapter 6).

If residential development does not pay its way—and research generally shows that it does not—then in-migrants represent a fiscal drain (Altshuler and Gomez-Ibanez 1993, Chapter 6). The secondary effects of incentive-induced growth thus could be negative, since most of the jobs will in the long run be filled by in-migration. The remaining jobs, filled by existing residents, should produce a fiscal surplus, since those residents will presumably be paying more taxes but consuming the same (or perhaps less) in services. But this surplus (from 22 percent of the jobs) will probably not be enough to offset losses from the remainder.

There is some evidence on the net fiscal effects of concomitant expansions in employment and population. A study of Montgomery County, Maryland, concluded that for manufacturing facilities, distribution centers, small office buildings, and even R&D facilities, the direct fiscal surplus from the business investment was insufficient (or just barely sufficient) to offset the negative fiscal effects of accompanying residential growth (Altshuler and Gomez-Ibanez 1993). Only large, white-collar office facilities generated a net surplus. Furthermore, Ladd and Yinger (1991) found that population growth produced an increase in the cost of city services. This is because as cities grow, labor and land costs rise, and congestion increases production costs; these effects outweigh the limited cost reductions achieved through economies of scale. The issue is not completely settled, however, due to the methodological issues that abound in performing a fiscal impact analysis.

This raises an obvious question: If a new manufacturing or distribution facility under normal conditions does not generally produce a large enough fiscal surplus to offset the fiscal losses produced by the residential development that follows that expansion, or produces only a slight net surplus, how could we expect *subsidized* business expansion to pay for itself?

The upshot is that it may well make sense to focus our attention on the direct tax effects of incentives. While pro-incentive or pro-growth advocates are fond of adding generous helpings of multiplier effects to their analyses, when we consider all of the evidence it seems likely that the fiscal consequences of these multiplier effects, and of the effects of population growth induced directly by the plant itself, are unlikely to be positive. (The exception is probably a project creating high-paying, white-collar jobs.) When combined with the fact that we also must ignore the direct public expenditure effects of business investment, because we can't measure it, the direct tax consequences of incentives almost surely provide a more favorable view of the fiscal effects of incentives than would a more comprehensive analysis. If the direct business tax effects are negative, it is quite unlikely that the overall effects are anything but even more negative.

The way for a community to attempt to ensure that the direct tax effects are positive is to a) make sure you don't give away all of your tax revenue to get the facility in the first place or b) make sure the facility stays around long enough to pay a significant amount of taxes, and c) provide incentives only in cases where the incentives are decisive. The trend is to provide ever more generous incentives, and we have already seen instances where states in effect give away everything, including the personal taxes of the employees (Michigan's Renaissance Zones, Pennsylvania's Keystone Opportunity Zones). And though almost everyone claims to be successfully applying a "but for" test in their discretionary incentive programs, given the asymmetry of information in negotiating subsidies, it is highly unlikely that this is the case.

So what do we know about the direct tax consequences of subsidies and incentives? We look first at the most publicized subsidies—the large, package deals offered to land a particular plant—and then at the tax incentives and tax cuts that function as entitlements, where most of the research has been focused.

THE PACKAGE DEALS

The large negotiated incentive packages represent the best case scenario for positive fiscal effects because there is a greater probability that the incentive package may be decisive. The community is presumably exercising discretion, not simply handing out incentives by formula to all comers, and there is at least some indication that the community would not get the business without incentives, in light of what the competing locations have to offer, in economic advantages as well as incentives. While the costs per job have escalated dramatically, proponents may argue that the costs are not really costs at all, because the firm and the employees (and all the multiplier effects) will generate tax revenues far exceeding the incentive cost.

Considerable attention has been paid recently to a paper by Greenstone and Moretti (2003) for the National Bureau of Economic Research that purports to demonstrate that communities benefit from offering subsidies to large plants. Greenstone and Moretti looked at a sample of major facility locations reported in *Site Selection* magazine, which identified not only the county that "won" the plant but the one or two runner-up counties as well. The authors found that the winner and loser counties had similar rates of income growth prior to the plant opening, but that the winner counties subsequently experienced a statistically significant boost in the rate of growth of wages and also of property values, as well as government revenues and expenditures. Princeton economist Alan Krueger, in a column in the *New York Times*, praised the study as "compelling" and claimed it showed that cities that offer generous incentive packages and win a large facility "seem to benefit from the arrangement" (Krueger 2003). The clear implication is that even incentives amounting to hundreds of thousands of dollars per job are worth the expense.

A closer look reveals that this study tells us less than it might appear with respect to the fiscal consequences of such deals. The results in terms of economic growth are not surprising; what they show is that, comparing similar counties, the one that gets a new plant does better than the one that doesn't—the growth trends in wage levels get a bump up. It would be surprising, in fact, if they didn't. Nor is it remarkable that both revenue and expenditure rose in the counties getting the economic boost from the new plant; one would expect that population growth would require additional services, and local governments must balance their budgets. Expenditures, at least in some categories, exceeded the increase in population, but we do not know if this reflects better services or higher costs of production. In sum, the results do not tell us whether the plants generated a fiscal surplus. There could well be higher taxes on residents and other firms to support the rising expenditures necessitated by the new plant and its employees.

What about the finding that property values increased? Greenstone and Moretti (2003) argue that the net effects of the new plant—the increased job opportunities and increased economic activity generally, as well as the cost and revenue effects of the subsidies and increased tax base—will be capitalized into property values. If property values rise, it indicates that the net effect of the new plant has been positive. In other words, the cost of the incentives was more than offset by the other benefits of the new facility. Note that Greenstone and Moretti do not claim that the fiscal benefits exceed the fiscal costs. Local government could well be facing increased expenditure demands that exceed the revenue gains, forcing higher tax rates for the same level of service; but as long as these fiscal losses are more than offset by other gains that translate into greater demand for land and housing, property values will rise.

Greenstone and Moretti (2003) acknowledge that they are looking at the local benefits of new plant location, and that state government is paying part of the incentive cost. This is not a minor point. In my extensive research on economic development subsidies with Alan Peters, we found that a typical package of state and local grants, loans, tax credits, and tax abatements granted to a manufacturing firm (and most of the plants in the G&M study were manufacturing) consisted in about equal portions of state subsidies and local subsidies (Fisher and Peters 1998). In enterprise zones, about 59 percent of the typical package in the 13 states we studied consisted of state incentives (Peters and Fisher 2002, p. 112). The important point here is that local property values may reflect most or all of the benefits of a plant location, but will definitely not reflect about half of the costs (more in enterprise zones), since state costs will not be capitalized at all into local property values. Furthermore, they assume complete capitalization of local incentive costs, which is quite doubtful. Previous studies of property taxes have generally found only partial capitalization. Their study therefore does not tell us, after all, whether the locality earns a fiscal surplus, nor does it tell us whether the overall benefits to the state as a whole exceed the state and local subsidy costs, which is the most important question.

So what does the Greenstone and Moretti (2003) study really tell us about the wisdom of incentive policy? We don't know the size of the winning and losing subsidy packages, nor do we really know if the subsidy offered by the winning county was decisive. We do not know whether the firm had already made up its mind where to go on the basis of economic considerations and was simply playing one community off against another to gain concessions. If the incentives didn't matter, they were not a good deal no matter how much wages and property values rose.

We do know that even these negotiated incentives are not always decisive. For example, a debate raged in Nebraska in the early part of this decade over a package of $75 million in tax breaks to induce Union Pacific Railroad (UP) to move 1,038 jobs from St. Louis to Omaha. While UP told Nebraska officials that they would not move the jobs without the incentives, they were telling a different story in St. Louis, where company officials stated that the move was motivated by "critical strategic considerations, not tax incentives," and that it made sense "from a synergy viewpoint" because the company's IT staff was already in Omaha (Hicks 2004). And in Iowa in the early 1990s, when citizens took county supervisors to court over a subsidy to a planned IPSCO steel plant, the company was asked if it would reverse its decision to locate in Iowa if the lawsuit were successful; it said it would not. The company admitted publicly that the incentives made no difference. It is not often that we are provided such insights into corporate behavior, but it would be foolish to imagine that such instances of large incentives being granted unnecessarily are rare.

Furthermore, these are short-run effects: the study looked at the first five years after a plant location. The long-run effect on property values may be lessened as the local housing market responds to the initial increase in demand brought about by the expansion of job opportunities. And the long-run effects could be wiped out altogether if the plant leaves. As my colleague Alan Peters has pointed out, many of the major disasters in the incentive wars have occurred after five years, including the United Airlines facility in Indianapolis that closed, leaving the city holding the bag for $320 million in subsidies.

More importantly, the results of these findings for a nonrandom sample of the largest package deals tell us little about the fiscal consequences of incentive competition in general, including the more modest one-time deals that are far more numerous, and including all of the entitlement incentives.

ENTITLEMENT TAX INCENTIVES AND TAX CUTS

Let's turn our attention now to the wide range of tax cuts and tax incentives that operate as entitlements. Here there is not even a pretense of the firm making a "but for" determination. There is simply a belief or hope that the tax cuts will stimulate some growth that would not have occurred otherwise. But here we also have a more researchable question: Do places that offer lower taxes, or tax incentives, grow faster than other places, controlling for all the other factors that influence investment and location decisions?

This question has been extensively researched. We need not review that literature here, except to say that some have argued that a consensus position has emerged that the interstate elasticity of economic activity with respect to taxes on business is somewhere between −0.1 and −0.6, with the most likely figure −0.2 or −0.3 (Bartik 1991; Wasylenko 1997). This position is not without its challengers. But let's proceed for now with the assumption that −0.2 or −0.3 is a reasonable estimate. This means, for example, that a 10 percent cut in taxes would produce a 2–3 percent increase in economic activity. What does this tell us about the fiscal gains or losses from incentives or tax cuts?

Bartik (1994) has argued that the fiscal effects of tax cuts are bound to be negative. He shows that tax revenues will increase approximately by the percentage increase in jobs induced by the tax cut, and decrease approximately by the percentage reduction in the tax rate. (The truly induced jobs produce revenue gains; the tax cut on all the jobs that would have been there anyway [the noninduced employment] produces revenue losses.) He then arrives at the formula for the net change in revenue per new job, expressed as a function of the elasticity E:

Revenue gain (or loss) per new job = revenue per job × (1 + 1/E).

For the revenue per job term, Bartik substitutes the national average state-local direct business tax revenue per job across all business sectors in 1989, which was about $1,620. Assuming an elasticity of −0.3, the average fiscal effect of a new job would then be −$3,780. Updating this estimate to 2003, we find that business tax revenue per job is now probably between $3,000 and $3,700, depending on which taxes are included.[1] Using Bartik's elasticity figure again (−0.3) and the lower revenue figure, annual revenue losses for each new, induced job would be about $7,000. If one agrees with Wasylenko (1997) that −0.2 is a more likely elasticity, and uses the higher revenue figure ($3,700), the fiscal losses more than double, to $14,900.

Let's be clear what these numbers mean. If a state embarks on a program of tax incentives that ends up attracting 100 new jobs that would not have been there but for the incentives, the state and its local governments should expect to have $700,000–$1,490,000 *less* in business tax revenues *each and every year* (assuming an elasticity of −0.2 to −0.3) than they would have had without the tax incentive program. All this to provide an estimated 77 jobs to people who have migrated to the state and 23 jobs to existing residents who otherwise would have been unemployed or not in the labor force.

The importance of Bartik's formulation is that it effectively undercuts the arguments of public officials and development practitioners that job creation is not only good policy, it is free policy—we can create jobs and add revenue at the same time. But let's look at the competition for business as if communities were offering sites at varying "tax prices," where a tax price is the cost to the business of a unit of public services. The problem for communities is that in this competition for capital, they are operating on an inelastic demand curve. Basic economic analysis tells us that when you cut price in the face of inelastic demand, you lose revenue.

States and communities that respond to the competitive environment by offering ever more generous incentives, as has been the pattern for the past two decades, on the grounds that this generosity will be rewarded with more investment, are in effect saying, "We lose a little more on each plant, but we're going to make it up in volume." Of course, larger incentives are more effective, but total fiscal losses rise proportionately. This is because the gains from additional induced jobs continue to be offset by ever larger losses from all the jobs that would have been there anyway but now are paying little in taxes. It can be shown that the percentage of new jobs that are actually induced can be found by multiplying the elasticity by the percentage cut in taxes (Peters and Fisher 2002, Appendix C). With an elasticity of −0.3 and a fairly typical incentive package amounting to a 30 percent cut in taxes, only 9 percent of the new jobs arriving in a community will be attributable to the tax cut. The incentives provided to the other 91 percent are a pure waste of money.

If we are evaluating the fiscal consequences of incentives, however, we would want a formulation that measures the effects of cuts in marginal tax rates on the gross flow of economic activity (annual establishment births, for example). Most of the research on taxes and business activity, however, has measured changes in the average level of business taxation and changes in the level of employment. My own research with Alan Peters (Peters and Fisher 2002, Appendix C) has shown that cuts in marginal tax rates have identical long-run effects to cuts in average tax rates only under the fairly restrictive condition that the marginal rate cuts are constant and permanent. But most incentives are neither; they are one-time grants or the equivalent in tax expenditures, or they are of limited duration, and generally front-loaded (the percentage abatement, for example, declining over time).

We have also shown that one cannot generalize from the fiscal effects of providing an incentive for one firm, to the fiscal effects of adopting an ongoing incentive program that will apply to the stream of establishments entering the community in all future years. Here communities face an additional problem (beyond the inelasticity of demand): the firms they do succeed in attracting don't stay forever. The argument for incentives rather than permanent cuts is made on fiscal grounds: they are front-loaded or temporary precisely because officials count on the firms paying the full rate in the future.

But local officials appear to routinely overestimate the longevity of business establishments. There is in fact a substantial gross flow of establishments into and out of communities every year. Data from the Census Bureau's Standard Statistical Establishment List show that on average during the early 1990s, establishment births and moves into a particular zip code (approximating an enterprise zone) averaged about 9.5 percent of the existing number of establishments per year; rates of establishment deaths or moves out were about 1.5 percentage points higher (Peters and Fisher 2002). Non-enterprise zone zip codes showed even higher rates of establishment births and deaths. Such high rates of turnover imply average lifespans that are not all that long.

There are only a few studies of the survival rates of business establishments. One study showed a median survival time of about 8.3 years for dependent establishments (branch plants) in goods-producing sectors (Boden 2000). This overstates the case to the extent that the survival distributions in the study cited were driven by large numbers of new, small businesses—the mean employment size was about 16—while incentives are generally focused on larger firms and branch plants. Studies have consistently found that the larger the initial employment size, the higher the survival rates. Data from the tax abatement program in Ohio, however, for 1,581 abatement agreements established between 1990 and 1997, shows that the median size establishment granted abatements for the creation of jobs was only about 70 employees, not as large as one might think.[2] Another study, moreover, indicated that the median survival rate even for larger establishments (over 50 employees) was only in the neighborhood of eight years (Joel Popkin and Company 1991). And this is at the national level, where only births and deaths matter. At the local level, relocations would reduce these rates.

What is the significance of this? Property tax abatements are often spread over an 8- to 10-year period, and states often grant generous tax credits that are not refundable and therefore cannot be used up in the first year but must be carried forward (sometimes for as long as 10 years), eliminating tax liability in all of those years. If the median life expectancy of a new establishment in a community is about 8 to 10 years, this means that over half of the establishments granted abatements or credits will no longer be around to pay the full tax rate.

Even these estimates of the direct revenue losses from tax incentives or business tax cuts are overly optimistic. The reason is that they are based on research showing the elasticity of business activity with respect to tax cuts, *holding all else constant*, including the level of public services. State and local governments must balance their budgets, so that business tax cuts, in practice, must be accompanied either by reductions in services or increases in taxes on other property or individuals. There has been substantial research showing that business activity is responsive to service levels as well, and some have even argued that tax *increases* accompanied by spending increases on nonwelfare services would have a *positive* effect on growth (see Bartik 1996; Fisher 1997). Thus, in the real world, incentive programs that come at the expense of public services would not generate even the modest levels of induced investment assumed above. The elasticities would be lower, probably close to zero, which means the direct fiscal effects are much higher (remember that with an elasticity of −0.1, the average annual loss rises to $33,500 per job). With a zero elasticity, of course, the net total fiscal effect is simply the total expenditure on incentives, since there are no induced jobs.

Some readers might say at this point, "But wait—you keep talking about elasticities of −0.2 or −0.3, or even lower, but those are interstate or intermetropolitan elasticities; we know that taxes have much larger effects on location within a metropolitan area." It is true that economists have long argued that taxes are most likely to alter location decisions within a given metropolitan area, since the other determinants of location (labor cost, utilities, access to markets) will be the same throughout the area, leaving room for differences in less significant costs (such as local property tax differentials) to tip the balance. It is also true that the empirical research has generally borne this out, though there are far fewer studies and a wider range of elasticities. But all this tells us is that incentives are most likely to work precisely where they are least justified—moving jobs around within the same labor market. And while the higher elasticities (above 1.0) mean that a particular locality may indeed gain revenue, this will come at the expense of its neighbors. Even worse, to the extent that the state contributes to incentive packages, state government will be paying cities to engage in a beggar-thy-neighbor strategy. Surely the sensible way to approach the fiscal issue is to ask whether a state and the state's local governments, in the aggregate, gain or lose. And the answer is that they lose.

Incentive programs in the last 20 years have assumed a life of their own; they are viewed as essential policy in good times and bad, in poor states and rich states. And state and local officials see themselves in a never-ending arms race. The results have been documented in terms of the escalating cost per job of the most publicized incentive battles for large facilities. But the same thing is happening, albeit much more quietly, with the more routine incentive programs that function as entitlements. In my research with Alan Peters we have modeled the state and local tax systems and incentive programs in 20 states, and were able to measure the average effective tax rate on a new plant built by a multistate manufacturing firm in each of these 20 states in 1990 and 1998. We also measured the effect of state and local tax incentives in lowering this effective rate. The results are shown in Figure 3.1.

The effective tax rate before incentives declined during this period by about half a percentage point, but the rate after incentives declined even more, by 1.3 percentage points. In just eight years, in other words, there was a 30 percent drop in the effective tax rate on new investment. Over this eight-year period, the average incentive package rose from about 10 percent of gross state-local taxes, to about 29 percent (Fisher 2002).

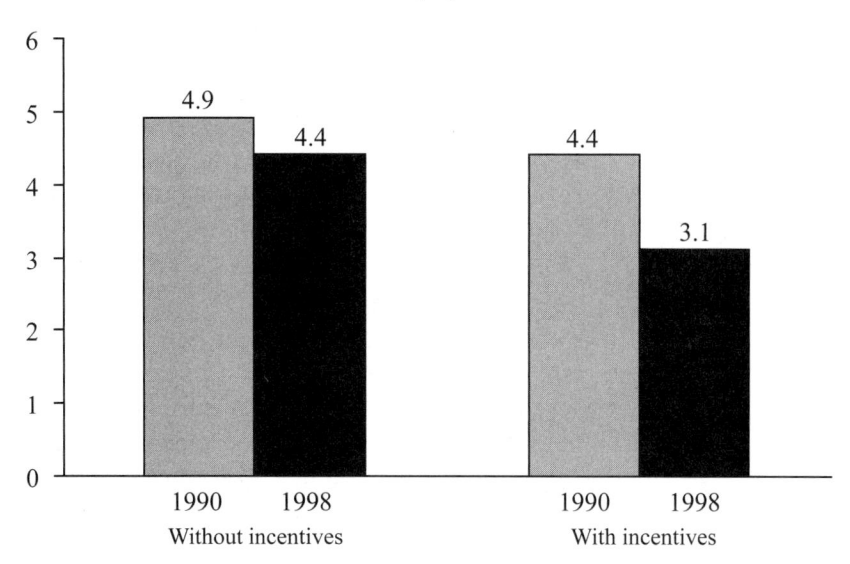

Figure 3.1 Effective Corporate Income Tax Rates on Manufacturing Investment in 20 States (%)

[Bar chart showing:
Without incentives: 1990 = 4.9, 1998 = 4.4
With incentives: 1990 = 4.4, 1998 = 3.1]

SOURCE: Fisher (2002).

THE LARGER CONSEQUENCES OF COMPETITION

We turn now to the effects of competition on tax policy more generally. It is clear from debates about tax policy in the last decade that competitiveness arguments are at the forefront.

How have these arguments changed business taxation and state/local taxes and budgets?

The Decline of the Corporate Income Tax

One of the most significant trends in the past 20 years has been the shift in apportionment formulas away from the standard three-factor towards formulas that weight sales more heavily.[3] As recently as 1980, only five states weighted sales more heavily; by 1999, this number had increased to 33 (Stark 2002). The most common formula in 1999 involved double weighted sales (24 states); four states used single-factor apportionment (100 percent on the basis of sales) exclusively, and another four allowed it as an option or allowed it for certain sectors. These measures are invariably touted as a means to make the state more attractive to exporting firms, and this argument continues to be used as more states consider moving towards single-factor apportionment.

The effects of single-factor apportionment are to reduce state tax revenues. Massachusetts, which adopted single-factor in 1996, lost an estimated $182 million in FY2001 as a result, while Illinois lost $95 million in FY1999 and Pennsylvania lost $89.7 million in FY2002 from their triple-weighted sales formula (Gavin 2001; Commonwealth of Massachusetts 2001; Commonwealth of Pennsylvania 2001).

What is the end result of the proliferation of incentives, the shift toward single-factor apportionment, and other measures that cut the effective state/local tax rate on business? The clearest picture emerges when we look at the decline in corporate income tax revenues as a share of total state/local tax revenue. Figure 3.2 shows that this share peaked near 10 percent in 1979–1980, dropped to around 8 percent through the rest of the 1980s, and then began a precipitous decline to around 6 percent during the most recent 6–7 years.

Corporate income tax revenues have also declined as a share of gross state product (GSP). Figure 3.3 below shows that this share declined substantially over the past 25 years, falling from 0.51 percent in 1980 to 0.27 percent by 2004.

During the past 25 years there has also been a decline in the average effective state/local corporate income tax rate, as measured by total state-local corporate income tax collections divided by corporate profits. These estimates are shown in Figure 3.4. The reason for the uptick in rates in 1999–2001 is not obvious.[4] The decade-to-decade trend remains pretty clear, however. The rate averaged 5.6 percent in the 1970s, 6.9 percent in the 1980s, and 5.1 percent from 1990 through 2002.

Is all of this decline in the corporate income tax due to competitive pressures to cut rates, pursue exporting firms through heavier weighting of sales factors, and adopt ever more generous credits and exemptions? No, it isn't. Some of the decline is due to the increasing use of pass-through entities: S corporations and limited liability companies (LLCs). One study estimated that the rise of LLCs appears to have reduced state corporate income tax revenue by about one-third (Fox and Luna 2003).

Figure 3.2 Corporate Income Tax as a Percent of Total State Tax Revenue: 1975–2005

Average share: 1975–1989: 8.6   1990–2005: 6.3

SOURCE: Data prior to 1991 from U.S. Advisory Commission on Intergovernmental Relations (1992, p. 120); data for 1991–2005 from U.S. Census Bureau (2006).

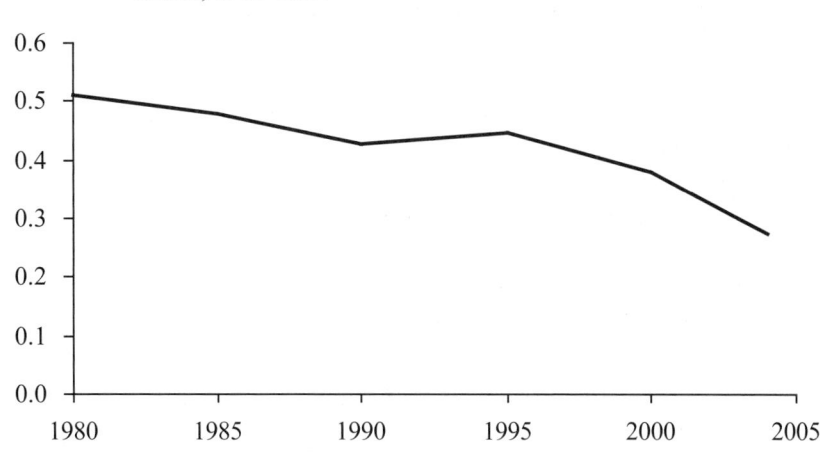

Figure 3.3 Corporate Income Tax Revenue as a Percent of GSP, All States, 1980–2004

SOURCE: Author's calculations. Data for GSP from U.S. Bureau of Economic Analysis (2005); data for corporate income tax revenue from U.S. Census Bureau (2006).

74 Fisher

Figure 3.4 Average Effective State and Local Corporate Income Tax Rate, 1970–2002 (%)

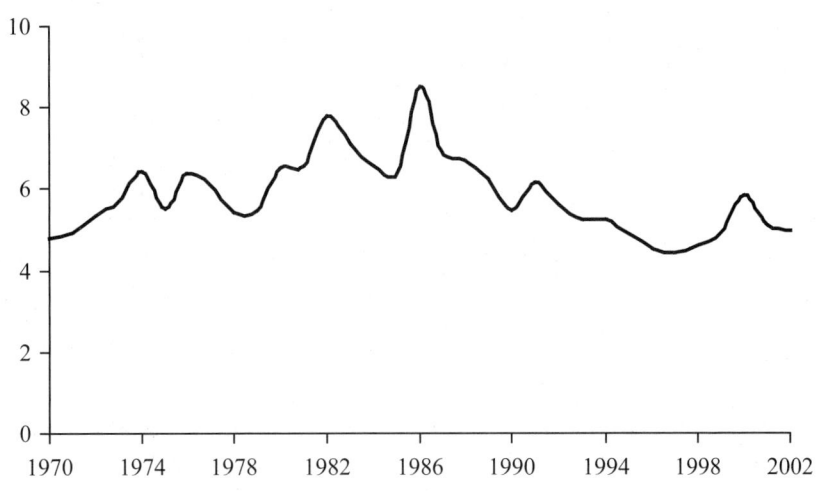

SOURCE: Maguire (2003).

Another factor that cannot be ignored is the increasing use of tax avoidance schemes. The most notorious of these are the passive investment companies (PICS) whereby a firm establishes a shell subsidiary in Delaware and transfers rights to the store name or logo or trademark to the subsidiary. The subsidiary then charges royalties to the parent firm's operating establishments across the country for use of this intangible property, effectively transferring profits from states where the firm actually has a presence (because the royalty expense is deducted from profits in those states) to Delaware, which does not tax royalty income (Mazerov 2003). Even here, competitiveness arguments are made. When the governor of Iowa proposed closing this loophole (which costs the state an estimated $25–$40 million annually), legislative leaders rejected the idea on the grounds that it was a tax increase on business, and the Iowa economy could not afford to drive business out of the state by increasing taxes. Profit shifting and other tax avoidance measures appear to have accounted for about a third of the decline in corporate tax revenue in Iowa from 1980 to 2004 (Fisher 2006).

The Shift Away from Business Taxes

State and local tax policy since 1980 has shifted the composition of taxes away from taxes with an initial impact on business. The share of state and local taxes paid by businesses declined from 46.5 percent in 1980 to 44.0 percent in 1990 and to 40.7 percent in 2000, before rising back to 42.5 percent in 2003 (as the recession and earlier income tax cuts eroded personal income tax revenues dramatically) (Bradley 2003). State and local taxes paid by business also declined as a percent of personal income, from 4.9 percent in 1980 and in 1990, to about 4.4 percent in 2000 and in 2003. The pattern is the same if one measures the burden relative to private sector GDP. Importantly, the taxes with an initial impact on business that have shown growth since FY2000 are overwhelmingly the taxes that are most likely to be shifted forward to consumers—property taxes (much of which are on rental property) and sales and excise taxes—and the payroll taxes, which are generally thought to be borne by employees (Bradley 2003).

The Increasing Regressivity of State and Local Taxes

Has the decline in the importance of the corporate income tax, and the shift away from business taxes generally, affected the distribution of the state local tax burden? We do know that state and local tax systems are, by and large, quite regressive. In 1989, the lowest 20 percent of families by income paid, on average, 10.2 percent of their income in state and local taxes, while the top 20 percent paid only 7.5 percent, and the top 1 percent just 5.5 percent. And indeed they have become more regressive in the past 15 years: by 2002 the effective tax rate on the bottom two quintiles had risen by about a percentage point. The effective rate on the top 20 percent, by contrast, had fallen slightly, from 7.5 percent to 7.3 percent, and the tax rate for the richest 1 percent had fallen from 5.5 percent to 5.2 percent (see Table 3.1).

What happened between 1989 and 2002? In the early part of the decade, many states raised taxes to solve budget shortfalls brought about by the recession. The tendency was to increase regressive taxes, mostly sales. When the economic boom of the latter 1990s started producing large surpluses, states cut taxes, but instead of rolling back the regressive increases of the early 1990s, they slashed the only progressive tax

Table 3.1 State and Local Taxes as Shares of Family Income

	Lowest 20%	Second 20%	Middle 20%	Fourth 20%	Top 20%	Top 1%
1989	10.2	9.4	8.8	8.4	7.5	5.5
2002	11.4	10.3	9.6	8.8	7.3	5.2
Change (%)	+1.2	+0.8	+0.7	+0.4	−0.1	−0.3

NOTE: Tax burdens are shown after the federal offset; that is, these are the net burdens on families after taking into account the deductibility of state and local taxes on federal returns for those who itemize (generally higher-income taxpayers).
SOURCE: Institute on Taxation and Economic Policy (2003, pp. 118–119).

at the state and local level—the personal income tax. The result was a substantial shift in tax burdens by the end of the decade from the highest to the lowest income taxpayers, and an increase in overall regressivity. This trend continued during the recession and budget crises of 2001–2003. Many states increased taxes during this period, but 62 percent of the state tax increases from late 2001 through 2003 were in regressive taxes. State sales and excise taxes were increased $9.9 billion during this period, while individual income tax increases amounted to $3.4 billion, and corporate income taxes to $3.7 billion (Johnson, Shiess, and Llobrera 2003). This trend did not continue into 2004–2005, however, as state revenues recovered. Over those two years, state personal and corporate income taxes were increased by about $1 billion but sales taxes were *cut* (by a similar amount). At the same time, 10 states increased tobacco taxes, which are quite regressive, by a total of about $1.6 billion (Nelson A. Rockefeller Institute of Government 2004, 2006).

Has competition for business played a role in these trends? While the corporate income tax is no longer a significant source of state revenue, there is evidence that the battleground has shifted to the personal income tax. Increasingly, one is hearing arguments that the top personal income tax rate is too high, or that personal income taxes in general must be cut in order to attract business. There has been little research directly addressing the question of whether or not interstate differences in personal income tax rates affect economic growth, but there is reason to be highly skeptical. For corporations, at least, even if they treated personal taxes as a labor cost—which is quite doubtful—differences in state income tax rates produce trivial differences in total business costs (see Fisher and Ditsler 2003). It simply defies logic that location choices would be altered by such small differences in the after-tax cost of living of a firm's employees, or that a corporation would move its facilities to a neighboring state so that its CEO could save a little in state income taxes. Yet these arguments are being made.

These trends have not produced major shifts in the composition of state-local tax systems, other than the decline in the corporate income tax. The typical state tax system relies primarily on a mildly progressive personal income tax and a regressive sales tax that includes a limited number of services in the tax base. Such a tax system (particularly if the income tax is not indexed) will become more progressive over time if left to its own devices, as inflation pushes people into higher tax brackets and the average income tax rate rises slowly, while the shift in consumption patterns from goods to services, combined with increasing internet purchases of goods, steadily erodes the sales tax base. Thus the effects of recent tax policies—cutting income taxes and business taxes in good times and raising regressive taxes in bad times—will not necessarily show up as a dramatic shift from income to excise taxes.

Other Shifts in State and Local Revenue Sources and Spending Priorities

It would be reasonable to hypothesize that the competition for business investment and jobs has had other effects on state and local budgets. Has it shifted revenues increasingly to current charges, which are among the most regressive of financing tools? In the 12 years from fiscal years 1991–1992 to 2003–2004, current charges as a share of own-source general revenue of state and local governments increased significantly, from 17.1 percent to 19.7 percent.[5] In no small part this was due to rising tuition at public universities; some 34 states raised tuition for the 2003–2004 year by more than 10 percent (Johnson, Shiess, and Llobrera 2003, p. 14).

Have state budgets increasingly focused on spending that more directly benefits business, such as infrastructure (streets, airports, water, sewer) and police and fire protection, and away from social services, education, and natural resources? While such effects may be occurring, we do not have a good counterfactual—what would spending priorities have been in the absence of the climate of competition? If these effects have been occurring, they have not yet revealed themselves in noticeable shifts in overall spending since the start of the 1990s.

THE ROLE OF COMPETITION FOR CAPITAL

What have we concluded so far?

- The one-time package deals negotiated by states and cities may or may not be a good deal fiscally for local governments or for state governments; the Greenstone and Moretti (2003) paper certainly has not established that they are, and there is good reason to believe many of these incentives have been granted unnecessarily.
- Entitlement incentives and tax cuts are quite costly to state and local governments, and this is probably where the bulk of economic development expenditure is found. Given the lack of responsiveness of economic activity to differences in taxation, state and local governments must spend large amounts of tax revenue for small gains in employment, and when the tax cuts are accompanied by service cuts it is likely that even these small gains disappear. Incentive wars and corporate income tax cuts in the name of economic development show no signs of abating.
- The corporate income tax is in danger of disappearing at the state level, and business taxes in general have declined somewhat in importance.
- State and local tax systems have become more regressive; tax cuts in the latter 1990s were almost entirely focused on the income tax, while tax increases during the recessions of the early 1990s and of 2001–2003 were concentrated on regressive consumption taxes. Governments are making increasing use of charges for services.

Let us not be too hasty, however, in attributing all of these fiscal effects to interstate and interlocal competition for capital. If we are looking for culprits, there are other plausible candidates. First of all, there are the "starve-the-beasters," to use Paul Krugman's term to describe the apostles of the strategy favored by Ronald Reagan's budget director,

David Stockman (Krugman 2003). The idea here is first to pass large tax cuts (because they are demonstrably popular) without specifying any service reductions, and then to slash spending on the grounds that we cannot afford to finance (selected) services. We shrink Leviathan by starving it. While this is arguably the underlying motivation behind Republican-led federal tax cuts since the early 1980s, it is clear that there are many in state legislatures who have been pursuing the same strategy in recent years.

If starving the beast is the underlying agenda, then competitiveness arguments are merely a convenient public rationale. A starve-the-beaster does not have to believe that tax cuts "work," though he may believe so. He has merely to convince others that this is a plausible argument.

Another potential culprit at the federal level, as Krugman (2003) points out, is the supply-sider. Here, tax cuts are favored on the grounds that by relieving the tax burden on investment, we will generate more of it, whether by expansion of existing firms or attraction of new ones. The economic growth that ensues will generate sufficient new tax base to ultimately pay for the tax cuts. The Bush administration has in fact built quite optimistic supply-side growth effects into its models for projecting the size of the federal deficit.

At the state level, supply-side arguments (that business tax cuts will pay for themselves) are even less plausible due to the openness of a state economy. One hears the supply-side arguments anyway; the fact that past tax cuts have not only failed to pay for themselves but are major contributors to the current fiscal crises of the states goes unacknowledged. The supply-side position is even, on occasion, bolstered by a demand-side argument—that putting more money into the hands of business and consumers via tax cuts will stimulate demand for the state's products and spur growth. This despite the obvious problem that states must balance their budgets, so that every dollar put into the economy through tax cuts is taken out by spending cuts. And if the spending leakages that occur with tax cuts are greater than the leakages associated with budget cuts, the demand-side effect could be negative.

A third potential culprit is the attack on income redistribution, otherwise known as class warfare. A substantial chorus of voices from the right has been calling for a reduction in progressive taxes, and they are fond of pointing out how much the rich pay (invariably focusing exclusively on the federal income tax as if that were the only tax anyone pays). Again, if this is the underlying motivation for cuts in taxes on business, then competitiveness arguments are merely a more publicly acceptable rationale, not the real reason. Attacks on progressivity are dressed up as policies to promote jobs for the unemployed. Incredibly, competitiveness arguments have even been put forth to advocate for cuts in state taxes on capital gains and for elimination of state inheritance taxes. Conservative think tanks have been promoting the idea that cuts in state personal income taxes, and capital gains taxes in particular, will stimulate venture capital investment and entrepreneurial activity *in that state*. Inheritance taxes are blamed for the closing of family businesses.

It is, of course, impossible to disentangle the effects of these four possible factors driving the reduction in business taxes: the perceived need to be "competitive," the starve-the-beast attack on the public sector, the supply-siders' notion of self-financing tax cuts, and the attempt to augment the success of the private economy in redistributing income upwards. There is abundant circumstantial evidence, however, that the starve-the-beast strategy is widely embraced on the right. There is also evidence for the attack on income redistribution, as can be seen by what has happened over the past 15 years to state and local tax systems. It is difficult to argue that the overwhelming trend towards increases in regressive taxes on consumption, coupled with reductions in progressive taxes on income and inherited wealth, can be explained solely by economic development concerns.

In the end, the most plausible hypothesis, I would argue, is that there is a complex of strategies and agendas and beliefs that have been working in concert (and, yes, there is evidence that this has been a coordinated effort, through such groups as the American Legislative Exchange Council) to produce increases in incentive packages and incentive entitlements, cuts in business taxes, and cuts in progressive personal taxes. The result is a fiscal crisis for state and local government (not to mention an enormous federal deficit) and an increasingly regressive tax system.

There are indeed those who truly believe the supply-side arguments, and those who truly believe the competitiveness arguments, and some of these folks may not also subscribe to the belief that any cut in government spending is a good thing, or that the rich need tax relief. Still, it is certainly very convenient and useful, if one is a starve-the-beaster or reverse Robin Hood, that there are such true believers, in right-wing think tanks and state legislatures and in the press, for they have been providing excellent cover. They keep the debate focused on questions such as, "Do tax cuts spur growth?" where one can always find an argument or statistic to support the position that they do. Journalists and public officials are, by and large, simply not equipped to sort out the valid claims from the spurious ones, and competitiveness and supply side assertions are simply repeated so often, and with such impunity, that the public comes to believe that these arguments are valid and are made in good faith.[6]

Whether or not competition for capital is in fact driving all of these fiscal changes (i.e., whether or not it is the real *cause*), it is clear that it is the driving issue whenever there are public debates about taxes and budgets. Advocacy organizations around the country—nonprofits working at the state and local levels on tax and budget issues, on child and family policy, on poverty, housing, education, and workforce development—continually find themselves up against the tax competitiveness argument. An alleged threat to competitiveness can effectively put a stop to attempts to fund social programs, to forestall the weakening of business regulation, or to adopt more progressive tax policies. Whether it is a useful counterstrategy to engage the debate on these terms—to continue to present the evidence on the tax competition issue, as if one is really just participating in a discussion about economic development policy among citizens and politicians with common goals and values—is a question for another chapter, or another day.

Notes

1. Total state and local taxes paid directly by business were $404.3 billion in fiscal year 2003, according to Cline et al. (2004). Private nonfarm employment was about 108,592,000, yielding taxes per job of $3,723 (USDOL n.d.).
2. Analysis by the author of the State of Ohio's enterprise zone agreement database.
3. Corporations must apportion their overall profits to the states in which they do business in order to determine what share of total profits is taxable in a given state. Each state has its own rules for apportionment, the traditional approach being three factor apportionment, where the firm takes a simple average of three ratios: property in state X divided by total firm property, payroll in state X over total payroll, and sales to state X over total sales. Single factor apportionment

uses only the sales ratio, and thus rewards domestic firms that export and penalizes foreign firms that sell in the state.
4. The federal corporate rate also rose in 1999, jumped up in 2000, then fell somewhat in 2001 and 2002, just as the state rate did. This suggests that the explanation lies in the determination of federal taxable income, not in changes in the way states taxed the part of that taxable income that was apportioned to each state. In other words, something happened to increase the share of corporate profits as measured by NIPA (the denominator in Maguire's tax rates) that becomes taxable income (which determines the numerator, along with tax rates, which we know did not rise). IRS corporate tax return data shows that the explanation does not lie in lesser use of deductions from net income in 1999 and 2000. Instead, a larger share of NIPA profits ended up as taxable income. In part, this was due to many more returns with net losses in 2000, which are combined with returns showing positive profits to arrive at aggregate NIPA profits (thus lowering the denominator), yet it is only the returns with positive profits that generate taxable income and taxes (the numerator). It is also possible that the IRS clamped down on abusive tax shelters in 1999 and 2000, notably the use of LILO (lease in, lease out) schemes, and it is taking a few years for corporate tax departments to find new ways to shelter profits.
5. U.S. Census Bureau, Annual Survey of Governments.
6. I recently spoke at a large public hearing on the state budget about the fact that our tax policies were driven largely by mythology, and was amazed to find that for most people this was the first time they had ever heard anyone argue that tax cuts might not be a good thing for the economy. I had heard the competitiveness argument, for cutting services rather than raising taxes, put forth twice by public officials just that day—in a newspaper report that morning and on a radio interview on the way to the hearing.

References

Altshuler, Alan, and Jose Gomez-Ibanez. 1993. *Regulation for Revenue: The Political Economy of Land Use Exactions.* Washington, DC: The Brookings Institution.

Bartik, Timothy. 1991. *Who Benefits from State and Local Economic Development Policies?* Kalamazoo, MI: W.E. Upjohn Institute for Employment Research.

———. 1994. "Jobs, Productivity and Local Economic Development: What Implications Does Economic Research Have for the Role of Government?" *National Tax Journal* 47(4): 847–861.

———. 1996. *Growing State Economies: How Taxes and Public Services Affect Private-Sector Performance.* Washington, DC: Economic Policy Institute.

Boden, Richard Jr. 2000. *Establishment Employment Change and Survival, 1992–1996.* Final report for the Office of Advocacy of the U.S. Small Business Administration, February.

Bradley, David. 2003. "Business Tax Burdens: Responding to the Ernst and Young Studies." Presentation to the 11th Annual Funding State Services Conference, Center on Budget and Policy Priorities held in Washington, DC, November 16.

Cline, Robert, William Fox, Tom Neubig, and Andrew Phillips. 2004. *Total State and Local Business Taxes: A 50-State Study of the Taxes Paid by Business in FY2003.* Washington, DC: Council on State Taxation.

Commonwealth of Massachusetts. 2001. Fiscal Year 2001 Tax Expenditure Budget, p. 36.

Commonwealth of Pennsylvania. 2001. Governor's Executive Budget 2001–2002, "Tax Expenditures," D:11.

Fisher, Peter S. 2002. "Tax Incentives and the Disappearing State Corporate Income Tax." *State Tax Notes* 23(9): 767–774.

———. 2006. "Revitalizing Iowa's Corporate Income Tax." *Iowa Fiscal Partnership*, April. Reprinted in *State Tax Notes* 40(8): 601–617.

Fisher, Peter, and Elaine Ditsler. 2003. "Tax Cuts and State Economic Growth: The Myths and the Reality." Policy brief. Mount Vernon, IA: The Iowa Policy Project, May. http://www.iowapolicyproject.org/2002-2004_reports_press_releases/030515-tax-cuts.pdf (accessed October 26, 2006).

Fisher, Peter, and Alan Peters. 1998. *Industrial Incentives: Competition Among American States and Cities.* Kalamazoo, MI: W.E. Upjohn Institute for Employment Research.

Fisher, Ronald. 1997. "The Effects of State and Local Public Services on Economic Development." *New England Economic Review* March/April: 53–66.

Fox, William, and LeAnn Luna. 2003. "Does the Advent of LLCs Explain Declining State Corporate Tax Revenues?" Unpublished working paper. Knoxville, TN: University of Tennessee.

Gavin, Robert. 2001. "Regional Report: States' Tax Plan Could Backfire—As Levies on Corporations Are Cut, The Incentives Lose Their Advantage." *The Wall Street Journal*, February 14, B:17.

Greenstone, Michael, and Enrico Moretti. 2003. "Bidding for Industrial Plants: Does Winning a 'Million Dollar Plant' Increase Welfare?" NBER working paper no. 9844. Cambridge, MA: National Bureau of Economic Research.

Hicks, Nancy. 2004. "Railroad's Tax Benefits at Issue." *Lincoln (Nebraska) Journal Star*, Feb. 10. http://www.journalstar.com/latest_reg/?story_id=121360 (accessed February 10, 2004).

Institute on Taxation and Economic Policy. 2003. *Who Pays? A Distributional*

Analysis of the Tax Systems in All 50 States. 2nd ed. Washington, DC: Institute on Taxation and Economic Policy.

Joel Popkin and Company. 1991. *Business Survival Rates by Age Cohort of Business*. Report for the U.S. Small Business Administration, Office of Advocacy, April.

Johnson, Nicholas, Jennifer Shiess, and Joseph Llobrera. 2003. "State Revenues Have Fallen Dramatically: Tax Increases So Far Have Failed to Fill the Gap." Washington, DC: Center on Budget and Policy Priorities, November 25. http://www.cbpp.org/10-22-03sfp.pdf (accessed July 24, 2006).

Krueger, Alan. 2003. "Economic Scene: A Study Finds Benefits for Localities That Offer Subsidies to Attract Companies." *New York Times*, December 11, C:2.

Krugman, Paul. 2003. "The Tax-Cut Con." *New York Times*, September 14, 6(Part 1).

Ladd, Helen, and John Yinger. 1991. *America's Ailing Cities: Fiscal Health and the Design of Urban Policy*. 2nd ed. Baltimore: Johns Hopkins University Press.

Maguire, Steve. 2003. *Average Effective Corporate Tax Rates: 1959 to 2002*. Washington, DC: Congressional Research Service.

Mazerov, Michael. 2003. *Closing Three Common Corporate Income Tax Loopholes Could Raise Additional Revenue for Many States*. Washington, DC: Center on Budget and Policy Priorities.

Nelson A. Rockefeller Institute of Government. 2004. *State Fiscal Brief*, November. Albany, NY: Center for the Study of the States, Nelson A. Rockefeller Institute of Government.

———. 2006. *State Fiscal Brief*, January. Albany, NY: Center for the Study of the States, Nelson A. Rockefeller Institute of Government.

Peters, Alan, and Peter Fisher. 2002. *State Enterprise Zone Programs: Have They Worked?* Kalamazoo, MI: W.E. Upjohn Institute for Employment Research.

Stark, Kirk. 2002. "The Quiet Revolution in U.S. Subnational Corporate Income Taxation." *State Tax Notes* 23(9): 775–784.

U.S. Advisory Commission on Intergovernmental Relations. 1992. *Significant Features of Fiscal Federalism*, vol. 2. Washington, DC: The Commission, Table 62, p. 120.

U.S. Bureau of Economic Analysis. 2005. "Regional Economic Accounts." Washington, DC: U.S. Department of Commerce, Bureau of Economic Analysis. http://www.bea.gov/bea/regional/gsp/ (accessed November 22, 2006).

U.S. Census Bureau. 2006. "State Government Finances, State Government Tax Collections." Washington, DC: U.S. Census Bureau. http://www.cen-

sus.gov/govs/www/statetax.html (accessed August 28, 2005).
U.S. Department of Labor, Bureau of Labor Statistics (USDOL). n.d. Current Employment Statistics series. http://www.bls.gov/ces/home.htm#data (accessed December 15, 2006).
Wasylenko, Michael. 1997. "Taxation and Economic Development: The State of the Economic Literature." *New England Economic Review* March/April: 37–52.

4
How the EU Manages Subsidy Competition

Adinda Sinnaeve
European Commission

When asked whether subsidies are good or bad, economists generally give so many different answers that the conclusion can only be: it depends. It depends on the objective, the type of subsidy, the beneficiary, the economic context, etc. Precisely because it depends on many factors, the European Union (EU) has set up a control mechanism for subsidies, or state aid, as the EU calls it, with a view to distinguish the "good" from the "bad" subsidies and make sure that only good subsidies are granted. This raises two questions: how to determine what a good subsidy is, and how to organize a functioning control mechanism.

The following contribution aims to explain in a nutshell how the EU system works, what its main features are, and what alternative approaches could be developed. (For a general overview of the EC State aid rules, see, for example, Bilal and Nicolaides [1999]; Biondi, Eeckhout, and Flynn [2004]; D'Sa [1998]; Hancher, Ottervanger, and Slot [1999]; Heidenhain et al. [2003]; Nicolaides, Kekelekis, and Buyskes [2005]; Quigley and Collins [2003]; Sinnaeve [2001].)

SYNOPSIS OF EU STATE AID CONTROL

Why State Aid Control?

State aid control in the EU has existed for almost half a century now. Its inclusion in the EC treaty was quite remarkable and novel as there were no other examples of comparable state aid disciplines at the time.

Among the reasons for introducing state aid control one could first refer to general economic arguments against subsidies: the risk of a subsidy race, where EC member states might outbid each other and transfer problems from one country to another. This would not only be a waste of public money, but in the long term, if companies rely too much on state intervention, it could weaken the competitive position of European industry.

The inclusion of state aid rules in the EC treaty is also closely linked to the establishment of a common market, where goods and services can circulate freely. After the gradual abolition of tariff and nontariff barriers to trade, the granting of state aid is one of the few remaining tools for national governments to protect their national industry. Barriers to trade that have been dismantled in the integration process should not be replaced by other barriers in the form of state aid. Therefore, strict control is necessary also from a common market perspective. At the same time, as markets become more integrated the distortive effects of state aid are more visible and more directly felt by competitors in other member states, thus requiring state aid disciplines.

Finally, it is important to underline that the state aid provisions were inserted in the competition chapter of the EC treaty. The logic of the treaty is to ensure undistorted competition regardless of whether distortions are caused by the behavior of businesses, for which the antitrust rules were adopted, or by the action of the state. State aid control should thus be seen in the light of its role to avoid unjustified distortions of competition. (For a comparison of EU and the United States in the application of competition policy against state intervention in the market, see Ichikawa [2004, p. 555].)

The Definition of State Aid

The treaty uses a rather wide definition of state aid. (For an overview of recent developments regarding the definition of state aid pursuant to Article 87 [1] EC Treaty, see Winter [2004, p. 475].) It includes all advantages selectively granted by the state or through state resources that distort competition or threaten to distort it and affect trade between member states, e.g., grants, loans at nonmarket conditions, state guarantees, all types of tax advantages, and the sale of land at nonmarket conditions. This notion is broadly comparable, although not identical, with that of a subsidy under the WTO rules.

The selectivity criterion (i.e., whether an aid measure is specific or selective) is determined at the level of each member state. This implies that if member states apply different levels of taxes, this is not considered to be state aid. If, however, they lower the tax rate or grant other types of tax advantages only to certain sectors, certain types of enterprises (such as small and medium-sized enterprises [SME] or coordination centers for multinational companies), or enterprises located in a certain area within the territory of a member state, this would constitute state aid and must respect the relevant conditions.[1]

The Substantive Rules of State Aid Control

What does the EU control mechanism look like? The treaty starts from the principle that state aid is incompatible with the common market, unless it falls under one of the exceptions of the treaty (Article 87). The Commission has the power to decide whether or not this is the case. The exceptions are formulated in a very general way (they refer, for example, to broad concepts such as the development of regions with an abnormally low living standard or serious underemployment, and the development of certain economic activities). As a result, the treaty gives the Commission wide discretion to develop criteria for the approval of certain types of aid and design a state aid policy. This policy will necessarily evolve in the same way as the common market and the EU objectives.

The basic principles, however, remain the same: the aid should contribute to the achievement of EU objectives in such a way that the distortion of competition is justifiable. Aid by definition distorts competition. The reason why it can nevertheless be authorized lies in the fact that it promotes other EU objectives, such as regional development, R&D, employment, etc., which outweigh the distortion in a proportional way. In other words: if market forces alone are sufficient to attain the EU objective, no aid should be granted, but where the benefits to the EU as a whole exceed those that would result from undistorted competition, authorization is justified.

It is clear that these general principles need to be embodied in more operational criteria. The Commission has therefore translated the principles into concrete assessment criteria, which are laid down in frameworks and guidelines.[2] These quasi-legislative texts define the conditions under which aid projects can be authorized for different types of aid, specifically aid for regional development, promotion of SME, employment, R&D, environmental protection, training of workers, restructuring of enterprises in difficulties, and provision of risk capital—to mention the most important objectives. They aim at ensuring greater legal certainty for member states and companies, predictability, and equal treatment.

For each of these horizontal objectives, a number of precise conditions define under which circumstances aid can be granted. Normally a maximum aid intensity will be determined. This is the maximum amount of aid, expressed as a percentage of the eligible costs. These percentages are further modulated according to the size of the aid beneficiaries (small enterprises can, as a rule, receive higher amounts of aid) and the region where they are located (higher aid is allowed in poorer regions). (On regional aid, see also Battista [2005]; Nicolaides [2003, p. 543]; and Wishlade [2003].) For example, a company setting up a new plant in a poor Portuguese region can receive a higher aid amount than if it had established its new plant in the Netherlands. If the company is a small enterprise, it can also get an SME bonus. If, however, a member state wants to grant the company a straight tax break without any condition, this will normally not be authorized by the Commission because there is no direct counterpart for the aid (such as new investment or job creation).

State Aid Procedures

In procedural terms, Article 88 of the EC treaty establishes a mechanism of prior control, based on the notification obligation and the standstill clause. (On state aid procedures, see Sinnaeve and Slot [1999, p. 1153].) Member states have to notify in advance all their aid projects to the Commission and may only implement them after the Commission has given its green light.

Simple cases are decided after a preliminary examination within two months starting from the receipt of a complete notification. For more complex cases that raise doubts about their compatibility with the common market, the Commission will open a formal investigation after the preliminary examination. In this second phase, all interested parties, in particular the aid beneficiary and its competitors, have the opportunity to present their comments on the aid project.

If member states do not respect these procedural obligations, the aid is granted unlawfully and the Commission can at any time start an investigation, e.g., following a complaint by a competitor or ex officio. If the Commission finds that the unlawful aid is incompatible with the common market, it will order its reimbursement, with interests. Aid grantors (and aid beneficiaries) thus run a serious risk if they do not follow the rules.

SOME REFLECTIONS BASED ON THE EU EXPERIENCE

Strengths of the EU System

One of the main strengths of the EU regime is obviously the fact that it has the legal and institutional framework for conducting state aid control; it has the following necessary means at its disposal to make the control system work:

- an independent authority (the Commission) to set and enforce the rules under the control of the EC Court of Justice.
- the legal and administrative mechanisms to organize the system of prior notification and authorization.
- flexibility, that is, the option to adapt the rules if changes in the economic environment or in the priorities of the EU require so. For example, if Europe underinvests in R&D, that will be taken into account when the rules on aid for R&D are revised; if on the other hand certain sectors suffer from overcapacity or serious structural problems, a more restrictive aid policy will be adopted (see, for example, European Commission [2002]). When member states recently started to use the provision of venture-capital as a tool to assist enterprises, the Commission adopted a communication in order to clarify in what circumstances such actions

would fall within the scope of the state aid rules and what conditions had to be respected (European Commission 2001).

- the necessary acceptance by all the actors involved (governments, industry, public at large) and the recognition that aid disciplines are needed in a common market like the EU. Of course, state aid control is also subject to criticism, but not more than any other policy. What contributes to this acceptance is the fact that the state aid regime still leaves sufficient room to member states for developing their economic policies including subsidies. There is no general interdiction of state aid; member states can still grant all types of aid (except export aid and local content aid, forbidden under the WTO rules), they only have to respect certain conditions. The more distortive the aid is, the stricter the conditions will be, but the approach is balanced and makes sense from a common market perspective.

Not all of these features of the EU regime are necessarily indispensable, but they certainly facilitate the functioning of the system.

Can the EU system then be called a success? Probably, since it has fulfilled the objectives rather well. The most distortive types of aid are under control. Very strict conditions are applied to

- operating aid, i.e., aid typically granted without any condition or counterpart, which relieves an enterprise of the expenses it would itself normally have to bear in its day-to-day management or its usual activities (*Siemens v. Commission* 1997).
- aid to large enterprises in rich areas of the EU.
- sectoral aid. The Commission's policy favors aid with horizontal objectives (e.g., SME development, R&D, and worker training) and takes a strict approach on sectoral aid, limited to particular sectors of the economy, such as steel.
- aid to enterprises in difficulty. While it used to be normal for the state to intervene in order to save jobs, such intervention now is only allowed under very strict conditions. The company must first provide a viable restructuring plan, and it must make a significant contribution and reduce its capacity on the market in order to compensate for the distortion. Furthermore, the one-time last-time principle applies according to which restructuring aid

is allowed only once. These conditions are important because restructuring aid is one of the most distortive types of state aid. The fact that both the Commission's decision and/or its nonimplementation can be challenged before the Court offers an additional guarantee in order to ensure that the said conditions are respected and enforced.

In brief, the most distortive types of aid are under control, and in addition, the rules normally also ensure that aid is not the main reason for a company to make certain decisions. For example, the aid allowed can rarely be so substantial that a company would decide to delocate merely because of that aid. Other factors, such as infrastructure, presence of trained workforce, general tax levels, and administrative procedures to be complied with, are more decisive. But if a company considers several alternative locations for a new plant, all of which meet its specific investment requirements, it may choose the site in a disadvantaged area, because it can get a comparatively higher aid amount there. This is fully in line with the EU's "cohesion policy."

Weaknesses of the EU System

Like any system, EU state aid control also has its weaknesses, some of which have been tackled already, others would require further reform action.

A first problem is the high administrative burden that results from the notification obligation. If the Commission had to assess every single measure, however small and unimportant, this would be unfeasible and an inefficient use of resources. Therefore, the obligation of prior notification has been softened. Member states can notify so-called aid schemes, which define the general conditions under which a certain type of aid will be granted. If the scheme complies with the rules, it will be approved for a certain number of years and the individual applications of the scheme do not need to be notified anymore. Furthermore, in recent years a number of block exemption regulations have been adopted for certain less distortive types of aid. (On the block exemptions, see Sinnaeve [2001, p. 1479].) They exempt, for example, aid for SME, and aid for employment or training of workers under well-defined conditions from the notification obligation. Block exemptions liberate the Commission from a number of routine cases, so that the Commission can concentrate on the more problematic cases. However, they also shift part of the responsibility to the aid grantors, which now have to control themselves whether their aid projects fulfill the conditions of the block exemption. Therefore, in order to avoid a weakening of the control system, increased ex-post monitoring, as well as the vigilance of competitors, who can complain to the Commission or go to national courts if the conditions of a block exemption are infringed is of utmost importance.

Block exemptions are also a good illustration of a second difficulty, that is, finding the right balance between the need for legal certainty, with simple and predictable rules, and the risk that such predefined rules leave no room to take account of the merits of each individual case. In theory the Commission has a wide discretion to decide in every case whether a subsidy is good or bad. However, member states and enterprises call for clear and transparent assessment criteria, which also ensure equal treatment. The Commission has over the years replied to this justified request by establishing rather precise rules for most types of aid. Once established, these rules bind the Commission and thus in practice considerably reduce its discretionary power. This leads to a situation where member states feel obliged to consider only aid measures fitting within the established criteria, even if other creative new projects might be equally defendable or even more efficient to achieve the objectives. Vice versa, the Commission cannot prohibit measures that fulfill the criteria of its block exemptions or guidelines, even if a particular case does not seem very convincing. This permanent tension between individual discretion and legal certainty is, however, inherent to all legislation and unavoidable. Like any legislator, the Commission is challenged to find the right balance in this respect.

A third difficulty worth mentioning is the fact that the EU control mechanism is not designed to ensure that aid measures are economically efficient. This fact should probably not be called a weakness, as it is simply the consequence of how the system was conceived: State aid policy is part of competition policy and its first aim is to limit distortions of competition. The paradox is that the most distortive aid may also be the most efficient in terms of achieving the goal of the aid provider. For example, tax holidays are likely to attract investments, but they distort both competition and the level playing field between enterprises too much to be acceptable in a common market. Conversely, aid schemes that do not create significant distortions might get a Commission approval, even if they are not so efficient, such as because the aid is too small to have an effect (a small tax advantage for the recruitment of new workers may not create any jobs which would not have been created anyhow). The Commission is reluctant to take a position on the efficiency of a proposed aid measure, also in view of the division of powers between member states and the Commission. Ultimately it is up to member states to decide how they pursue an economic policy adapted to their own situations and spend—or waste—money.

This does not mean, however, that efficiency plays no role in the assessment of state aid. If aid were completely inefficient it would not normally be authorizable, as it could hardly be considered to be in the interest of the EU. To some extent efficiency requirements are thus incorporated in the conditions for authorization. They ensure, for example, that 1) for any aid there must be a significant counterpart from the company, such as job creation; 2) the enterprise must make a substantial own contribution (aid can never finance the whole project); and 3) if aid is granted for investment or job creation, the investment or the jobs must effectively be maintained for a certain number of years. But these criteria are defined at a general level and are not conceived to select the most efficient measure in a particular case. The Commission thus will not analyze whether other measures might be more appropriate and more efficient than state aid. That is left to member states.

In this respect the question may be raised whether more prior and ex post assessment should be done before and after aid is granted. For example, member states should more often make a study concerning what type of economic measures would be most appropriate before having recourse to state aid. Currently this indispensable preliminary question is often ignored. Similarly, during the operation of an aid scheme, a study of its impact could be useful so that adjustments could be made in case the objectives are not reached. But here a time problem exists: aid schemes have a limited duration of normally five years. Before the effects can be seen and a study can be completed, the scheme often already comes to an end. In any event, it could be argued that, as a minimum, some kind of ex post assessment on the effects of aid measures should be required. That way, aid grantors could benefit from the experience when considering new aid measures or the extension of existing ones. At the same time the Commission would be better equipped to evaluate and adapt its own policy. The Commission has recently made attempts to encourage member states to carry out such assessments, as with the "Scoreboard project," which is published online.[3] The Commission also is reflecting on how to introduce more economic analysis in its assessment of state aid (Hancher 2005, p. 425). However, leaving aside some ad hoc initiatives, it can be argued that so far, not enough emphasis is put on this aspect.

A final problem is the volume of illegal aid. It must be recognized that a significant number of aid measures is still granted without authorization (Nicolaides 2002, p. 249). This is explained partially by the fact that local and regional aid providers especially lack awareness of the rules or infringed the notification obligation because they believed that their measure did not constitute state aid—given the relative unclarities left by the state aid definition it is often far from obvious what is aid and what is not. It may also be the result of a deliberate decision of the granting authority to take the risk.

Many of these cases are discovered by the Commission, either because competitors complain or because politicians publicly announce what action they took to stimulate the local industry. But certainly a number of aid measures will always remain unknown. Is this a real problem? One should not overestimate it. First, if there is a big distortion and a real competition problem, this cannot be hidden. Competitors will know and will complain to the Commission. Secondly, there is a powerful remedy: if the illegal aid does not fulfill the conditions for ex post authorization, the Commission will order its recovery, with interests. And reimbursement can go back for 10 years. The recovery procedure may be long and cumbersome, because it is the member state who has to recover from the beneficiary and the latter may exhaust all remedies under national law against the reimbursement. But the jurisprudence of the EU is such that ultimately reimbursement will have to take place. And although repayment can, of course, not always fully redress the distortion of competition, especially after several years, the recovery rules are an important deterrent to prevent the granting of clearly incompatible aid. Moreover, compared to the WTO rules, for example, they definitely increase the efficiency of the EU system. The recovery tool is therefore, despite some weak points, a strength of the EU state aid policy.

THE EU SYSTEM AS A MODEL?

Since the EU experience is overall quite positive, the question arises of whether and how it could be a model for other jurisdictions. Again, the answer should probably be: it depends. One has to recognize that EU state aid control is linked to the common market and competition policy. The system as such can therefore probably only be successfully transposed to groups of countries or regions with a comparable level of economic integration and also the political will to entrust an independent authority with the power to determine the common interest of all members, with all the repercussions this may have on economic, social, environmental, and other policy areas.

Such groups of countries exist. For example, the EFTA Surveillance Authority fulfills the same role as the European Commission for Norway, Iceland and Liechtenstein (in the past also for Austria, Finland, and Sweden) (Antoniadis 2002, p. 157). This example proves that EU state aid control is not unique.

Another interesting, somewhat different example of subsidy control is that, of the 14 accession candidates, 10 meanwhile became members of the EU on May 1, 2004.[4] In view of the importance attached to state aid policy, the EU concluded with these countries, well before accession, bilateral agreements on the basis of which they were required to respect the State aid regime of the EU, as a kind of preparation for accession. The practical implementation of this obligation was not easy, since none of the accession candidates had any experience with State aid control. They all set up separate State aid authorities from scratch and created the necessary legislative framework to comply with this new task. Obviously this process was not completely successful for all countries, but it proved its value, not only as a transitional solution in the run up to EU accession, but also as a model for state aid control at the national level. It has shown that state aid control, not by a supranational authority but at the national level, can work, provided the state aid authority has the necessary legal framework, administrative capacity and functional independence from the grantors of state aid. The state aid authorities should function in a comparable way as competition authorities. In federal states, such a system might be an option in order to avoid interstate or even intercity bidding wars.

Organizing state aid control by an independent state aid authority does not necessarily mean that the system must be a copy of the EU, which is admittedly rather heavy. Both in terms of procedural enforcement and of substance, a "light" version can be imagined. For example, procedurally one could exempt all the less-important cases and set such a threshold that only the big cases are subject to control, in order not to overload the system. One could also replace the general prohibition with exceptions after prior authorization by its opposite: all aid is allowed unless it is forbidden. Or one could replace it by a system where enterprises or other regions have a right to complain if they suffer from subsidies granted elsewhere (a sort of actionable subsidies within a certain jurisdiction). In regard to the substantive rules, one could envisage only some basic, minimum criteria (e.g., define specific objectives for which aid can be granted and the conditions which the recipient must achieve, put a cap on the aid amount, etc.), or detailed rules for the most problematic types of aid.

The alternative to organize state aid control without a separate state aid authority, for example, through legislation by which all aid grantors are bound, is probably more difficult. In such regime, the rules would have to be agreed by national, regional, or local governments, which would weaken the whole mechanism and in practice be very difficult if the rules should go beyond some minimum conditions. Furthermore, in a system without independent authority to apply, with a certain margin of discretion, the predefined rules to a concrete case, there would be no flexibility. The rules would have to be exhaustive, and their regular update in function of economic developments would be cumbersome. Moreover, the question arises as to who would control and enforce the rules? Presumably, in the absence of a central state aid authority, the rules should be enforceable through the courts, but that would again create problems. Therefore, this alternative seems to be less promising.

Ultimately, to what extent the EU system can be a model depends thus on the situation and the objectives one pursues. Creating an independent authority to set and enforce the rules is certainly a big step but an easier starting point for a well-functioning system. However, other less ambitious options should not be disregarded, even if they would just consist of some general minimum requirements, as that would still be better than having no rules at all.

CONCLUSION

To make a proper evaluation of the EU system, one would in fact have to compare the current regime with a situation without any state aid control. Only such a hypothetical comparison would demonstrate the full impact of the system.

While it is obviously not possible within the scope of this chapter to go through this exercise, it may be expected that, in broad terms, it would reveal that:

- The EU system strikes a reasonable balance between limiting distortions of competition caused by aid, and allowing measures that promote EU objectives; since all aid, and especially the most distortive types of aid, are subject to conditions, the distortions are kept to an acceptable level.

- Since the rules are rather precise and transparent, many cases will never be proposed in the first place. Member states are generally well aware of the basic principles; therefore, they will plan their interventions accordingly and not propose any "unworthy" projects. Any discussion with the Commission will then more be on the details of the project than on the broad characteristics. An important part of the impact of the EU system therefore lies in all the potentially distortive measures that were never even considered, or were withdrawn when it became apparent that no approval could be expected.

To conclude, the EU regime perhaps is not perfect, but it works well and there seems to be no reason why many elements of it would not be useful also in a different context.

Notes

The views expressed in this article are the author's own and should not be attributed to the European Commission.

1. For the definition of an SME, see European Commission (2003). On the application of the definition of state aid to tax measures, see Luja (2003) and Rossi-Maccanico (2004, p. 229).

2. An overview of the currently applicable rules can be found at http://europa.eu.int/comm/competition/state_aid/legislation (accessed August 9, 2006).
3. http://europa.eu.int/comm/competition/state_aid/scoreboard/ (accessed August 9, 2006).
4. On May 1, 2004, Cyprus, the Czech Republic, Estonia, Hungary, Latvia, Lithuania, Malta, Poland, Slovakia, and Slovenia joined the EU. Bulgaria and Romania are expected to join in 2007. Turkey and Croatia are also candidate countries. See Schütterle (2002, p. 79; 2005, p. 255).

References

Antoniadis, Alexandra. 2002. "The EFTA Surveillance Authority's Practice in the Field of State Aid." *European State Aid Law Quarterly* 2: 157–182.

Battista, Jasmin. 2005. "Latest Developments in Regional and Horizontal State Aid." *European State Aid Law Quarterly* 3: 407–413.

Bilal, Sanoussi, and Phedon Nicolaides, ed. 1999. *Understanding Aid Policy in the European Community: Perspectives on Rules and Practice*. The Hague: Kluwer Law International.

Biondi, Andrea, Piet Eeckhout, and James Flynn, ed. 2004. *The Law of State Aid in the European Union*. Oxford: Oxford University Press.

D'Sa, Rose M. 1998. *European Community Law on State Aid*. London: Sweet & Maxwell.

European Commission. 2001. "Communication on State Aid and Risk Capital." *Official Journal of the European Communities* C 235, 21.08.2001: 3–11.

———. 2002. "Communication on the Modification of the Multisectoral Framework on Regional Aid for Large Investment Projects with Regard to the Establishment of a List of Sectors Facing Structural Problems." *Official Journal of the European Communities* C 263, 01.11.2003: 3–4.

———. 2003. "Recommendation of 6 May 2003 Concerning the Definition of Micro, Small, and Medium-Sized Enterprises." *Official Journal of the European Communities* L 124, 20.05.2003: 36–41.

Hancher, Leigh. 2005. "Towards an Economic Analysis of State Aids." *European State Aid Law Quarterly* 4(3): 425–433.

Hancher, Leigh, Tom Ottervanger, and Piet Jan Slot. 1999. *EC State Aids*. 2nd ed. London: Sweet & Maxwell.

Heidenhain, Martin, ed. 2003. *Handbuch des Europäischen Beihilfenrechts*. München: Beck.

Ichikawa, Yoshiharu. 2004. "The Tension between Competition Policy and State Intervention: the EU and US compared." *European State Aid Law Quarterly* 4: 555–571.

Luja, Raymond. 2003. *Assessment and Recovery of Tax Incentives in the EC and the WTO: A View on State Aids, Trade Subsidies and Direct Taxation.* Antwerp: Intersentia.

Nicolaides, Phedon. 2002. "Control of State Aid in the European Union: Compliance, Sanctions and Rational Behaviour." *World Competition* 25(3): 249–262.

———. 2003. "Regional State Aid: An Assessment of Community Rules and National Measures." *European State Aid Law Quarterly* 4: 543–551.

Nicolaides, Phedon, Mihalis Kekelekis, and Philip Buyskes. 2005. *State Aid Policy in the European Community. A Guide for Practitioners.* The Hague: Kluwer Law International.

Quigley, Connor, and Anthony M. Collins. 2003. *EC State Aids Law and Policy.* Portland, OR: Hart Publishing.

Rossi-Maccanico, Pierpaolo. 2004. "State Aid Review of Member States' Measures Relating to Direct Business Taxation." *European State Aid Law Quarterly* 2: 229–251.

Schütterle, Peter. 2002. "Implementing of the EC State Aid Control—An Accession Criterion." *European State Aid Law Quarterly* 1: 79–86.

———. 2005. "State Aid Control in the Western Balkans and Turkey." *European State Aid Law Quarterly* 2: 255–263.

Siemens v. Commission. 1997. ECJ, Case C-278/95 P, 1997 [ECR] I-2507.

Sinnaeve, Adinda. 2001. "Block Exemptions for State Aid: More Scope for State Aid Control by Member States and Competitors." *CMLRev.* 38(6): 1479–1501.

Sinnaeve, Adinda, and Piet Jan Slot. 1999. "The New Regulation on State Aid Procedures." *CMLRev.* 36(6): 1153–1194.

Winter, Jan A. 2004. "Re(de)fining the Notion of State Aid in Article 87(1) of the Treaty." *CMLRev.* 41(2): 475–504.

Wishlade, Fiona. 2003. *Regional State Aid and Competition Policy in the European Union.* The Hague: Kluwer Law International.

5
Solving the Problems of Economic Development Incentives

Timothy J. Bartik
W.E. Upjohn Institute for Employment Research

How can economic development incentives best be reined in? I agree with most students of this issue that economic development incentives are often wasteful. But this chapter maintains the position that some incentives are socially beneficial.[1] The challenge is to design reforms that encourage dropping wasteful incentives and keeping those that are socially beneficial.

To design incentive reforms, we must first agree on the causes of current U.S. incentive practices. This is the focus of the next section. What are the social benefits and costs of incentives? Why are incentives so often wasteful? Answering these questions allows us to address the problems leading to wasteful incentives, while encouraging beneficial incentives.

My conclusion is that some incentives are beneficial for two reasons: 1) because corporations are becoming more footloose, they are becoming more responsive to incentives; and 2) increased local employment rates yield social benefits. However, incentives are often wasteful for two reasons: 1) local policymakers often overestimate the benefits of incentives, and 2) the local debate over incentives is dominated by business interests. Unlike some students of this issue, I do not think that incentives are excessive because a state government ignores an incentive's "spillover costs" for other states.

Based on this analysis, I conclude that incentive reform should focus on improving the local decision-making process for incentives. Local decisions about incentives will be improved by a more democratic process with full information, a budget constraint on incentives, better benefit–cost analysis, incentive designs that target new business activity that brings social benefits, and performance requirements. Federal policy can encourage better information about incentives, help finance efficient incentives in economically distressed regions, and encourage cooperative economic development policy in metropolitan areas that cross state lines.

THE FORCES LEADING TO INCENTIVES

Before discussing the forces leading to incentives, I should define what I mean by incentives. In this chapter, I focus on the type of incentive that looks most like legalized bribery of the rich: cash or near-cash assistance provided on a discretionary basis to attract or retain business operations owned by large businesses. Such cash or near-cash assistance includes property tax abatements, discretionary credits under the state's corporate income tax, low-interest financing, and free land or buildings. This type of incentive deserves the most attention because, out of the total resources for economic development, such incentives comprise the largest share. For example, in Michigan such incentives are about three-quarters of all resources devoted to economic development programs (Bartik, Eisinger, and Erickcek 2003).[2]

Other incentives to large businesses are close substitutes for cash assistance. Incentives to attract or retain large businesses may also include customized services, which help meet the needs of an individual business, such as information on potential sites, help with state or local regulations, customized training for new or existing employees, and expedited provision of site-related public infrastructure, such as access roads. Customized services are sometimes almost equivalent to cash; for example, in some cases "customized training" is writing a check to the company to train its own employees. Another close substitute for discretionary cash incentives are business tax breaks provided as an "entitlement" under state or local tax laws, such as investment or employment expansion tax credits that go by legal right to all businesses that meet the tax law's criteria. Discretionary tax incentives, such as property tax abatements, may become so routine that they are almost equivalent to "entitlement" tax breaks. Reforms to cash incentives for large businesses may lead to increased use of these other incentives.

Economic development programs also provide assistance to new businesses and small and medium-sized businesses, including many high-tech businesses, which is intended to be an "incentive" for the growth of such businesses. Assistance to small and medium-sized businesses includes cash assistance, such as loans or equity finance, and grants for research and development. Assistance to small and medium-sized businesses may also include customized services, such as information on how to start up a business, or make an existing one more profitable (e.g., industrial extension services, and small business development centers). Reforms to incentive programs for large businesses may also affect these other programs.

Is there a good rationale for state and local governments to offer economic development incentives to attract or retain large businesses? Is there a good rationale for why such incentive use appears to be rising over time? One plausible rationale is that incentives are increasingly perceived as a necessary cost incurred to produce social benefits. It seems increasingly plausible that incentives might help attract or retain business, and thereby produce benefits such as greater employment rates and a stronger state and local fiscal situation. I will argue that these statements are true, but that incentives' costs are often large while incentives' benefits are often modest.

Incentives may increasingly affect business location decisions because businesses are increasingly footloose. As shown in Figure 5.1, over the past 100 years, transport and communication costs have declined. Cheaper transport of inputs and outputs, and the greater ease of using communications and computers to coordinate business activities at distant locations, allows business activities to be sited at a wider variety of locations. Because businesses have many more sites that are acceptable options from a transport and communications perspective, businesses are much more sensitive to local costs, such as wages and taxes. Wages are a larger share of costs than taxes, but taxes and the incentives that offset them are more immediately controllable by government.

Declining transport and communication costs help explain why research increasingly shows a statistically significant but modest effect of state and local tax rates on economic development. Reviews of the literature suggest that the long-run elasticity of a state or metropolitan

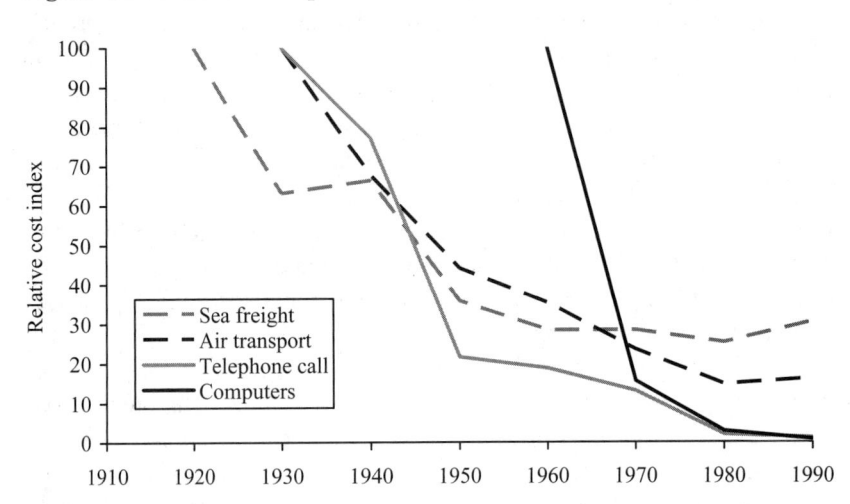

Figure 5.1 Relative Transportation and Communication Costs

[Chart showing relative cost index from 1910-1990 for Sea freight, Air transport, Telephone call, and Computers, all declining over time]

NOTE: The figure sets transport and communication costs equal to 100 for the first year for which such cost data are available in the UN report. Each type of cost therefore uses a different base period. This allows all the data to be placed on one graph.

SOURCE: These data are derived from United Nations Development Programme (1999, p. 30). This particular presentation was developed by Rodrigue, Comtois, and Slack (2004).

area's business activity with respect to state and local taxes is between −0.2 and −0.3 (Bartik 1991a, 1992; Wasylenko 1997), which means that a 10 percent reduction in effective state and local business tax rates (for example, a reduction of the state corporate income tax rate from 5.0 to 4.5 percent, accompanied by similar reductions in other state and local business taxes), with state and local public services held constant, will increase the long-run level of local business activity by 2 or 3 percent.[3]

Such an effect on business activity is not huge. If the state and local tax cuts are financed by cutting public services, the result may be lower business activity. The elasticities are not large enough to produce a Laffer Curve, in which cuts in tax rates would raise the tax base enough to increase revenue. The estimates imply that the gross cost of creating a job through lower business tax rates is a sacrifice of $10,000 annually per job in lower business tax revenue. The higher business tax base would offset only about a quarter of this "static" revenue loss, resulting in a net cost of creating a job through lower business tax rates of about

$7,000 per year in foregone business tax revenue. At a 10 percent real discount rate, the present value cost in foregone business tax revenue is $70,000 per job created.[4] Still, for state or local officials searching for some way to affect the local economy, lowering taxes seems one of the few options.

These figures are for business tax cuts for an entire state or metropolitan area. Research suggests that a business tax cut by an individual suburb within a metropolitan area, holding the taxes of other jurisdictions constant, has much larger effects, perhaps 10 times as great per dollar of incentive. That is, a 10 percent cut in an individual suburb's business taxes, such as a cut in the business property tax rate from 2 percent to 1.8 percent, will increase that individual suburb's business activity by 20 percent, largely by capturing business activity from other jurisdictions in the same metropolitan area. These larger effects make sense because individual jurisdictions within a metropolitan area are closer substitutes for one another than different states are for one another, as jurisdictions within the same metropolitan area offer more similar access to markets and inputs. The research is mixed on whether business tax cuts for large central cities have significant effects on business location (Bartik 1991a, 1992; Haughwout et al. 2003).

What implications do these estimated effects of state and local business tax cuts have for the effects of incentives? Few studies directly estimate the effects of incentives. However, under the assumption that a "dollar is a dollar," tax incentives for a large business should have similar effects on its location decisions to an equal dollar-sized business tax cut. Therefore, the effects of incentives on the probability of a particular branch plant locating in a state should, on average, be such as to yield the same expected gross dollar cost per job as business tax cuts. For example, the highest incentive offers, according to Fisher and Peters (2002), are equivalent to an annual subsidy of about $2,800 per worker inside some enterprise zones.[5] To be consistent with the business location literature, reducing business taxes via an incentive offer of $2,800 per job for a branch plant, compared to no incentive offer, would increase the probability of a new branch plant choosing the state by about 0.3.[6] This implies that for every 10 plants offered such an incentive, the incentive would be decisive for about 3 of them. The incentives given to the other 7 plants would have no effects on business location or employment growth. The only effect would be an extra cost to state and local governments of these unneeded 7 incentives. Unless economic developers can somehow determine which of the 10 plants "needs" the incentive to tip its location decision, this loss on 7 of the 10 plants is a necessary cost to tip the location decision of the other 3 plants. For smaller, more "normal" incentives, an even lower percentage of location decisions would be tipped by incentives. Fisher and Peters' figures imply that the mean state/local economic development incentive outside of enterprise zones is equivalent to an annual subsidy of about $300 per worker. Such an incentive would be expected to affect the location decision of only 3 out of 100 subsidized companies.[7]

The benefits of greater job growth in a metropolitan area occur in the form of earnings increases for local residents who get jobs as the local employment rate increases, earnings increases for local residents who move up to better-paying jobs with a tighter local labor market, local property value increases, profit increases in local businesses that have a head start in serving a larger local market, and tax base increases for state and local governments.[8] These benefits must be netted against costs of greater local job growth, including the value of the foregone nonwork time for local residents who gain jobs, the costs of additional public services required by expanding employment and population, and environmental costs.

We have reasonable estimates of the magnitude of these benefits and costs and how they are affected by differences in local conditions and the type of job growth (Bartik 1991a, 1993). A 1 percent increase in local employment is associated in the long run (more than five years) with an increase of 0.8 percent in local population, implying that 8 out of 10 new jobs in a metropolitan area go to persons who otherwise would have lived elsewhere. This 1 percent job increase is also associated with a 0.2 percent increase in the local employment rate (employment to population ratio), as local residents increase their labor force participation as they acquire better job skills with their greater job experience. One percent extra job growth in the long run is associated with average real wages moving up by 0.1 to 0.2 percent, but due entirely to local residents moving up to better-paying occupations; the real wages of particular occupations are unchanged, with occupational wages just matching increases in local prices. At low unemployment rates, when jobs are easy to get, the value of time spent unemployed, which economists call the reservation wage, may be 90 percent of the market wages, which would imply a cost of foregone nonwork time of 0.18 percent in a low unemployment labor market due to 1 percent extra job growth.

The required public services due to growth should, in the long run, increase about the same as the tax base for employment growth that is accompanied by the same population growth and involves no occupational upgrading. But as detailed above, the employment growth due to the "labor demand" shock caused by economic development policies will raise employment rates and increase real wages due to occupational upgrading. If employment rates go up, tax revenues should increase faster than public spending needs for three reasons: 1) business growth by itself brings tax revenue greater than public services, estimated as $1.70 in taxes per dollar of required public services according to one source (Oakland and Testa 1996); 2) increased employment rates should reduce required state spending for transfers, reducing welfare spending by about 6 percent for a 1 percent increase in employment growth (Bartik and Eberts 1999), and unemployment benefit outlays by about 3 percent (Bartik 1991b); and 3) increased employment rates will raise personal tax revenues per capita, by a percent equal to the percent increase in the employment rate. Increases in real wages, such as those caused by the occupational upgrading due to increased labor demand, will also raise personal tax revenues, which should go up approximately proportionately with the increased real wages. In the short run, public service costs associated with growth will go up less than the percentage increase in employment and population if there is excess capacity in local infrastructure. On the other hand, if new infrastructure is required, and the depreciation cost of the current infrastructure is not reflected in local budgets, then most estimates suggest that additional public service costs will significantly exceed new tax revenues in the short-run (Altshuler and Gomez-Ibanez 1993).

One percent extra employment growth will increase local property values by 0.4 percent. However, the present value of the increased earnings from growth are at least triple the size of the property value gains (Bartik 1991a, 1994b). In addition to increases in property values due to increased land demand, the value of "brownfield" property that is cleaned up as part of an economic development project may also go up due to removing this development barrier. Other local asset values will also change: locally owned businesses that have some comparative advantage in selling to a local market will increase their profits, whereas locally owned businesses that sell to an external market may lose profits due to increased wages and rents.

Other than brownfield clean-up, most environmental effects of growth are likely to be negative, but will vary greatly with project details. In addition, changes in community character that accompany growth may be viewed negatively by the original local residents.

The net effects of greater job growth are likely to be progressive, as lower-income groups are more likely to be initially nonemployed or employed in low-wage jobs. Therefore, most estimates suggest that the lowest income quintile probably has earnings gains that are three or four times greater, in percentage terms, than the earnings gains of the average family, and income gains that are around twice as great, in percentage terms, as the real income gains of the average family (Bartik 1994b). However, the actual dollar effects on earnings and income of the lowest income quintile are less than that of the average family, as many low-income individuals are disconnected from the labor market (Bartik 2001, Table 5.3). The progressivity of increased job growth is considerably less than the progressivity of redistributive social programs, which deliver their greatest dollar benefits to the lowest income quintile (Bartik 1994b).

The bottom line from this analysis is that for an average incentive project in a low unemployment local labor market, benefits and costs are of similar magnitude (Bartik 1991a, p. 183). The chapter's appendix and its accompanying table present some illustrative calculations. There is sufficient uncertainty about the estimated effects of taxes on growth, and growth on local economic variables, that whether the net benefits are positive or negative is unclear. Benefits and costs will vary greatly with project particulars.

Social benefits of incentives are greater if the project overcomes "market failures" that impede the use of local resources.[9] For example, social benefits are greater if the project helps overcome involuntary unemployment or underemployment that impedes workers from being employed or being employed in higher-wage jobs. Social benefits will be greater if local employment rates increase more, or local residents move up to higher-paying jobs to a greater extent, or if the local labor market is more depressed. An increasing local employment rate provides more earnings benefits to local residents, reduces the need for social services to the nonemployed, and reduces the public services costs and environmental costs associated with increased population. An increase in higher-paying jobs for local residents increases earnings benefits, and increases fiscal benefits by reduced social services and increased taxes. In a more depressed local labor market, the nonemployed will be more desperate for jobs and have lower reservation wages.

Social benefits will also be greater if the current public infrastructure is underutilized, which allows increased employment and population growth to increase tax revenue without a commensurate increase in public infrastructure costs. This is more likely in a local area that has been sufficiently economically distressed that it has lost population and employment from some previous peak. Social benefits will also be greater if the project overcomes regulatory and other barriers that prevent brownfields from being productively used.

But policymakers should also be aware that social benefits of growth will be much reduced under any of the following circumstances: low-unemployment local labor markets; lower wages of the new jobs; fewer local workers for the new jobs; significant public infrastructure or environmental costs. For example, estimates suggest that if the job growth is in industries that pay 10 or 15 percent less than the average industry controlling for worker characteristics, then the job growth may produce no earnings benefits for local residents (Bartik 2004b). If there are zero earnings benefits from additional employment growth, and consequently little if any fiscal benefits, it is highly unlikely that an incentive package will pass a benefit-cost test unless it has extremely low costs per job created.

Therefore, incentives can affect business location, and increased job growth can yield important social benefits. We would expect informed state governments, or metropolitan agencies concerned with economic development, that are maximizing the well-being of all their residents, to only offer incentives if the benefits outweigh the costs. These calculations would consider that only a fraction of incentive offers would prove decisive, and only a fraction of newly created jobs would go to local residents. Policymakers would consider the circumstances of the local economy, the environmental costs or benefits, the quality of the new jobs, and who is hired for those new jobs. So, what is the problem?

The problem is that many incentives currently being offered in the United States have costs that exceed benefits. For example, in 2001 Chicago awarded large incentives to the Boeing Corporation for relocating its headquarters, even though the jobs would go to relocated workers, which eliminates many of the labor market benefits.

One cause of wasteful incentives is ignorance. Policymakers assume that all growth is good. They assume that all incentive offers are decisive. It is often assumed that benefits can be measured by looking at the earnings and tax base associated with the new business activity. This assumption forgets that only a portion of the new jobs go to local residents and the unemployed, and that new public expenditures will be required.

But there may be reasons for ignorance. As Upton Sinclair (1935) said, "It is difficult to get a man to understand something when his salary depends upon his not understanding it." Local economic development decisions have been dominated by local business interests, including Chambers of Commerce, newspapers, banks, and real estate developers. From these groups' perspectives, the benefits of economic development are the increase in the value of their property, including the value of local business assets, and this increase in local capital values is closely related to the earnings and tax base increase of the new plant. Furthermore, the costs of the incentives, including the incentives that do not work, will be borne largely by the general public. There is truth to the observation by Logan and Molotch (1987, pp. 50–51) that, "For those who count, the city is a growth machine, one that can increase aggregate rents and trap related wealth for those in the right position to benefit."

Unlike some analysts of incentives, I do not think the fundamental problem is that a state government (or a metropolitan-wide economic development authority) fails to take into account the negative effects of its incentives on other states. If all states had rational incentive regimes, on the margin investors in each state would be charged a tax rate net of incentives that would reflect the marginal public service and environmental costs, net of any employment benefits, that the investment caused. Under those conditions, a state's incentive that attracts a marginal plant that would have otherwise gone to another state causes no net cost for that other state. Of course, states don't usually have rational incentive regimes, and so it is likely that attracting this marginal plant would cause net social costs (or benefits, depending upon the net effect in the other state) for the state that otherwise would have received this investment. But this "externality" is not the fundamental problem, rather it reflects the fundamental problem: each state lacks, from its own self-interested perspective, a rational incentive regime that maximizes the interests of all state residents.

Critics who argue that incentives negatively affect other states also argue that states are offering incentives so excessive that the social costs of attracting these new plants exceed the social benefits. If this is the case for all states, then if state X attracts a plant that would have gone to state Y, state X is doing state Y a favor by saving it from a wasteful incentive.

This analysis so far has considered economic development decisions by a state or an entire metropolitan area, and asks whether a state or metropolitan area acting rationally has the proper incentive to consider all benefits and costs. The analysis is different when we consider economic development decisions for an individual suburban jurisdiction. For an individual suburban jurisdiction attracting a new plant, the main effects on the jurisdiction itself are effects on the jurisdiction's tax base and the jurisdiction's environmental quality. The net fiscal costs of providing public services to additional households attracted by the new business activity will mostly be incurred by other jurisdictions in the metropolitan area, or by the state government, as most workers in an individual suburban jurisdiction do not live there. The employment benefits of increased employment rates and promotions to better-paying occupations will also mostly be received by residents of other jurisdictions. The decisions of individual suburban jurisdictions about incentives have no strong reason to fully reflect all these social costs and benefits.

ALTERNATIVE INCENTIVE REFORMS

Given this economic context, what incentive reforms are desirable? This section evaluates the merits of possible reforms. Although some reforms are mutually exclusive, others could be combined.

Maintain traditional state and local policies towards business, but remain competitive in the global economy. State and local governments would maintain their traditional business tax systems and not offer any incentives or other business cost reductions to improve the local business climate. As mentioned previously, this traditional system imposed state and local taxes on business that exceeded the public services to business, with $1.70 in business taxes per dollar of public services to business (Oakland and Testa 1996).

For most state and local areas, I doubt whether this alternative will prove politically viable. The mobility of business is increasing. Most state and local areas will sometimes experience high unemployment that will lead to public demands for action, and this high unemployment will also increase the benefits of growth. There is enough evidence that business taxes and incentives affect local growth that business interests will be able to argue for reduced taxes or increased incentives to reduce unemployment. The argument for doing something will win out over the argument for doing nothing.

Localism. Rather than competing for mobile capital, local areas could "just say no," eliminate incentives for mobile corporations, and rely on locally generated capital. The best articulation of this approach is in Michael Shuman's (2000) book, *Going Local,* although this approach appeals to many American community activists. Shuman advocates community corporations with voting shares controlled by local residents, with these community corporations making the local economy more self-sufficient by producing goods and services that replace imports of goods and services from other local areas.

The main problem with this approach is that greater reliance on local capital and local production would significantly reduce an area's real per capita income. There are static and dynamic gains from trade and capital mobility. Local areas should be free to pursue this option, but local residents should understand the costs.

Develop unique local assets that yield economic rents. Local areas can develop unique assets that make their area significantly more valuable to large businesses than these businesses' next best alternative, so that these large businesses receive what economists call an "economic rent" from the local area. This "economic rent" would allow business taxation in excess of public service costs without offering incentives to attract or retain these large businesses. One unique local asset would be a unique cluster of industries that increases productivity by resulting in more new ideas, and greater availability of specialized inputs such as workers with special skills (Rosenfeld 2002a,b). Another unique local asset would be distinctive local amenities that attract what Florida (2002) calls the "creative class," the professional and technical workers who enhance productivity for many high-tech businesses.

The problem is that for most local areas, it is difficult to develop unique industry clusters or local amenities. Businesses will have many options of similar metropolitan areas that offer advantages from industry clusters and local amenities. There are then no economic rents for local areas to exploit, and offering incentives must at least be seriously considered.

Lower overall business tax rates. Faced with businesses with many location options, localities can respond by lowering overall business tax rates rather than offering special incentives. This low-tax alternative to incentives is favored by many conservative critics of incentives.

The problem is that this change would significantly reduce tax revenue, forcing difficult choices on state and local governments about raising household taxes, or cutting public services or transfers. These problems would be particularly acute in economically distressed local areas.

Lower marginal tax rates on new business operations. Rather than cutting business tax rates across the board, state and local areas could give tax credits or deductions for business investment or employment expansion. Compared to overall business tax reductions, this results in less of a short-run or medium-run revenue loss. Reductions in taxes on new business operations are similar to incentives, but would be provided as an entitlement to all businesses meeting the law's criteria, rather than in a discretionary manner to approved businesses.

Providing tax breaks as an entitlement, rather than at discretion, in theory encourages a state or local government to analyze the impact of the tax break in toto. In practice, such tax breaks are not reviewed closely. In addition, entitlement tax breaks, compared to discretionary tax breaks, do not allow the advantages of being selective, such as selecting projects in which assistance is more likely to tip the location decision, or the location has greater benefits.

Make discretionary incentives truly selective. As mentioned before, many discretionary incentives are provided so automatically to projects that they become equivalent to a tax break provided as an entitlement. Economic developers can be forced to become selective by requiring the number of incentives be capped, or better, that the dollar volume of incentives be capped. Criteria can be required for selecting incentive winners from incentive applicants, such as evidence that this incentive will tip the location decision, and benefit-cost analyses of the projects. Michigan's "MEGA" program, for example, which provides large tax credits to attract or retain businesses, has limits on the annual number of projects. It requires that all projects present data showing that a non-Michigan site would be more profitable without the incentive, and that all projects be subject to fiscal impact analysis.[10]

Capping incentive volume limits incentive costs. Political debate on the incentive cap may lead to a broader debate about the incentive regime. Whether government officials can determine if the incentive is needed to tip the location decision is more questionable. However, requiring businesses to legally certify, with official financial figures, that without the incentive the business would have located elsewhere, might discourage some egregious cases where clearly the incentive was irrelevant to the location decision. Finally, models can be developed to provide reasonably accurate estimates of the labor market and fiscal benefits of a new facility.

Transparency. The details of incentives and incentive offers can be required to be clearly publicly disclosed. This disclosure promotes broader public debate. If the incentive offers are reported in a consistent fashion nationally, the disclosure may also give economic developers a more accurate knowledge of what alternatives are open to business location decision makers, which should improve the bargaining position of economic developers. Businesses already know what they have been offered by different local areas, but economic developers do not. The national collection of this information would allow better research on incentives. Finally, transparency is essential for any incentive regulation by the federal government or supranational organizations. The European Union requires public disclosure of incentives by its member states, and disclosure and transparency are encouraged by international trade agreements.

Metrowide economic development programs, not within-metro competition. State governments can require that incentives not be provided by individual local governments, but only by the state as a whole or by metrowide organizations or coalitions. As discussed previously, local governments that are a small part of the local labor market will not consider many important social effects of business growth when offering incentives, such as the labor market benefits throughout the metropolitan area, and the fiscal effects of increased metropolitan population. This makes it unlikely that incentive policies conducted by small individual local governments will be optimal. A metrowide perspective would seem to be a minimum requirement for incentive policy to consider the full range of economic and fiscal effects. One limitation of state governments in this regard is that some metro areas cross state boundaries, a subject considered below.

Better benefit-cost analyses. State legislatures can require that all economic development incentive offers be subject to a prospective benefit-cost analysis to estimate whether their incentive offers are efficient. This analysis would estimate employment benefits, including what proportion of the new jobs would likely go to local residents, particularly unemployed local residents; wage effects, including the wage rate paid on the jobs for workers of given credentials versus current local jobs held by local residents with similar credentials; fiscal effects, including local as well as state effects, effects on required public expenditure as well as taxes, and analysis of the capacity of existing infrastructure to accommodate job growth; and environmental effects. If the estimates are high quality, they increase the likelihood of the right incentive choices. Even imperfect estimates would encourage debate on some relevant issues about incentives.

Job quality and other project standards. As suggested by Greg LeRoy and the organization "Good Jobs First," as well as others, states could require that all projects awarded incentives meet some minimum standard for job quality (LeRoy 1999; Nolan and LeRoy 2003; Purinton et al. 2003). In theory, concerns about job quality are already addressed as one component of the benefit-cost analysis. Decisions should be based on the net benefits of the incentive, not just on whether the project met a job-quality standard. However, as a check on the incentive decision-making process, it might be wise to identify in advance some minimum standards for projects, under the assumption that projects failing to meet standards would be unlikely to pass a benefit-cost test. Projects that did not meet these minimum standards would have to go through a special review process to be approved. These minimum standards would give economic developers a summary of what types of projects they would be encouraged to pursue, and would give the public and policymakers extra assurance that there is some selectivity involved in the benefit-cost analysis process. Benefit-cost analysis is too often a "black box" dominated by technical experts. Standards may help clarify what the analysis process is trying to do.

More up-front incentives. Studies indicate that corporate executives use very high real discount rates in making investment decisions, averaging 12 percent (Summers and Poterba 1992). For business location decisions, this implies that the portion of the property tax abatement provided 10 years from now is almost completely irrelevant to the location decision, because the business decision maker is focused on shorter-term profit objectives. On the other hand, most studies suggest that governments should use social discount rates much lower than 12 percent. To serve the public interest, governments should have a longer time horizon than corporate executives.

As a result, it is possible to have a greater effect on business location decisions at a lower cost by providing a greater proportion of the incentive up front. Up-front incentives also force state and local political leaders to immediately deal with incentives' costs, rather than pass on costs to their successors. However, providing more up-front incentives brings to the forefront the issue of whether the incentive can be recovered if the location decision does not provide the promised benefits, for example, if the company relocates. To provide more incentives up front, a greater proportion of the incentive can be provided as customized training or infrastructure, or tax incentives can be made larger but shorter term.

Clawbacks. The net benefits of an incentive regime increase when some of the incentive can be recovered if the business receiving the incentive does not provide the planned social benefits, for example, if the business relocates or the number of jobs created falls short of projections.[11] This can be dealt with by legally binding "clawback" provisions, which recover some portion of the up-front incentives if the business does not meet performance goals. State use of clawback provisions is increasing, with the number increasing from 9 to 17 between 1992 and 2002 (Peirce 2002). It is believed that local use of clawbacks is also increasing. Surveys of local governments show that 59 percent of local governments claim they "always" require a performance agreement as a condition for incentives, and an additional 30 percent of local governments claim they "sometimes" require a performance agreement (Bartik 2004a).

The main potential problem with clawbacks is that if they are unduly onerous, they may be a disincentive to attracting businesses. However, if they are designed with incentives so they are clearly related to the social benefits associated with the business, then businesses that expect to make a long-term investment in the community should not perceive clawbacks as a huge disincentive to their location decisions.

Redesign incentives to focus more on the social benefits of business growth.[12] As discussed above, the largest portion of the social benefits of growth arise from increasing local employment rates. Increasing such rates provides the unemployed with greater job experience, puts upward pressure on local wages, and increases local taxes more than public spending needs. Local employment rates are most likely to go up when the new business hires the unemployed, and least likely to go up when the new business hires in-migrants. The rates may go up when the new business hires local residents who are already employed, as this creates a job vacancy that may be filled by the local unemployed.

Therefore, incentives will be more targeted on the projects with greatest social benefits if the amount of the incentive is based on whom the business hires. Incentives should be somewhat greater for projects that hire local residents, and considerably greater if the business hires the unemployed.[13] More benefits of greater employment experience occur in the first year of employment, so it would be justifiable for greater incentives to be provided for the initial hiring of the unemployed and their first year of employment, and somewhat smaller incentives for subsequent years. In addition to targeting incentives on projects that provide greater social benefits, such incentives will encourage businesses to do more hiring of the unemployed. Such hiring incentives will be more effective if tied to local programs that attempt to screen and train potential hires from among the unemployed, which I discuss next (Bartik 2001, Chapter 8). Finally, tying incentives to the provision of social benefits is an automatic "clawback," as the incentive that is not paid until the benefit is delivered does not need to be "clawbacked" if the benefit is not delivered.

Tie incentives to participation in "first source" hiring programs.[14] Many local governments have some nominal requirement for local hiring by businesses receiving incentives, but frequently these requirements are unenforced because of fears of discouraging business locations. A few cities, such as Portland (Oregon), with its now-defunct JobNet program, and Berkeley, with its First Source program, have tried to encourage local hiring without adversely affecting business locations. These programs combine a moderate requirement—that businesses "consider" hiring workers referred by the program—with a public service to help businesses overcome the many difficulties they face in finding productive workers to fill jobs with few formal credential requirements. Studies suggest that one-quarter of new hires in small and medium-sized firms are producing less than 75 percent of what the employer anticipated after six months on the job (Bishop 1993). These difficulties may occur in part because job performance is so dependent on "soft skills," such as showing up at work on time and getting along with co-workers and customers, and these soft skills are hard to observe in the normal hiring process. Because normal hiring so often is disappointing to employers, a program that can train and screen qualified workers, who are then considered for hiring by employers receiving incentives, can potentially help businesses find productive workers. Local public agencies may have some comparative advantage over private businesses, particularly private businesses from out of town, in working with neighborhood groups, churches, and social service agencies to find productive workers for jobs with low credential requirements. Local public agencies may also be better able than businesses to mobilize resources for training from local workforce agencies and the local community college.

Focus incentives on in-kind up-front services such as customized training and access roads and other infrastructure. Customized training and infrastructure are incentives that inherently are concentrated up front and therefore have the advantages of up-front incentives mentioned previously, including a greater effect on location decisions per present value dollar of incentive. They also can be at least partially clawed back, without legal proceedings, as the infrastructure and most of the trained workers will remain in the local area even if the business relocates or downsizes. Customized training can be designed to increase the likelihood that a greater proportion of those trained and hired are local residents who otherwise would be unemployed (see Batt and Osterman [1993] and Osterman and Batt [1993] for some examples in North Carolina's customized training programs). Finally, both customized training and infrastructure can be justified as making public services more effective, rather than unjustifiably treating some businesses more favorably than others. For example, public infrastructure, such as highways, is supposed to be provided in response to demand. Providing access highways as part of an incentive package is only an "incentive" because the access highway is expedited to the top of the "to do" list. It could be argued that making the provision of highways more responsive to changes in demand makes government more responsive. It could also be argued that training programs can increase their quality by becoming more customized to the needs of both those receiving the training and those organizations that will demand the skills of those trained.

Federal intervention in incentive policy. In theory, federal intervention could be used to require or encourage all of these recommendations for more effective incentive policy. However, absent some rationale for why there is a national interest in incentive policy, there is no reason to think that federal intervention will be any wiser than state and local incentive policies. There is some reason to think that federal intervention would make things worse. The federal government has less knowledge about local labor market institutions, which might be important, for example, in designing customized training programs. The federal government will also have less of other "local knowledge": less knowledge about job needs of different groups, the hiring practices of local employers, the problems caused by particular environmentally contaminated properties, the capacity of particular local infrastructure, etc. In addition, the federal government is likely to be less responsive to local needs. Because the benefits and costs of incentive policies depend on the details of the local labor market and local fiscal structure, effective policymaking depends on an intimate knowledge and responsiveness to these details. Federal intervention is at a disadvantage.

Federal government intervention in incentive policy is particularly likely to be casually reckless if it is free of cost constraints, accomplishing its goals by regulating or taxing state and local incentives it wants to prevent rather than subsidizing incentives it wants to encourage. For example, some have proposed having Congress ban or heavily tax incentives (Minge 1999; Burstein and Rolnick 1995). As argued previously, some incentives have social benefits, and assuming the "federal incentive tax" was not easy to evade, a uniform tax would discourage these beneficial incentives. For example, an economically distressed city may find that economic development incentives are part of the best policy package for its economic revitalization. If a federal incentive tax prevents these incentives, that distressed city may have to adopt an inferior revitalization package—for example, one that tries to make the city competitive by lowering overall business tax rates and making cuts in redistributive public services. However, in practice I would suspect that most federal incentive taxes would be easy to evade, so this policy would serve little purpose except political posturing.

In theory, federal intervention could be more selective than a uniform federal incentive tax, which would make the intervention more beneficial. For example, Congress could only impose the federal incentive tax on incentives provided by affluent local areas. However, I am skeptical that Congressional intervention would be so enlightened.[15] If Congress is able to gain revenue, or at least not lose revenue, by regulating state and local economic development activities, I suspect that this unfettered intervention would be just as likely to discourage efficient economic development programs as inefficient programs.

Federal intervention in incentive policy is more likely to be effective if it is 1) targeted on instances where there is a clear national interest in state and local incentive policy, and 2) accomplished through federal subsidies rather than taxes and regulation, which forces some awareness of costs by federal decision makers. Three types of federal interventions appear justified based on national interests. First, federal dollars should continue to be provided for initiatives that seek to target economically distressed areas, such as Empowerment Zones and the New Markets Initiative. The rationale for this intervention is that there is a national interest in promoting a more progressive income distribution, which such initiatives help accomplish. Second, federal dollars should be provided for rigorous prospective and retrospective benefit-cost analyses of economic development incentives. In the process of evaluating these incentives, such study will disclose exactly what incentives are being offered in different states. The incentive offers from the different states should be compiled by the federal government into a database that would be publicly available. The rationale for this intervention is that information on what incentives are being offered, and these incentives' effectiveness, is a public good with benefits to economic developers and the public in all states. Third, federal dollars should be provided to help fund metrowide economic development organizations, with extra funding for metrowide economic development organizations that extend across state boundaries. The federal government has some advantage over the states in encouraging cooperation that might benefit an interstate metro area as a whole.

CONCLUSION

Wasteful economic development incentives should be dealt with largely by opening up the incentives policy process at the state and local level to broader public participation and debate. To promote more effective public participation, we should continually improve our data on and analyses of the benefits and costs of incentives. Broader public participation and better analysis should lead to the specific reforms that are discussed in this chapter.

Such a reformed incentive policy would only offer incentives selectively, subject to an overall budget constraint. Incentive offers would be coordinated at the metrowide or state level. Full public information would be available on all incentive offers and their results. Incentive offers would be subject to a prospective benefit–cost analysis, have some minimum standards for job quality, and have provisions for recovering incentives if performance goals were not achieved. Incentives would focus on encouraging more hiring of the unemployed, for example, through hiring subsidies and customized training grants. Economic development incentives should be seen as a part of an overall policy to improve local labor markets. Economic development incentives should be used to increase labor demand for those local residents who are unemployed or underemployed. Such local demand policies should be coordinated with local labor supply policies, which would provide the training and education needed for local residents to succeed in these new and better jobs. In addition to overcoming barriers to the efficient working of local labor markets, economic development incentives should be used to overcome barriers preventing the use of brownfields, and to encourage use of underutilized public infrastructure.

A "bottom-up" approach to reforming incentives, by working at the state and local level to improve incentive policy, is likely to be more effective, more durable, and more democratic than a heavy-handed "top-down" approach of using federal intervention to prevent certain practices. Federal policy can be more helpful by providing financial support for "bottom-up" reform: subsidizing better benefit-cost analyses and information on incentives, encouraging stronger coordination of incentives at the metro level, and targeting assistance on economically distressed local areas.

Incentive reforms are preferable to incentive abolition, as there are real economic forces that in some cases make incentives a desirable policy. Attempting to abolish incentives will lead to even more wasteful policies to create a "good business climate."

If one believes the government can take wise action, it is sensible to allow state and local governments the flexibility to use incentives. We should have a reasonable faith in state and local governments as "laboratories of democracy." State and local experimentation in economic development incentives can lead to better public policies if the public has the information and participation needed to allow for incentive reforms.

Appendix 5A

Plausible Calculations of Medium-Term Benefits and Costs of Economic Development Incentive Programs for a State or Metropolitan Area

This appendix presents in table form plausible medium-term flows of benefits and costs associated with an economic development incentive program. The table is an expansion and updating of calculations I have previously presented in Bartik (1991a, 1992, 1994b, 2004a) and Bartik, Eisinger, and Erickcek (2003). The incentive program considered is for a state or a metropolitan area. The benefits and costs estimated are for the residents of the state and metropolitan area, and their governments and businesses. Benefits and costs to the federal government, or to persons, businesses, or governments outside the state or metropolitan area, are not considered. The benefits and costs are calculated as annual flows over some medium term after the incentives are provided, say, five years. Some table entries also speculate about shorter-term or longer-term benefits and costs. Benefits and costs are calculated in two ways: 1) as percentages of annual state or local personal income for a 1 percent once-and-for-all labor demand increase to state or metropolitan area employment, with this 1 percent employment increase induced by incentives of average effectiveness; and 2) as real dollars, using prices of 2003, per job induced by incentives of average effectiveness. This appendix will go through Table 5A.1 line by line, explaining how each line is calculated based on the research literature and various data sources.

The gross incentive costs (line [1]) are derived assuming the response of state or metropolitan employment with respect to an incentive will be equivalent in gross costs to the foregone business tax revenue to induce increased local activity if the elasticity of local employment with respect to state and local business taxes is −0.25. As derived in Note 4, the gross foregone business tax revenue per induced job (line [1], column B) is $dR/dJ = (JdT)/dJ = T(1/E)$, where dR is the gross change in business tax revenue due to a reduction in business taxes, J is the number of jobs, dJ is the number of induced jobs, T is the business tax rate calculated as state and local business taxes per job, dT is the change in that tax rate, and E is the elasticity of state and local employment with respect to the business tax rate, which is assumed to be −0.25, a compromise between the −0.3 preferred in the literature review of Bartik (1992) and the −0.2 preferred by Wasylenko (1997). Business tax revenue per job is calculated as detailed in Note 4. Line (1)(A) is derived in similar manner, using the

Table 5A.1 Estimated Benefits and Costs of Economic Development Incentives

Category	Benefits/costs as % of local personal income for 1% induced employment growth (column A)	Benefits/costs in annual real 2003 dollars per induced job (column B)
(1) Incentive costs	−0.218	−9,699
(2) Fiscal effects		
(2.1) Induced revenue from additional business tax base	0.055	2,425
(2.2) Net incentive cost = (1) + (2.1)	−0.163	−7,274
(2.3) Net long-run fiscal effects of equal employment and population growth	0.000	0
(2.4) Gross effects of extra jobs on revenue from business tax base	0.011	485
(2.5) Required public services for extra jobs	−0.006	−285
(2.6) Net fiscal effects of "profit" on extra business tax base = 2.4 + 2.5	0.005	200
(2.7) Reduced social spending and unemployment benefits due to higher employment rates	0.019	845
(2.8) Sales/income taxes on increased personal income of local residents = 3.8	0.018	795
(2.9) Property taxes on increased real estate values	0.008	343
(2.10) Short-run fiscal effects: Positive if underutilized infrastructure, negative if growth requires expensive new infrastructure	Uncertain	Uncertain
(2.11) Net quantifiable fiscal effect = 2.6 + 2.7 + 2.8 + 2.9	0.049	2,183

(3) Labor market effects

(3.1)	Gross real earnings gains for local residents	0.317	14,104
(3.2)	Extra real earnings on new job	0.916	40,766
(3.3)	Subtracting out earnings of in-migrants = 80% of (3.2)	−0.733	−32,613
(3.4)	Net earnings of local residents on new jobs = 3.2 + 3.3	0.183	8,153
(3.5)	Increase in real wages due to promotion of local residents to better-paying occupations = 3.1 − 3.4	0.134	5,950
(3.6)	Loss of social spending transfers = 2.7	−0.019	−845
(3.7)	Net increase in real income of local residents before taxes = 3.4 + 3.5 + 3.6 = 3.1 + 3.6	0.298	13,258
(3.8)	Sales/income taxes on increased income of local residents	−0.018	−795
(3.9)	Increase in income of local residents after taxes = 3.7 + 3.8	0.280	12,463
(3.10)	Reservation wages in low unemployment local area = 90% of 3.4	−0.165	−7,338
(3.11)	Reservation wages in high unempl. area: assumed zero	0.000	0
(3.12)	Net labor market benefits in low unemployment area = 3.9 + 3.10	0.115	5,125
(3.13)	Net labor market benefits in high unemployment area = 3.9 + 3.11	0.280	12,463
(3.14)	Shorter-run or longer-run labor market benefits: probably greater in short-run, less in long-run	Uncertain	Uncertain

(4) Real estate effects

(4.1)	Gross gains in real estate values, as annual income flow	0.077	3,426
(4.2)	Increased annual property tax	−0.008	−343

(continued)

127

Table 5A.1 (continued)

Category	Benefits/costs as % of local personal income for 1% induced employment growth (column A)	Benefits/costs in annual real 2003 dollars per induced job (column B)
(4.3) Net gain to property owners	0.069	3,083
(5) Locally-owned business effects: Profit increase at businesses serving local market, decrease at export-base businesses.	Uncertain	Uncertain
(6) Environmental/congestion effects: likely to be negative unless project involves restoring brownfields	Uncertain	Uncertain
(7) Community effects: Some loss in community character and increased rents for local residents for growth beyond original community size, some gain for growth that restores community's customary size	Uncertain	Uncertain
Total quantifiable effects		
(8.1) In low unemployment local labor market = 1 + 2.11 + 3.12 + 4.3	0.016	692
(8.2) In high unemployment local labor market = 1 + 2.11 + 3.13 + 4.3	0.181	8,030

equation that the foregone taxes as percentage of income to induce 1 percent employment growth will be $= 100(dT/Y) = ([1\%$ employment growth$/E](T/Y)$, where T is now business taxes in dollar terms, Y is personal income, and state/local business taxes as a percent of personal income are assumed to be 5.46 percent, based on calculations in Bartik (1991a, p. 180).

Lines (2.1) through (2.2) present a side calculation showing fiscal effects and net incentive costs if the only fiscal effects considered are the extra business tax revenue from enhancing the business tax base. This extra business tax revenue is simply the business tax revenue associated with the induced jobs. Line (2.1)(B) is business tax revenue per job in 2003 dollars, based on calculations in Note 4, as the (B) column expresses everything per one induced job. Line (2.1)(A) is 1 percent of average business tax revenue as a percent of personal income, because the (A) column expresses everything per 1 percent in induced extra employment. Line (2.2) then shows a supposed "net incentive cost," which, however, is erroneous because it omits all the fiscal effects from the public services associated with the extra business tax base, as well as the taxes and public services associated with the extra households, and the effects of higher employment on the need for social services and revenue from the property tax. This erroneous calculation is the style of calculation frequently done by advocates for incentives who claim that such incentives "pay for themselves." Line (2.2) shows that such incentives clearly don't pay for themselves even if we only look at the business tax base gains.

To simplify the analysis of the full fiscal effects, I start from the baseline of the long-run fiscal effects of employment growth and population growth when both increase by the same percentage. This baseline is straightforward to analyze, and the actual net fiscal effects of the incentive-induced growth are then analyzed as effects of deviations from this baseline. Line (2.3) assumes that if state and local public services are constant returns to scale in the long run, as indicated in Fisher (1996) and Inman (1979), a balanced increase in employment and production should produce equal tax revenue and public service needs. But of course we don't expect that induced jobs will bring about the same percentage increase in population. Based on Bartik (1991a, 1993), we expect that for a given percentage increase in induced employment, the percentage increase in population will be about four-fifths as much. So we analyze the fiscal effects as if for every 1 percent in induced jobs, we have four-fifths of 1 percent in increased population. The fiscal effects then are a combination of a "balanced" increase of four-fifths of 1 percent in both employment and population, which should have zero fiscal effects in the long run, and the fiscal effects of the "extra" one-fifth of 1 percent of jobs. The effects of these extra jobs are the effects of these extra jobs on the business tax base and required public services, as well as the effects of the extra jobs, via a higher employment rate, on the taxes and transfers associated with higher earnings for local residents, considered in the section on labor market effects.

Line (2.4) calculates the business taxes from the extra jobs as one-fifth of the business taxes from the business tax base associated with all the jobs, from line (2.1). Line (2.5) is based on Oakland and Testa's (1996) calculation that business tax revenue is 70 percent greater than public services directly required by businesses. Line (2.7)(A) is based on estimates from Bartik and Eberts (1999) that 1 percent employment growth reduces welfare caseloads by 6 percent, and estimates by Chernick and McGuire (1999) that own-source state and local spending on social services is 1.3 percent of personal income; social services spending is assumed to decline by the same percent as welfare caseloads. This yields a decrease in social services spending as a percent of income of −0.008 percent. This may seem small compared to overall earnings gains of 0.317 percent (see line (3.1) below), but growth is only modestly progressive; about 4.2 percent of the total earnings gains from stronger regional labor demand goes to the bottom income quintile, which is not much more than their share of income (Bartik 2001, Table 5.3). In addition line (2.7)(A) is based on estimates (Bartik 1991b, Table 2) that 1 percent extra local employment growth in the short run reduces unemployment payments by 3.4 percent. Based on 1995 statistics from O'Leary and Wandner (1997, p. 733), and 1995 personal income data from the Regional Economic Information System, UI benefits are 0.33 percent of personal income, so a 3.4 percent reduction in such payments will reduce unemployment benefit payments by 0.011 percent of personal income. Adding 0.011 percent to the 0.008 percent reduction in social spending yields the 0.019 percent figure shown in line (2.7)(A). Line 2.7(B) is derived from (A) by using ratios. Line (2.8) is based on the taxes associated with the extra earnings of local residents, and will be discussed further when the labor market section of the table is discussed. Line (2.9) is based on the property taxes on the increased real estate values associated with growth and is discussed further in that section. Line (2.9) is based on case studies by Altshuler and Gomez-Ibanez (1993) that show that new required infrastructure frequently vastly exceeds tax revenue from growth; because existing infrastructure will eventually require replacement, this suggests that depreciation charges for existing infrastructure are understated.

Line (3.1)(A) is based on estimates reported in Bartik (1991a, p. 163) on effects of growth on real earnings, expressed as a percent of personal income by assuming earnings are 73.5 percent of personal income (Bartik, 1991a, p. 163). Line (3.1)(B) uses ratios to calculate this on a per job basis. Lines (3.2) through (3.5) attempt to divide line (3.1) into various components: gains for workers newly employed, vs. gains for workers already employed who get better jobs. Line (3.2) attempts to replicate what a naive benefit-cost analysis would assume about earnings gains: they are equal to the earnings on the induced jobs. Line (3.2)(B) is based on dividing total earnings by total employment, using 2002 data from the Regional Economic Information System. Line (3.2)(A) uses ratios to calculate this as a percent of personal income. Line (3.3) subtracts out the earnings of in-migrants to get the effects on local residents who get jobs in line (3.4). The rationale for subtracting line (3.3) is twofold: 1) this analysis takes a local perspective in which only the original residents count, and 2) the analysis in Bartik (1991a) suggests that the well-being of in-migrants is not substantially affected by extra jobs in this local area, as the in-migrants would otherwise move to a similar local area. After subtracting line (3.4) from line (3.1), the remaining earnings gain must be from local residents moving up to better paying jobs. The residual calculation for line (3.5) appears roughly consistent with data from Bartik (1991a) on how employment growth affects occupational upgrading for local residents. The loss of transfer income in line (3.6) was previously derived for line (2.7). Line 3.8 is based on estimates from Citizens for Tax Justice that state and local personal sales and income taxes in 1995 averaged 6 percent of income for households in the middle income quintile (Ettlinger et al. 1996, Appendix 1, p. 51). In line (3.10), the reservation wage figure of 90 percent is used in Bartik (1991a) based on a review of the reservation wage literature. The assumption that reservation wages are zero for the unemployed in high unemployment areas is arbitrary. This assumption might be justified, even if nonwork time has some value for the unemployed, as seems likely, if unemployment has sizable social costs such as increased crime or increased social problems for the children of the unemployed. Lines (3.12) and (3.13) emphasize how different the labor market benefits are based on different assumptions about reservation wages. Line (3.14) reflects that estimates suggest that the earnings effects reported in this table for local residents are probably greater in the short run and less in the long run than the medium-run figures used here (Bartik 1991a; Bartik 1994b). The question mark for line (3.14) suggests that it is unclear how this would affect a present value analysis compared to simply using the medium-run annual flow benefits and costs reported in the table.

Line (4.1)(A) comes from Bartik (1994b, Table 3) and is based upon estimates by Bartik (1991a) that 1 percent employment growth increases real estate values by 0.451 percent. A 10 percent real discount rate is used to convert changes in capital values to annual flows. Line (4) (B) is derived from (A) using ratios. Line 4.2 is based on Table 3.13 of the 2001 American Housing Survey, which estimates that the median residential property tax rate for owner-occupied housing is 1 percent of value (U.S. Census Bureau 2001).

The line (5) discussion assumes that only locally owned businesses should be considered in this local benefit-cost analysis. This is consistent with this analysis focusing on the perspective of the state or metropolitan area, and ignoring effects on the federal government, or other state or metropolitan areas. Growth will clearly increase nominal wages and prices, as shown in Bartik (1991a), which reduces profits for businesses selling to outside markets. But businesses with some comparative advantage that they can maintain as the area grows (e.g., a local newspaper) will likely increase profits due to growth, as discussed in Bartik (1991a). For more discussion of environmental effects of local economic development, and of brownfields, see Bartik (2004b).

The line (7) entry assumes that in a world with imperfect mobility, changes in a community's "character" that bring it away from the originally chosen amenity package of the area's households, with the accompanying wage and price changes, will reduce utility of the area's original residents, as these original residents must have preferred the original amenity package given prevailing wages and rents. For more on this type of model, see Bartik (1991a, pp. 73–76), and Bartik (1986).

There is considerable uncertainty in these figures; for example, I could come up with a rationale for adjusting the incentive cost figures and the earnings gains numbers up or down by 50 percent or more. Stating the numbers in this table to three, four, or five digits is an aid to calculation, but is a misleading indication of how much we really know. Therefore, it would be relatively easy to come up with a scenario under which quantifiable net benefits of economic development in a low unemployment area are negative.

Notes

This chapter reprinted by permission. See Bartik (2005).

1. I have previously written about incentives in Bartik (1990; 1991a; 1993; 1994a,b,c; 1996a,b; 2001; 2003; 2004a,b), as well as in Bartik, Erickcek, and Eisinger (2003). My comments on the benefits and costs of incentives from a state and local perspective are reasonably consistent. As I will footnote later, my comments on federal intervention in incentives have some inconsistencies.
2. The following Michigan programs are cash or near-cash incentives to large businesses: property tax abatements, one-third of tax increment financing, MEGA tax credits, brownfield tax credits, Renaissance zones, and federal Empowerment Zone/Enterprise Community funding. Together these programs comprise $531 million of the $706 million in annual Michigan economic development resources. Michigan also spends $13 million on customized job training, $60 million in federal community development block grants on infrastructure development for economic development in nonurban communities, and $48 million on business recruitment and retention. The remainder of Michigan economic development

Solving the Problems of Economic Development Incentives   133

resources are devoted to small business development, high-tech research, and manufacturing extension.

3. Although this is the general consensus, not all scholars agree that state tax effects on business location are significant. The most prominent scholarly critic of the notion that state taxes affect business location is McGuire. McGuire admits, however, that her position is inspired in part by fears of how state policymakers will respond to the conclusion that taxes affect business location. According to McGuire:

> ... I confess to being somewhat (perhaps very) irrational in my interpretation of this literature. With respect to the interstate and interregional studies, despite the number of studies with significant coefficients, I find it difficult to be convinced that taxes are an important factor in explaining differences in business location decisions and economic activity between states or regions. In part I believe the discrepancy between my conclusion and that of many other scholars of the topic is due to our different perspectives. I came to this topic through the tax-study, blue-ribbon-commission route. I have seen firsthand state policymakers grasping for straws. I simply do not think that the evidence allows us to comfortably advise lawmakers that reducing the corporate income tax rate or the personal income tax rate will revive a flagging state economy. (McGuire 2003)

4. This calculation is as follows: the tax elasticity of private employment with respect to state and local business taxes (E) is defined as $(dJ/J)/(dT/T)$, where J is the number of jobs, dJ is the change in the number of jobs, T is the tax rate, and dT is the change in the business tax rate. The percentage change in revenue from a tax cut, dR/R, will approximately equal $dT/T = dJ/J$.

Substituting and rearranging, one obtains, for the net foregone revenue cost per job created, $dR/dJ = (R/J)[1 + (1/E)]$. R/J is state and local business tax revenue per job, which was about $1,634 per job in the United States as of 1989. With a value of -0.25 for E, one obtains $dR/dJ = -\$4,902$. Updating by the change in consumer price index from 1989 to 2003 gives a figure in 2003 dollars of $(184/124)4,902 = \$7,274$. The figure of $1,634 for state and local business taxes per private employee comes from three sources. Total state and local tax revenue in fiscal year 1989 was $469 billion (U.S. Census Bureau 1991, p. 21). One estimate of the business share of state and local taxes is 31 percent (ACIR 1981, revised version of table A-1; figures for 1977). Private nonagricultural employment in the United States averaged 89 million during fiscal year 1989 (U.S. Department of Commerce 1991, S-10). These figures could be updated using more recent data, but most of the studies were estimated using earlier data, so use of this historical data is probably better. The elasticity used is a compromise between the -0.3 preferred in the literature review by Bartik (1992) and the -0.2 preferred by Wasylenko (1997). The Consumer Price Index figures come from the U.S. Bureau of Labor Statistics. I used an identical calculation in Bartik (2004a, 1992). The dynamic calculation here only looks at effects of taxes on the business tax base, and ignores extra public expenditures required by a higher business tax base, and extra taxes and required public expenditures because of a larger household tax base.

The cost in static tax revenue is $dR = JdT$, which, per job created by lower business tax rates, is $JdT/dJ = T(1/E)$ = (business tax base per job) (1/0.25). Using the same figures the loss in static revenue from a business tax cut in 2003 dollars is $9,699 = 1,634(184/124)(1/0.25)$.

5. Derived from Fisher and Peters (2002, Table 3.7). This takes their present value of incentives per job in the highest subsidy city and state of $22,678 in 1994, translates this into an annual equivalent by multiplying by the 10 percent discount rate used by Fisher and Peters, and then adjusts to a 2003 value using the Consumer Price Index, or $(1984/148.2) \times (0.10)(22,678) = 2,816$.
6. An annual subsidy of $2,816 per job will yield a gross cost of $9,699 per induced job, as previously calculated, if the proportion of induced jobs (p) satisfies the equation $p = \$2,816/\$9,699 = 0.29$.
7. These calculations are based on Fisher and Peters' figures for the mean value of "general incentives" per job in 1994, translated into an annual equivalent and updated to 2003 dollars.
8. What about migrants? I explore this in Bartik (1991a, Chapter 3). The argument is that persons on the margin of migrating in, or migrating out, do not have their opportunities substantially affected by changes in the characteristics of this one local area. If the local area had remained unchanged, with no growth, the persons who would have otherwise migrated in would choose other, similar metropolitan areas. Similarly, the individuals whose outmigration is averted by growth are by definition close to indifferent between staying or moving.
9. For more "market failure" analysis of state and local economic development policy, see Bartik (1990, 1994c) or Courant (1994).
10. This fiscal impact analysis is imperfect. The fiscal impact analysis only looks at state revenues, and not at state expenditures, or local taxes and expenditure. In addition, a full benefit-cost analysis would include labor market benefits. See Bartik, Erickcek, and Eisinger (2003) for a more detailed discussion of MEGA.
11. More extensive discussion of clawbacks is found in Peters (1993) and Weber (2002).
12. This is advocated by Bartik (2001) and Schweke and Woo (2003).
13. Favoring the unemployed in jobs associated with business subsidies would seem likely to be acceptable discrimination from a legal perspective. Favoring local residents is more open to question.
14. More on "First Source" programs is in Anderson (1999); Bartik (2001, Chapter 9); Molina (1998); and Schweke (1999).
15. I have been inconsistent over the years in my comments on federal regulation of incentives. I have sometimes been tempted by the notion that the federal government should intervene to prevent the wasteful incentives of state and local areas with low unemployment. In the current political environment, I am pessimistic that an intervention that comes at no federal cost, such as taxing incentives, would be so benign as to simply target wasteful incentives.

References

Advisory Commission on Intergovernmental Relations (ACIR). 1981. *Regional Growth: Interstate Tax Competition.* Report A-76. Washington, DC: ACIR.

Altshuler, Alan A., and Jose A. Gomez-Ibanez (with Arnold M. Howitt). 1993. *Regulation for Revenue: The Political Economy of Land Use Exactions.* Washington, DC: The Brookings Institution.

Anderson, Barbara. 1999. "First-Source Hiring Agreements." *Accountability: The Newsletter of the Business Incentives Clearinghouse* 1(3): 1. Washington, DC: Corporation for Enterprise Development.

Bartik, Timothy J. 1986. "Neighborhood Revitalization's Effects on Tenants and the Benefit-Cost Analysis of Government Neighborhood Programs." *Journal of Urban Economics* 19(March): 234–248.

———. 1990. "The Market Failure Approach to Regional Economic Development Policy." *Economic Development Quarterly* 4(4): 361–370.

———. 1991a. *Who Benefits from State and Local Economic Development Policies?* Kalamazoo, MI: W.E. Upjohn Institute for Employment Research.

———. 1991b. "The Effects of Metropolitan Job Growth on the Size Distribution of Family Income." Upjohn Institute staff working paper no. 91-06. Kalamazoo, MI: W.E. Upjohn Institute for Employment Research.

———. 1992. "The Effects of State and Local Taxes on Economic Development: A Review of Recent Research." *Economic Development Quarterly* 6(1): 102–110.

———. 1993. "Who Benefits from Local Job Growth, Migrants or the Original Residents?" *Regional Studies* 27(4): 297–311.

———. 1994a. "What Should the Federal Government Be Doing About Urban Economic Development?" *Cityscape* 1(1): 267–292.

———. 1994b. "The Effects of Metropolitan Job Growth on the Size Distribution of Family Income." *Journal of Regional Science* 34(4): 483–502.

———. 1994c. "Jobs, Productivity, and Local Economic Development: What Implications Does Economic Research Have for the Role of Government?" *National Tax Journal* 47(4): 847–861.

———. 1996a. "Eight Issues for Policy Toward Economic Development Incentives." 1996. Paper presented at the conference, "Economic War among the States," sponsored by Minnesota Public Radio and Ford Foundation, held in Washington, DC, May 21–22.

———. 1996b. "Strategies for Economic Development." In *Management Policies in Local Government Finance*, J.R. Aronson and E. Schwartz, eds. 4th ed. Washington, DC: International City/County Management Association Press, pp. 287–312.

———. 2001. *Jobs for the Poor: Can Labor Demand Policies Help?* New York: Russell Sage Foundation, and Kalamazoo, MI: W.E. Upjohn Institute for Employment Research.

———. 2003. "Thoughts on American Manufacturing Decline and Revitalization." Upjohn Institute staff working paper no. 03-96. Kalamazoo, MI: W.E. Upjohn Institute for Employment Research.

———. 2004a. "Evaluating the Impacts of Local Economic Development Policies on Local Economic Outcome: What Has Been Done and What Is Doable?" In *Evaluating Local Economic and Employment Development*, Alistair Nolan and Ging Wong, eds. Paris: Organisation for Economic Co-operation and Development, pp. 113–141.

———. 2004b. "Local Economic Development Policies." In *Management Policies in Local Government Finance*, J. Richard Aronson and Eli Schwartz, eds. 5th ed. Washington, DC: International City/County Management Association, pp. 355–390.

———. 2005. "Solving the Problems of Economic Development Incentives." *Growth and Change* 36(2): 139–166.

Bartik, Timothy J., and Randall Eberts. 1999. "Examining the Effects of Industry Trends and Structure on Welfare Caseloads." In *Economic Conditions and Welfare Reform*, Sheldon H. Danziger, ed. Kalamazoo, MI: W.E. Upjohn Institute for Employment Research, pp. 119–158.

Bartik, Timothy J., Peter Eisinger, and George Erickcek. 2003. "Economic Development Policy in Michigan." In *Michigan at the Millennium*, Charles Ballard, Paul Courant, Doug Drake, Ron Fisher, and Elizabeth Gerber, eds. East Lansing, MI: Michigan State University Press, pp. 279–298.

Batt, Rosemary, and Paul Osterman. 1993. "Workplace Training Policy: Case Studies of State and Local Experiments." Working paper no. 106. Washington, DC: Economic Policy Institute.

Bishop, John. 1993. "Improving Job Matches in the U.S. Labor Market." *Brookings Papers on Economic Activity* 1(1993 Microeconomics): 335–390.

Burstein, Melvin, and Arthur J. Rolnick. 1995. "Congress Should End the Economic War Among the States." 1994 Annual Report Essay in *The Region*. Minneapolis, MN: Federal Reserve Bank of Minneapolis.

Chernick, Howard, and Therese J. McGuire. 1999. "The State, Welfare Reform, and the Business Cycle." In *Economic Conditions and Welfare Reform,* Sheldon H. Danziger, ed. Kalamazoo MI. W.E. Upjohn Institute for Employment Research, pp. 275–303.

Courant, Paul. 1994. "How Would You Know a Good Economic Policy If You Tripped over One? Hint: Don't Just Count Jobs." *National Tax Journal* 47(4): 863–882.

Ettlinger, Michael P., John F. O'Hare, Robert S. McIntyre, Julie King, Neil Miransky, and Elizabeth A. Fray. 1996. *Who Pays? A Distributional Analysis of the Tax Systems of All 50 States*. Washington, DC: Citizens for Tax Justice.

Fisher, Peter S., and Alan H. Peters. 2002. *State Enterprise Zone Programs: Have They Worked?* Kalamazoo, MI: W.E. Upjohn Institute for Employment Research.

Fisher, Ronald C. 1996. *State and Local Public Finance*. Chicago: Irwin.

Florida, Richard. 2002. *The Rise of the Creative Class*. New York: Basic Books.

Haughwout, Andrew F., Robert P. Inman, Steven Craig, and Thomas Luce. 2003. "Local Revenue Hills: Evidence from Four U.S. Cities." NBER working paper no. 9686. Cambridge, MA: National Bureau of Economic Research. http://papers.nber.org/papers/w9686 (accessed September 13, 2006).

Inman, Robert P. 1979. "The Fiscal Performance of Local Governments: An Interpretative Review." In *Current Issues in Urban Economics,* Peter Mieszkowski and Mahlon Straszheim, eds. Baltimore: Johns Hopkins Press, pp. 270–321.

LeRoy, Greg. 1999. "Counterpoint: We Are Making Progress!" *Accountability: The Newsletter of the Business Incentives Clearinghouse* 1(12). Washington, DC: Corporation for Enterprise Development.

Logan, John, and Harvey Molotch. 1987. *Urban Fortunes: The Political Economy of Place.* Berkeley, CA: University of California Press.

McGuire, Therese J. 2003. "Do Taxes Matter? Yes, No, Maybe So." *State Tax Notes*, June 9.

Minge, David. 1999. "Reforming Incentives through Federal Action." *Accountability: The Newsletter of the Business Incentives Clearinghouse* 1(6). Washington, DC: Corporation for Enterprise Development.

Molina, Frieda. 1998. *Making Connections: A Study of Employment Linkage Programs*. Washington, DC: Center for Community Change.

Nolan, Anne, and Greg LeRoy. 2003. *Get Something Back! How Civic Engagement Is Raising Economic Development Expectations in Minnesota*. Washington, DC: Good Jobs First.

Oakland, William, and William Testa. 1996. "State-Local Business Taxation and the Benefits Principle." *Federal Reserve Bank of Chicago Economic Perspectives* 20(1): 2–19.

O'Leary, Christopher J., and Stephen A. Wandner, eds. 1997. *Unemployment Insurance in the United States: Analysis of Policy Issues*. Kalamazoo, MI: W.E. Upjohn Institute for Employment Research.

Osterman, Paul, and Rosemary Batt. 1993. "Employer-Centered Training for

International Competitiveness: Lessons from State Programs." *Journal of Policy Analysis and Management* 12(3): 456–477.
Peirce, Neal. 2002. "State, Local Corporate Subsidies: A New Coalition for Accountability." Syndicated column for Washington Post Writers Group, August 5. http://www.napawash.org/resources/peirce/Peirce_8_12_02.html (accessed October 17, 2006).
Peters, Alan. 1993. "Clawbacks and the Administration of Economic Development Policy in the Midwest." *Economic Development Quarterly* 7(4): 328–340.
Purinton, Anna, Nasreen Jilani, Kristen Arant, and Kate Davis. 2003. *The Policy Shift to Good Jobs: Cities, States and Counties Attaching Job Quality Standards to Development Subsidies.* Washington, DC: Good Jobs First.
Rodrigue, Jean-Paul, Claude Comtois, and Brian Slack. 2004. "Transport Geography on the Web." Hofstra University, Department of Economics and Geography. http://people.hofstra.edu/geotrans (accessed September 13, 2006).
Rosenfeld, Stuart. 2002a. *A Governor's Guide to Cluster-Based Economic Development.* Washington, DC: National Governors Association.
———. 2002b. *Just Clusters: Economic Development Strategies that Reach More People and Places.* Carrboro, NC: Regional Technology Strategies.
Schweke, William. 1999. "Linking Incentives and Employment Programs." *Accountability: The Newsletter of the Business Incentives Clearinghouse* 1(3): 1. Washington, DC: Corporation for Enterprise Development.
Schweke, William, and Lillian G. Woo. 2003. "There Are Job Creation Alternatives to Traditional Business Incentives: A New Direction for North Carolina." Unpublished manuscript. Washington, DC: Corporation for Enterprise Development.
Shuman, Michael. 2000. *Going Local: Creating Self-Reliant Communities in a Global Age.* New York: Routledge.
Sinclair, Upton. 1935. *I, Candidate for Governor: And How I Got Licked.* New York: Farrar and Rinehart. Repr., Berkeley, CA: University of California Press, 1994.
Summers, Lawrence, and James Poterba. 1992. "Time Horizons of American Firms: New Evidence from a Survey of CEOs." In *Capital Choices: Changing the Way America Invests in Industry*, Michael Porter, ed. Washington, DC: Council on Competitiveness.
United Nations Development Programme. 1999. *Human Development Report 1999.* New York: Oxford University Press.
U.S. Census Bureau. 1991. Government Finances: 1988–89. Washington, DC: Government Printing Office.
———. 2001. "American Housing Survey, 2001." http://www.census.gov/

hhes/www/housing/ahs/ahs01_2000wts.html (accessed October 17, 2006).
U.S. Department of Commerce. Bureau of Economic Analysis. 1991. "Survey of Current Business." http://bea/pub/0101cont.htm (accessed November 30, 2006).
Wasylenko, Michael. 1997. "Taxation and Economic Development: The State of the Economic Literature." *New England Economic Review* (March/April): 37–52.
Weber, Rachel. 2002. "Do Better Contracts Make Better Economic Development Incentives?" *American Psychological Association Journal* 68(1): 43–55.

6
Negotiating the Ideal Deal

Which Local Governments Have the Most Bargaining Leverage?

Rachel Weber
University of Illinois at Chicago

It is easy to criticize local governments' use of financial incentives for business retention and attraction. Critics say that incentives cost more than the public benefits they create and redirect monies from other important public goods like infrastructure and education. They argue that incentives poison interjurisdictional relations, contribute to sprawl, favor large businesses over small, strain the planning capacity of local government, and are subject to the worst kinds of cronyism and abuse (for an inventory of such abuses, see LeRoy [2005]).

However, calls for both federal legislation that could eliminate the practice of incentives (Burstein and Rolnick 1994) and regional truces that could reduce their use have been largely ignored. Public officials and fiscal watchdogs alike admit that, despite their general distaste for incentives and the competitive interjurisdictional relations they have created, such programs are difficult to condemn across the board. Incentives, along with zoning and land use regulations, are one of the few sources of leverage that local governments possess in their negotiations with developers and businesses.

Local governments use these economic development tools in different ways and to different effect. Whereas some jurisdictions are held hostage to demands of businesses and sign off on expensive long-term commitments, other states and cities negotiate better agreements. Some local governments have used incentives strategically to influence both the site-location decision as well as the magnitude of private investment. These dealmakers absorb relatively little risk and commit relatively little up-front investment in relation to the public benefits created.

In other cases, however, "subsidy programs and deals have become so astronomically expensive that they can only be fairly described as 'soak the taxpayer' scams" (LeRoy 2005, p. 34). Anecdotes of states and cities spending (or foregoing tax revenues) upwards of $500,000 *per job created* abound.

What is a "good deal" from the public sector's perspective, and why do some states and cities craft better deals than others? This chapter provides some insight into the context in which the public sector and private business negotiate agreements; it also describes the elements of a well-designed deal from the public sector's perspective.[1] The final section identifies the different sources of bargaining leverage from which local governments and business draw in order to partially explain the observed variation in deal structure.

BARGAINING ENVIRONMENT

Regulatory Context

Development incentives and regulatory environments matter less to businesses when deciding between distinct regions of the country. Proximity to key markets and suppliers, labor and transportation costs, and the whims of corporate executives are more important at this stage. Once the business has narrowed its choice of location to a particular region, however, it begins to consider the tax burden and physical characteristics of potential sites. The site location decision could be a relatively private affair, whereby the company purchases land, hires a developer and employees, and pays whatever taxes are levied on its property, employees, sales, and income. Aside from obtaining the requisite building permits and complying with existing zoning and environmental regulations, the business could have little direct contact with the public sector.

Protracted negotiations ensue only if expectations are raised, that is, either the business wants something more from local government, or the local government wants something more from business. What exactly comprises *more* is contested because public and private responsibilities in economic development are not fixed and unchanging. The principle, for example, that a city should not be responsible for the development costs of individual businesses (because this falls squarely within some kind of proprietary private realm of responsibility) is difficult to support given the historical reality of public assistance for business. The courts have tried to resolve the issue by requiring local governments to document and prove the "public purpose" inherent in every act of targeted assistance (Schoettle 2003). But 200 years of incentive use in the United States have stretched the public purpose doctrine beyond recognition, blurring the boundaries of public and private roles and making it impossible to defer to principle or precedent (Sbragia 1996). Every case, therefore, must be negotiated on its own merits.

State governments have historically limited city taxing and spending power to curtail the cronyism, wasteful expenditures, uncontrolled borrowing, and general profligacy associated with municipal financial governance (Frug 1980). But they have also authorized municipalities to engage in development negotiations and, beyond an initial grant of authority, have often provided little to no guidance to them in terms of what to offer and expect from subsidized businesses (Briffault 1997). Even within the same state, local governments lack uniform criteria for allocating funds toward business attraction and retention. The variation in deal structure reveals multiple local economic development "regimes" and cultures that have evolved over time, with little interference from higher orders of government.

Depending on one's perspective, this reliance on negotiated strategies at lower levels of government is either the result of a historic oversight, whereby such practices had become entrenched before they could be regulated, or the intentional by-product of a federalist system of governance. Cities and states have fought to preserve their autonomy from higher levels of government and have, in the case of economic development, exhibited a preference for more informal and decentralized strategies. The economic theory of jurisdictional competition advanced by Tiebout (1956) and developed by Peterson (1981) provide *post facto* support for this kind of decentralization by arguing that a combination of independence in public strategy and choice in private location decision will lead to regulatory outcomes that are aligned with citizen preferences in a dynamic equilibrium.

Interests

Businesses and governments are not likely to agree on what constitutes the "ideal deal" due to the conflicting nature of their interests. Business wants to maximize profits, and can best do so when local governments agree to absorb risks and pay for costs that the business would otherwise shoulder (e.g., taxes, infrastructure, job training). Public interests are more complex, broad, and diffuse: improving the general welfare of citizens through the provision of tax-funded services.[2] Public officials can achieve this objective if they strengthen their economic base (retaining and attracting business) with minimal expenditure. Because strengthening an economic base is a formidable and unmanageable goal, public economic development practitioners tend to "shoot low" and focus their efforts on a tangible outcome: attracting businesses to their locale (Rubin 1988).

While it may initially appear that one party's benefit is always the other's burden, a gray area exists where mutual gains may be had. This is because public and private interests are interdependent: both parties need the other in order to attain their objectives. Businesses rely on a public service infrastructure, property security, and a stable business environment whereas governments depend on tax revenues, employment, indirect and induced spending, and the physical development businesses provide. A deal that allows a firm to add more staff will help it to grow to meet increasing demand for its products while a municipality in need of jobs for its un- or underemployed population also values these jobs. The notion of a "spillover effect" captures and complicates the interdependence of public and private interests. Development subsidies selectively mitigate some of the costs of doing business for individual firms, but advocates contend that assisting individual projects will lead to areawide improvements and the sharing of public benefits.

Deal structure depends on both parties' ability to persuade the other that their interests are symbiotic and served equally well by the agreement. If a business is able to convince local governments that their interests overlap entirely ("what's good for General Motors is good for Detroit"), governments may be excessively accommodating and assume many of the costs of private land development and infrastructure. If a municipality can convince a business that it is getting a special deal on land in an up-and-coming inner-city neighborhood, that business is less likely to demand generous tax incentives.

Power

Despite their interdependence, local governments and businesses do not always negotiate on equal footing. Local governments are handicapped by the fact that they are embedded in space and not footloose like business. Because they are constrained by interjurisdictional competition for private investment, public entities are dependent on private business to pay for basic services and infrastructure (Peterson 1981). They may be more likely to offer compromises so that deals end closer to the business' initial proposal.

Businesses are also better able to control critical information flows during negotiations (Markusen and Nesse 2007). The financial gap companies seek to fill to make a project feasible may be much smaller than they would have the public sector believe. Business tries to assure local governments that the deal would not take place without public assistance (the "but for" condition) (Persky, Felsenstein, and Wiewel 1997). However, they can also bluff about the other sites they are considering and demand more than is really necessary because management has access to relevant information about the firm's own cost structure and hurdle rates to which local governments are not privy (LeRoy 2005; Weber 2002). Government agencies never know the extent to which the business is serious about selecting a location; even if the business has made up its mind, it does better to keep the local government nervously anticipating a change of heart.

Moreover, the private sector starts from an organizational advantage. Local governments often lack flexibility; in order for public administrators to change their initial offers of infrastructure provision, for example, they often have to go back to their city councils or legislatures and engage in a time-consuming process of backroom lobbying (Rubin 1988). Even though local officials try to limit the range of interest groups who can participate in the debate over these issues, community organizations, labor unions, and watchdog groups may try to expose the terms of the deals and insist on protracted public discussion. In contrast, most corporate officials control information and negotiate in a bare-knuckled manner, hire consultants and lawyers to help them do so, and rely on internal decision-making structures for expedited action.

Local governments have only recently learned how important good negotiation skills are to protecting their interests. They are subjecting their spending on economic development to more scrutiny and relying on more accountable forms of assistance by looking to the legal framework that governs the performance of private sector contracts for guidance. This changed behavior is not the result of some enlightened attitude—with fewer own-source funds, fewer intergovernmental transfers, and increased community outrage at "corporate welfare," cities have to been forced to be more selective about the businesses and project expenses they finance.

WHAT IS A GOOD DEAL FOR THE PUBLIC SECTOR?

In many ways, the quality of a deal can only be evaluated *post facto*. Did the local government get what it wanted (business retention, jobs, tax revenues) without paying "too much"? At a minimum, the marginal benefits should equal or exceed the marginal costs (including any foregone revenues and additional costs associated with the development) after a reasonable period of time (Bartik 1991; Ledebur and Woodward 1990). But local governments may not have to wait years to evaluate the quality of their deals. Even before the ink has dried and the deal is cut, certain kinds of incentive design are more likely to lead to better outcomes for the public sector.[3] In such deals, the benefits and burdens of public financing are more fairly calibrated, contractual safeguards exist to help governments manage risks, and relevant information is disclosed.[4]

Ex Ante Decision Analysis

Local governments should have some idea of what they want out of a deal before negotiations even begin. Contracts that rely on very loose parameters of fulfillment are considered "incomplete" and provide parties with opportunities to exploit gaps. The state of Minnesota, for example, requires all state agencies and municipalities to develop explicit benchmarks for awarding subsidies.[5] These public purpose benchmarks include standards for job creation as well as for the wages of any new jobs. Job retention is only considered a legitimate criterion "where job loss is imminent and demonstrable." The law requires each incentive-granting agency to submit their benchmarks to the state's Department of Employment and Economic Development and for the department to publish them annually.

With a better sense of their bargaining goals, local governments can better evaluate the costs and benefits of their subsidy programs. Few cities and states actually know the real cost of what they are giving away or what they are getting in return. In a survey of local economic development practitioners, only 24 percent reported any systematic or quantitative means of analyzing deals (Reese 1993). By comparing the present value of anticipated public costs (e.g., foregone revenues and additional expenditures on services, such as schools and infrastructure) to the present value of expected benefits (e.g., increased jobs, revenues generated by salaries of new employees, and multiplier effects) *ex ante*, standard methods of cost-benefit analysis can provide a ballpark estimate of how much the public benefits will cost. The more intangible design amenities, real estate improvements, and environmental mitigation may be valued by comparing them to their market equivalents.

Performance Standards

Local government can make their assistance to private business conditional by including legally binding provisions in the contracts that specify public benefit projections. For example, business may have to commit to creating a certain number of jobs, not relocating within a specified time period, and compliance with higher environmental or design standards. Many state statutes now require contracts to specify a particular wage rate, often based on a percentage of the federal minimum wage or regional averages (see Purinton [2003] for an inventory of jobs standards). Contracts may also stipulate that businesses provide health care benefits to the new or retained employees.

The contractual agreement can specify a reasonable time period for which the business must maintain operations in the locality or create a certain amount of jobs in exchange for its assistance. A Connecticut statute governing a below-market rate loan program states that "Business is prohibited from relocating during the term the loan is outstanding or for 10 years after receiving assistance, whichever is longer."[6] Without a so-called "benefit period," a subsidized company will have an indefinite amount of time in which to fulfill its promises.

At the same time, savvy governments are not excessively rigid in their attempts to embed capital; they understand that it can be difficult to hold firms to their promises about the future given the vagaries of the global economy (Weber 2002). Corporate managers make location decisions in the context of great uncertainties and attempt to rein in the factors they can control: debt levels, capital spending, overhead, and staffing—all of which influence the places where they locate.

Local administrators are left with the challenge of protecting their assets while anticipating the uncertainties inherent in a turbulent business environment. They do this by designing incentives that calibrate the number of jobs or investment to a subsidy *ex post* and by making investments in places, as opposed to individual firms. Unlike an outright grant of funds, performance-based programs provide no assistance to a company *until* it meets specified levels of performance. For example, a firm receives an income tax benefit once it has hired a certain number of workers at a designated minimum wage. The incentive can increase as the number of employees hired grows. The $2.5 million incentive package negotiated between Bismarck, North Dakota, and Coventry Healthcare contained a provision whereby the company agreed to receive progressively larger payments for the subsequent phases or groups of employees hired (Hanson 2002). The city waited to make its largest payment until the final group had been hired.

This kind of payment clause protects the jurisdiction's investment in case the company encounters setbacks or falls behind in its hiring schedule. Performance-based incentives may be less popular with businesses, as they typically prefer to receive lump sum payments to cover development and other start-up costs. With proper monitoring, however, they are easier for the public sector to enforce and respond better to unforeseen exigencies.

Enforcement Mechanisms

Spending time and effort to write detailed contracts and then ignoring the subsidized businesses after funds have "changed hands" is not an effective economic development strategy. If businesses do not comply with the terms and conditions of the agreement as stated, they may have "breached" their contracts. Some contracts include a notice provision to inform the municipality of any changes in the operations of the business, such as the initiation of any lawsuits or bankruptcy proceedings, which might adversely impact the subsidized project.

In other cases, the public sector must devise monitoring requirements. Local governments typically include one of two types of monitoring techniques. The first type places the onus of oversight on the public sector but requires that specified documents be available for public inspection and audit. A more effective type of provision creates an affirmative obligation on the part of the business to provide necessary information rather than to merely allow local governments to ask for the right of inspection. Kansas City, for example, double checks self-reported data from firms against information derived from the city's employee earnings tax (Weber 2002). Companies are given a grace period of about two to three years to meet the specified standards.

Penalties are less important when municipalities use performance-based incentives from the start. If a state or city withholds funds until the recipient company has demonstrated that it has lived up to its obligation, there is no need to recapture funds because of nonperformance further down the road.

If public funds do change hands up front, however, nonperformance provisions, remedies, and damages should be written into the contract. These provisions generally fall into five categories (Ledebur and Woodward 1990):

1) Recisions: canceling a subsidy agreement if job and revenue projections are not met.

2) Clawbacks: recovery of all or part of subsidy costs if performance goals are not met.

3) Recalibrations: adjustment of subsidy to reflect changing business conditions.

4) Penalties: additional charges (e.g., the interest accrued on the public's investment) for nonperformance or relocation.

5) Debarment and suspension: prohibiting the noncompliant company from receiving incentives in the future.

A written contract should represent the complete understanding between parties because informal promises do not hold up well in court. If accountability mechanisms are clear, reasonable, and obvious from the start of negotiations, firms may voluntarily repay the incentive if they renege on their promises, obviating the need for any formal legal enforcement.[7] In 2003, for example, Philips Semiconductor honored its clawback agreement by paying back $13.1 million in tax breaks to the City of Albuquerque, New Mexico, after it closed its plant. United Airlines agreed to pay back almost $32 million in prorated clawback fines (of the $300 million in tax breaks it had received from Indiana government agencies) after it failed to live up to its promise to invest $800 million by 2001 (*Wall Street Journal* 2002). Accountability mechanisms reduce the uncertainty and potential for arbitrary behavior that plague incentives on both sides of the bargaining table.

WHAT KINDS OF GOVERNMENTS NEGOTIATE GOOD DEALS?

Nonetheless, many local governments continue to fear that the above-mentioned contractual mechanisms will lower the value of the incentive for the business if the business perceives future tussles with the law, a lack of flexibility on the part of the public sector, and additional reporting requirements and compliance costs. Many states and cities resist the use of the contractual protections mentioned above and enter into deals where they accept the bulk of project risks for little return. When the state of West Virginia loaned over $64 million to Anchor Hocking to help the company keep its plant open and provide jobs to its employees, it failed to state these goals in the actual loan documents. When the company closed its plant, the absence of a specific goal, coupled with a contractual provision allowing prepayment of the loan without penalty, led the court to conclude that the firm had satisfied its obligations by paying off the loan (*West Virginia v. Anchor Hocking* 1988).

Conversely, some governments take a rigid bargaining position, refusing to negotiate altogether or make any concessions. The assumption of fundamental interest conflict (i.e., zero-sum bargaining) underpins the notion that firms seek only to extract wealth from the locale and that cities try to extract as much as they can from the firm. Such adversarial assumptions lead local governments to adopt overly protective regulatory strategies: for example, exactions on corporations disproportionate to the costs associated with new development. Such behavior may discourage business activity. Although perceptions of its impact vary in hindsight, the city of Cleveland experienced an investment "strike" following then-Mayor Dennis Kucinich's refusal to subsidize a large retail redevelopment in the absence of a living wage guarantee.

Why do some states and cities negotiate safeguards to manage risks and assure performance while others potentially jeopardize their fiscal health? Why do others adopt overly demanding and rigid postures? This last section seeks to generalize about the features of local governments that may influence their bargaining leverage.

Leverage implies some situational advantage—those who have it have less to lose if the deal falls through. Although space-bound governments start off from a bargaining disadvantage, any locality that has discretionary power to grant or deny requests for changes in density, tax burdens, and zoning has a modicum of bargaining leverage. This is because property development and industrial relocation offer businesses opportunities to increase their profits. The subsidies themselves are perceived to be a source of leverage, which is one of the reasons why local governments continue to offer them.[8] If municipalities had no leverage, businesses would have no need to negotiate with them.

However, the more assets particular places possess, the more leverage and decisional independence they are likely to acquire. This is why those governments with better market positions (relative to their competition as potential business locations) appear to have the ability to be better negotiators. If the private sector needs the municipality more than the municipality needs the business, many of the risks of development can be migrated back to the private sector. The shifting of need occurs in urban areas that are built-out with relatively little available land for development. For example, the attractiveness of Chicago as a location for retail development has allowed the city to require that developers receive tax increment financing (TIF) incentives on a "pay-as-you go" basis instead of front-funding subsidies with bond proceeds (Weber 2003). Structuring the deal this way means that the developer initially pays for the costs of the project and is only reimbursed as the municipality collects the incremental property taxes. This places the onus on the developer (to generate new property tax revenues) instead of on the municipality (to float bonds secured with the incremental tax revenues).

Moreover, in higher income locations with strong tax bases, residents may prefer slower growth, choosing less congestion over more development (Elkins 1995; Goetz 1990). Slow growth measures have been adopted by many municipalities (particularly those on the coasts) and, in these places, citizens have rejected ballot measures that would raise taxes to support new large-scale development. These jurisdictions can afford to be selective, either refraining from the practice of offering incentives or including extensive public benefits requirements in their incentive contracts. They can devalue the threats of businesses in favor of other political objectives. In contrast, poorer places may have to offer more to induce much-needed development and help private investors overcome perceived and actual development risks (Rubin and Rubin 1987).

The desirability of a locale is reflected in the value of its land. Indeed, those municipalities with a valuable land inventory (i.e., publicly owned properties) are able to extract benefits from potential developers (Elkins 1995). With the Yerba Buena development in San Francisco and California Plaza in Los Angeles, the respective cities took on more risks but were able to secure from private developers expensive new cultural facilities and public spaces (Sagalyn 1997). They used the power of rising land values and a scarcity of developable sites to negotiate for additional developer contributions to their ambitious mixed-use projects. Because of the desirability of these sites, the municipalities crafted deals in such a way that the developers were able to achieve their anticipated rates of return. Expensive homes provided the tax base needed to pay for the bulk of city services so that the overall tax burden on businesses was not considered so high as to require abatements.

For these reasons, one might expect to see those local governments with higher initial levels and rates of growth in a superior bargaining position relative to those more desperate for private investment. Indeed, jurisdictions such as Berkeley (CA), Westchester County (NY), and Cambridge (MA) include public benefit requirements, such as job quality standards, in their incentive contracts. These jurisdictions are not as concerned about their competition because they know their highly educated residents and positive reputations are already a draw for particular kinds of business.

But not all such governments play their (upper) hands. For example, New Jersey, a wealthy, high-tax state, just passed a law that would allow it to borrow to pay for incentive grants in any year when the state legislature does not appropriate the money. A recent report found that several high-profile deals between New York City and businesses contained "employment cushions" that allowed companies to lay off employees without such actions breaching their contracts (Good Jobs First 2004).

Nor does this rationale explain why many lower-income jurisdictions are proponents of more accountable deal making. Good Jobs First lists the 43 states, 41 cities, and 5 counties that attached job quality standards to at least one development subsidy (Good Jobs First 2003). On this list, many poor, fiscally challenged jurisdictions stick out—Detroit, St. Louis, and Rochester, to name a few.

Factors unrelated to the wealth of their residents appear to be at play. Elkins (1995) finds that more progressive strategies were adopted by municipalities with higher unemployment rates. Perhaps, it has been argued, some poor municipalities experience such high degrees of political activism that local governments are pressured into good behavior (see, for example, Reese and Rosenfeld [2001]; Elkins [1995]). If this is the case, local officials there may propose incentives with more community benefits requirements.

Recent examples of the success of grassroots coalitions in getting community benefits agreements signed in cities such as Los Angeles and Milwaukee attest to the role of third parties in influencing government behavior (Good Jobs First 2006). In the past decade, a community-based movement for corporate accountability has arisen to monitor economic development deals and expose incidents of subsidy abuse. These groups have organized an increasing number of petition drives and referenda to place subsidies and performance measures on local ballots. Their power also lies in their ability to raise community awareness of the deal terms, which may shame companies and the local governments that subsidize them into better behavior. If minorities participate to a high degree in such movements, it may explain why Reese (1998) finds that the larger the minority presence in a municipality, the more likely it was to include contractual requirements of community benefits.

Even if a municipality has bargaining leverage (e.g., due to a scarcity of developable sites and concomitant market appeal), there must be opportunities for exploiting this bargaining advantage. Such opportunities arise only when government and business engage in specific political processes to coordinate interests on specific matters of public policy (Kantor 2002; Elkins 1995). For example, wealthy residential suburbs may not craft ideal deals because they have little available land for new commercial or industrial development and wish to maintain their community's exclusivity. No deals would come to the table so there would be no opportunity to use the leverage that the suburb would, in all likelihood, possess.

Ideal deal-making is likely to arise out of what economists call "repeated games"—similar experiences that build staff's negotiation skills, spur community activism around these issues, and lead to ordinances and statutes that expressly require such mechanisms. This is one of the reasons why larger cities and states (with better-paid staff and more use of sophisticated planning and decision analysis techniques) tend to be better negotiators. Competing with larger cities may induce smaller places in the metro area to mimic their good behavior. One study found that the more strategic municipalities were located in close proximity to cities of similar sizes or were suburbs of a central city (Reese 1998). In contrast, depopulated, low-tax, rural areas have been known to give away the store to lure branch plants.

Local governments comprise part of the distinctive civic cultures of economic development. Some adopt ideal deal structures because they are in keeping with a broader "good government" culture that respects values such as transparency and accountability. Others adopt better deal structures because they are desperate for anything that promises short-term outcomes and willing to try anything and everything (i.e, the "shoot anything that flies" approach). Reese and Rosenfeld (2001) note the importance of differentiating between these two motivations.

Empirical studies have found the use of accountability mechanisms more prevalent on the West Coast and in the Northeast (Elkins 1995; Reese 1998), but that their use cuts across political persuasions. Some of the most conservative, pro-business local regimes have passed the most stringent laws requiring the use of these contractual safeguards. In Indianapolis, for example, it was Republican mayor Stephen Goldsmith who insisted that all new jobs pay at least 90 percent of the area average wage level in order to qualify for property tax assistance, and the city has a reputation for auditing firms and enforcing clawbacks (Weber 2002). In 1996 alone, the Indianapolis Metropolitan Development Commission cancelled tax abatements to five companies who failed to live up to their pledges of job creation (Phillips 1996). Ideal dealmaking is not, apparently, politically partisan.

CONCLUSION

Without empirical research it is difficult to determine which specific factors will predict which political jurisdictions negotiate better deals. It is also difficult to examine whether ideal deals actually lead to ideal outcomes. Although using performance standards is certainly better than giving away subsidies for free, local governments still draft contracts too loosely and enforce them too weakly to get the most from their public investments (Weber 2002).

Often economic development practitioners give up before they start. They figure that even when they write comprehensive contracts, there is no guarantee that businesses will stick by their promises. Indeed, public officials have the power to bargain and persuade, to make concessions, provide incentives and reduce or eliminate local taxes or restrictions, but they do not have the power to compel businesses to move into or remain in the jurisdiction. Drafting contracts takes place within a larger context of suburban, regional, and international competition for business and the context in which it operates has become increasingly unstable and unpredictable.

This fact, however, is no excuse for being a poor negotiator. Specialized real estate investments can help embed footloose firms in the locality and create spillover benefits in terms of jobs, additional investments, and tax revenues. Indeed, sunk costs may be able to soften the market pressure firms feel to traverse the globe in search of the cheapest factors of production. However, the irony is that the more the public sector subsidizes those sunk costs and effectively absorbs part of the development expenses, the less firms have financially at stake in their own investment decisions. Public risk bearing allows firms to be more, not less, mobile. A recent survey by *Site Selection* magazine found that since 1996, corporate migration within the United States "has soared, roughly doubling to more than 11,000 moves a year" (cited in Uchitelle 2000). Widespread use of business attractive incentives has no doubt contributed to some of this movement.

Better public use of these tools, especially a reliance on more performance-based incentives and legal protections to govern breach, remedies, and damages if businesses do not perform as promised, may give businesses pause before they consider yet another corporate relocation. But these contractual provisions will only be effective if more municipalities and states adopt them as routine operating practice. If all governments raise standards in a coordinated manner, accountability mechanisms will not hamper the ability of individual governments to "bid for business"—a habit that has proven hard to break although one whose implementation still needs improvement.

Notes

1. This chapter focuses on those incentives that are negotiated on a case-by-case basis at the discretion of the local government. Other kinds of programs, sometimes called "statutory" incentives, are offered "as a right" if a business meets certain preset eligibility requirements. An example of the latter case is an investment tax credit program that allows any business that meets eligibility requirements to deduct a certain amount from its annual income tax bill. In such a case, no negotiation is necessary.
2. Of course, public agencies must often be reminded of their responsibility to serve wider, public interests—a role that interest groups, fiscal watchdogs, and community organizations take on.
3. Parts of this section are based on a handbook for state and local officials, *The Ideal Deal: How Local Governments Can Get More for Their Economic Development Dollar* (Weber and Santacroce forthcoming).
4. "Ideal deals," as they are labeled in this chapter, closely resemble what other authors have referred to as "Type II developmental strategies" or "programs in which local jurisdictions require private developers to provide a service or public benefit in exchange for development rights" (Goetz 1990, p. 171; see also Elkins 1995).
5. Minnesota Statutes 116J.994.
6. Connecticut Development Authority, Master Guarantee Agreement, Participatory Loan Program 1995. See also Connecticut Public Act No. 93: 218.
7. In a recent interview in *Site Selection Magazine,* a vice president of Toyota denied that states and cities with accountability mechanisms were "crossed off" the list of possible plant locations (Bruns 2004). He advised, "If you're going to

use clawbacks, put them in up front. Don't put them in at the last minute, when you think you have a deal and all of a sudden the lawyers get involved with all these clawbacks nobody talked about. The problem with clawbacks is . . . (i)t's just another bureaucracy to deal with. But I understand why states sometimes use them—with some companies you're not sure of their history and can't test their track record."

8. Scholars have long questioned just how much leverage subsidies provide given that they often comprise a small percentage of total relocation and start-up costs (Fisher and Peters 1998).

References

Bartik, Timothy J. 1991. *Who Benefits from State and Local Economic Development Policies?* Kalamazoo, MI: W.E. Upjohn Institute for Employment Research.

Briffault, Richard. 1997. "The Law and Economics of Federalism: The Rise of Sublocal Structures in Urban Governance." *Minnesota Law Review* 82: 503–534.

Bruns, Adam. 2004. "Growing Where You're Transplanted." *Site Selection,* January. http://www.siteselection.com/issues/2004/jan/p024/ (accessed October 4, 2006).

Burstein, Melvin, and Arthur Rolnick. 1994. "Congress Should End the Economic War among the States." *Federal Reserve Bank of Minneapolis 1994 Annual Report.* Minneapolis, MN: Federal Reserve Bank of Minneapolis.

Elkins, David. 1995. "Testing Competing Explanations for the Adoption of Type II Policies." *Urban Affairs Review* 30(6): 809–839.

Fisher, Peter, and Alan Peters. 1998. *Industrial Incentives: Competition among American States and Cities.* Kalamazoo, MI: Upjohn Institute for Employment Research.

Frug, Gerald. 1980. "The City as a Legal Concept." *Harvard Law Review* 93: 1059–1154.

Goetz, Edward. 1990. "Type II Policy and Mandated Benefits in Economic Development." *Urban Affairs Quarterly* 26(2): 170–190.

Good Jobs First. 2003. *The Policy Shift to Good Jobs: Cities, States and Counties Attaching Job Quality Standards to Development Subsidies.* http://www.goodjobsfirst.org/pdf/jobquality.pdf (accessed July 18, 2006).

———. 2004. *Know When to Fold 'Em: Time to Walk Away From NYC's "Corporate Retention" Game.* New York: Good Jobs New York.

———. 2006. *Community Benefits Agreement Victories.* http://www.goodjobsfirst.org/accountable_development/community_benefit_vic.cfm (accessed July 18, 2006).

Hanson, Mark. 2002. "Counting on Accountability." *Bismarck Tribune,* October 31, A:1.
Kantor, Paul. 2002. "The Local Polity as a Pathway for Public Power: Taming the Business Tiger during New York City's Industrial Age." *International Journal of Urban and Regional Research* 26(1): 80–98.
Ledebur, Larry, and Douglas Woodward. 1990. "Adding a Stick to the Carrot: Location Incentives with Clawbacks, Recisions and Recalibrations." *Economic Development Quarterly* 4(3): 221–237.
LeRoy, Greg. 2005. *The Great American Jobs Scam: Corporate Tax Dodging and the Myth of Job Creation.* San Francisco: Berrett-Koehler Publishers.
Markusen, Ann, and Kate Nesse. 2007. "Institutional and Political Determinants of Incentive Competition: Reassessing Causes, Outcomes, and Remedies." In *Reining in the Competition for Capital,* Ann Markusen, ed. Kalamazoo, MI: W.E. Upjohn Institute for Employment Research, pp. 1–42.
Persky, Joe, Dan Felsenstein, and Wim Wiewel. 1997. "How Do We Know That 'But for Incentives' the Development Would Not Have Occurred?" In *Dilemmas of Urban Economic Development: Issues in Theory and Practice,* Richard Bingham and Rob Mier, eds. Thousand Oaks, CA: Sage Publications, pp. 246–290.
Peterson, Paul. 1981. *City Limits.* Chicago: University of Chicago Press.
Phillips, Michael. 1996. "Localities Force Firms to Keep Promises." *Wall Street Journal,* June 26, A:2.1.
Purinton, Anna. 2003. *The Policy Shift to Good Jobs.* Washington, DC: Good Jobs First.
Reese, Laura. 1993. "Decision Rules in Local Economic Development." *Urban Affairs Quarterly* 28(4): 501–513.
———. 1998. "Sharing the Benefits of Economic Development: What Cities Utilize Type II Policies?" *Urban Affairs Review* 33(5): 686–711.
Reese, Laura, and Raymond Rosenfeld. 2001. *The Civic Culture of Local Economic Development.* Thousand Oaks, CA: Sage Publications.
Rubin, Herbert. 1988. "Shoot Anything That Flies; Claim Anything That Falls: Conversations with Economic Development Practitioners." *Economic Development Quarterly* 2(3): 236–251.
Rubin, Irene, and Herbert Rubin. 1987. "Economic Development Incentives: The Poor (Cities) Pay More." *Urban Affairs Quarterly* 23(1): 37–61.
Sagalyn, Lynne. 1997. "Negotiating for Public Benefits: The Bargaining Calculus of Public-Private Development." *Urban Studies* 34(12): 1955–1970.
Sbragia, Alberta. 1996. *Debt Wish: Entrepreneurial Cities, U.S. Federalism, and Economic Development.* Pittsburgh: University of Pittsburgh Press.
Schoettle, Ferdinand. 2003. "What Public Finance Measures Do State Constitutions Allow?" In *Financing Economic Development for the 21st Century,*

Sammis White, Edward Hill, and Richard Bingham, eds. Armonk, NY: M.E. Sharpe, pp. 27–49.

Tiebout, Charles. 1956. "A Pure Theory of Local Expenditures." *Journal of Political Economy* 64(5): 416–424.

Uchitelle, Louis. 2000. "Shifting Workplace: Renewed Corporate Wanderlust Puts a Quiet Brake on Salaries." *The New York Times,* July 24, A:1.

Wall Street Journal. 2002. "United Airlines to Pay Indiana about $32 Million." *Wall Street Journal,* January 2, A:9.

Weber, Rachel. 2002. "Do Better Contracts Make Better Economic Development Incentives?" *Journal of the American Planning Association* 68(1): 43–55.

———. 2003. "Tax Increment Financing in Theory and Practice." In *Financing Economic Development for the 21st Century,* Sammis White, Edward Hill, and Richard Bingham, eds. Armonk, NY: M.E. Sharpe, pp. 53–69.

Weber, Rachel, and David Santacroce. Forthcoming. *The Ideal Deal: How Local Governments Can Get More for Their Economic Development Dollar.*

West Virginia v. Anchor Hocking. 1988. No. 87-C-759-1 (N.D.W.V. filed June 3, 1988).

7

Do Better Job Creation Subsidies Hold Real Promise for Business Incentive Reformers?

William Schweke
Corporation for Enterprise Development

INTRODUCTION: AN IMAGINARY DIALOGUE ON BUSINESS INCENTIVES

Typically, business incentive reformers win the intellectual arguments about the downsides of business incentives, but state and local policymakers refuse to stop providing incentives. The following imagined dialogue between a "wonk" reformer and a business recruiting "buffalo hunter" captures the "back-and-forth" of such a conversation. But there is one big difference: *this* conversation may offer a way out of the present impasse.

Wonk: Business incentives are a waste of money, nationally speaking. They only make sense if they are designed to correct a market failure or really move private investment into poorer communities. The typical recipient of public largess does not need the money to do the deal. They are instead shaking down the jurisdiction for what they can get. Continued incentive use also perpetuates an unceasing incentives "arms race" between jurisdictions and a virtual "war between the states."

Buffalo Hunter: That is easy for you to say. It might be high-minded of you to take such a perspective, but I have to think "state" and "local." These are my constituencies and my customers. Sometimes an incentive can land a deal for my state and create some much-needed jobs.

Wonk: That's noble, but this is a game that you cannot win ultimately. If you also roll back your regulations and tax base to court footloose firms, it can lead to a "race to the bottom." Eventually, you will inevitably fall behind in the incentives competition: you match your peers, and then come up with a new fiscal gimmick only to see it copied by others. It just pushes the price tag up and up. Plus, there is also the danger of the "winner's curse": you land the deal, but end up paying way too much for it. Essentially, the company holds all the cards because only it knows what will tip the deal one way or the other.

Buffalo Hunter: Fine, but I can't just sit on my hands. If I'm heading down the wrong path, get the Feds to stop me. Regulate subnational subsidy use, like the European Community does. Or get the World Trade Organization to pay more attention to America's implicit industrial policies and crack down on the most egregious of these.

Wonk: That's not really the point. Just looking at the deals themselves, you should be a smart investor, not a chump. When negotiating you need to be sure to add stronger performance standards, increase transparency, conduct independent cost-benefit analyses, and so forth. It will help you to be more cost-effective with your incentives and weed out the bad programs.

Buffalo Hunter: Maybe, but my constituents can't eat "good government." Telling them I avoided some bad deals only goes so far. They want jobs.

Wonk: Of course they do, but the most important way to create jobs and wealth is to invest wisely in early childhood and K-12 education, research and development, higher education, infrastructure, and workforce retraining. Modernize the tax structure and provide professional and predictable regulation.

Buffalo Hunter: I completely agree, but it takes so long to generate the jobs and enterprises that are yielded by these public investments. Plus, it is kind of invisible, compared to cutting ribbons at the construction site of a new 100-job project.

Wonk: Well, what if I were to tell you that I have a viable alternative to the limited promise of that ribbon cutting ceremony? What if I can give you an option that generates real returns in one year or less? It is guaranteed to foster development in all counties of a state—not just the most affluent places, such as the metro areas (though it can help them, too). It is a game that everybody can play and win. It can really aid small businesses and help those workers and communities that are losing jobs today. The option that I propose is a smarter approach: growth tax credits and direct grant incentives for targeted job creation.

Buffalo Hunter: I'm listening. Please continue.

Such, in microcosm, is our current policy and political situation regarding business incentive reform. We are making headway. More cities and states are adopting performance standards, disclosure, and other accountability mechanisms. But, at the same time, the costs of incentives and the expectations of business for public dollars are constantly escalating.

We also win most of the policy arguments. Most technical policy experts believe that state and local business incentive competition is a zero sum (and at times a negative sum) game. Incentives are a waste of money, nationally speaking. They typically subsidize companies for jobs that they were already going to create. Incentives are unfair to firms that do not receive the subsidies. They divert scarce public dollars from wiser investments in the workforce or infrastructure. And they frequently fail to even generate a positive fiscal impact. But sadly, state and local policymakers keep on providing them, thereby weakening the tax base and escalating the costs of the incentives customarily offered. Ultimately, the only way to turn this situation around is via Congressional action and complementary litigation on Interstate Commerce grounds.

What can be pursued at the subnational level? Several things. We should strengthen performance standards, accountability, and disclosure. In addition, reform advocates must advance and provide evidence for the thesis that the best climate for private investment and job creation is not one loaded with incentives, but one with good schools, quality higher education, a modern infrastructure, predictable and professional regulation, research and development, a fair but not excessive tax system, amenities, and good public services and governance. More policy attention to entrepreneurship and the existing business base is needed as well.

Yet, there are problems, politically, with this approach. The citizens cannot "eat good government": they want jobs. Moreover, the payoff on many of the preferred foundational investments take time. Constituents and their elected leaders want "jobs now." Therefore, what is needed is a viable alternative to the ribbon-cutting that accompanies "successful" business attraction efforts.

We need an alternative that generates a return in one year or less, that is guaranteed to foster development in all parts of a state (not just the most affluent areas), and that is a game that every community can play and win. In short, we need to generate jobs in a fashion that dwarfs the output of the standard business capital subsidy.

That is essentially what I propose in this chapter. And I have two questions for all readers: 1) Could this be a "shut them up" alternative to the final points that business recruiters and chambers typically make—that although what we say is right, our alternatives to incentives (school reform, entrepreneurship, etc.) take too long to generate results, and although incentives may not be a good thing, they are a necessary option? And 2) Should we have our own subsidy preferences, which could build a new political constituency base for reform, beyond the usual suspects, based on rural areas, small and existing business, and economically struggling cities? Distilled into its essence: Could more fine-tuned job creation subsidies be a promising new direction for the business incentive reform field? It's a sort of "if you can't beat them then join them" notion.

I will start by describing the situation in my home state of North Carolina. Next, I describe my alternative business subsidy alternatives. The chapter closes with a few summary points and questions.[1]

THE NORTH CAROLINA CASE

The North Carolina economy is struggling. Compared to its state peers, it ranks as follows: unemployment rate (45th), short-term employment growth (44th), involuntary part-time employment (37th) and rural/urban disparity (47th). Nineteen North Carolina counties have jobless rates with more than 10 percent unemployment. Black unemployment was 10.7 percent in 2002; Hispanic was 10.8 percent. In the last few years, 121,000 manufacturing jobs have been lost. Obviously, the recent recession and a weak recovery have hit the state hard, and more jobs are desperately needed. And like most states, North Carolina has a weakened fiscal base. Further cuts in public services are strong possibilities.

When an economy is stalled like North Carolina's, state and local officials often try to jump-start economic renewal by using tax and other business incentives to attract footloose facilities. Their hope is that these will sweeten the deal and help their state or community stand apart from the other competitors who are also trying to entice private investment. Economic development professionals also believe that these subsidies will send firms the message that this jurisdiction is a good place to do business.

THE WILLIAM S. LEE ACT

Prior to the mid-1990s, North Carolina had not been known as an incentive-providing state. Its first entry in this all-too-crowded field was a grant program, with a number of strong job quality and environmental standards. But, as the competition for trophy facilities heated up and the state lost out on some high-profile projects, its policymakers felt compelled to enter the sweepstakes. Created in 1996, the William S. Lee Quality Jobs and Business Expansion Act has been the principal incentive tool used by the state of North Carolina for business recruitment and expansion. Businesses may qualify for the Lee Act tax credits by

- creating new jobs,
- investing in machinery and equipment,
- incurring the expenses of training workers,
- undertaking research and development efforts, and/or
- establishing a headquarters or central administrative offices.

The act has been amended repeatedly since its inception in order to update and refine its tier targeting approach and to make the credits available for specific projects. It has three main goals:

1) help existing firms stay competitive by encouraging modernization and investment in new technologies,
2) encourage new investment in North Carolina's economy from both new and existing industries, and
3) ensure that economic growth reaches all people in all parts of the state, particularly distressed rural counties and high-poverty urban areas.

Counties are divided into five economic distress tiers based on unemployment rate, per capita income, and population growth of the county. For many of the credits, the lower the tier of the county, the more favorable the incentive.

In summary, an official summary and assessment document on the law states the following:

> Before 1996, North Carolina made little use of tax incentives to lure businesses to the state. Even without incentives, North Carolina was consistently one of the top states in attracting industry. The array of credits authorized by the Lee Act was viewed as an experiment, to be evaluated in five years to determine whether the incentives were cost effective and actually affected behavior, or merely provided tax reductions to businesses that would have located or expanded in any case. In 1999, the General Assembly extended the 2002 sunset to 2006. (Luger 2003)

CONTROVERSY OVER INCENTIVES

The Lee Act was created by the North Carolina legislature as an *experiment* to see whether tax incentives could successfully create jobs and increase private investment, especially in economically distressed parts of the state. Recently, the North Carolina Department of Commerce's own commissioned research has concluded that only about 4 percent of the jobs claimed under the act were induced by the Lee tax credits and that most of the incentives and private investment are going to the *least distressed* areas of the state (Luger 2003, p. 1). The Corporation for Enterprise Development's (CFED) research further emphasized that the state had already cost North Carolina taxpayers $208 million with an ultimate liability of over $1 billion.[2]

Despite these damning findings and a fair amount of press coverage, the governor called a special session for the North Carolina General Assembly to approve specialized grant-based incentive packages for a handful of hot prospects.[3] The legislature complied with his wishes.

It is also important to note here that the focus of incentive policy has shifted from the Lee Act to another grant-based tool: the Job Development Investment Grant (JDIG). The Department of Commerce can award up to 15 grants annually to strategically important new and expanding businesses and industrial projects. The subsidy is deep—up to

70 percent of the personal state withholding taxes are derived from the creation of new jobs. JDIG has a performance-based dimension—money is only released when jobs are created. An offer by the state, along with the grant awarded to the firm, only occurs after a fiscal analysis has been conducted. Its purpose is to make sure that fiscal benefits exceed costs. Theoretically, these grants are only given to projects that would otherwise not locate in the state. JDIG has a cap on costs per job created and a cumulative annual ceiling of $10 million.[4]

Simultaneously, legislative leadership, worried about North Carolina's current economic misfortunes, including a high-profile 5,000-worker textile firm closing, created a Joint Select Committee on Economic Growth and Development. This committee is charged with examining the state's economic conditions and opportunities and developing new ideas. The governor's office has responded with a laundry list of actions, including—you guessed it—more incentives and a corporate tax cut.

Ironically, in December 2003, North Carolina was named the best business climate in the United States by *Site Selection* magazine (Arend 2006). This occurred approximately at the same time as the special session, which sought to earmark money for trophy projects like Merck, Reynolds, and Boeing.

At roughly the same time, bipartisan leadership in the general assembly asked CFED to develop some incentive reform models, which they hoped to include in the select committee's deliberations. As a result, we pursued three courses: 1) arguing for improved services for displaced workers, their families, and their communities (including rapid action on mortgage foreclosure mitigation); 2) crafting a variety of incrementalist refinements of the Lee Act and the other two grant-based incentives; and 3) developing more job creation–focused incentive alternatives.

We argued that the Lee Act was a noble experiment, but in our view, the results are clear: the experiment has failed. The William S. Lee Act has already cost North Carolina taxpayers $208 million. In these tough economic times, the state cannot afford to finance these failing tax giveaways any longer. It is time to end or seriously restructure the Lee Act.[5]

FOCUSING ON JOB CREATION: THE TWO MODELS

We have developed two new options for the state. Firms must elect to participate in one program or the other, not both.[6]

1) A new Job Growth Tax Credit, which would provide a 30 percent tax credit of the first $14,700 of wages paid to each additional employee over and above 102 percent of the baseline employment. In other words, the state would only subsidize additional employment for a firm. This incentive would be offered statewide to all sizes of business only in years of high unemployment.[7]

2) A Targeted Job Creation Grant Program, which would offer private employers direct wage and benefit subsidies in Tier 1 counties (the most economically disadvantaged) for hiring unemployed job seekers.[8]

It is important to state at the start that the term—job creation, hiring, wage, and employment subsidies—are sometimes used as equivalent expressions. In this chapter, they are not. A hiring subsidy refers to funds used to offset wage costs in the initial part of an employee's period of employment with a firm. A wage subsidy is one whose purpose is to raise an employee's income. This chapter focuses on job creation or employment subsidies. We are exploring ways to increase employment. This strategy may use wage subsidies, but the purpose is different. Both of our options try to create net new employment relative to the nation as a whole.

The Job Growth Tax Credit

The first option, the Job Growth Tax Credit, is a refinement of the New Job Tax Credit, one that is tailored to the state of North Carolina. During years in which the state's unemployment rate exceeds 5 percent, it would provide subsidies for employment only on the margin (and not finance all current employment). It would apply to for-profit firms that expand employment and be paid to the firms.[9] In so doing, the tax credit lowers the cost of labor for employers, hopefully spurring a substitution of labor for capital. The structure of the credit safeguards against a firm firing all of its current employees and hiring twice as many half-time workers who qualify for the tax credit and minimizes the advantages of hiring additional part-time workers.

Under this proposal, the credit would be available for firms that increase their employment beyond some percentage (say, 2 percent) over the base year's employment level; the base year is that year in which the state's unemployment first exceeds 5 percent. The credit would exist until the state's unemployment rate falls below 4.5 percent. Based on typical business cycles, we expect the credit to exist for multiyear stretches (probably three or four years at a stretch). Assuming that the baseline year is announced after January 1, the period in which the credit may be applied should be free of gaming behavior by firms; that is, firms will be unable to adjust their baseline employment to maximize their later tax credits. During that period, any firm that increases its employment *more than* the prescribed percentage will receive the credit. The multiyear period would help firms make investments that require more time, investments that support increased employment (e.g., expansion of a plant). The credit would be available for each year that the firm increases its employment above the targeted amount.

The design is antirecessionary and countercyclical. By encouraging expansions in employment during high unemployment periods, the state is rewarding firms that act, perhaps hastening the recovery. It is possible that firms may delay expansions until recessionary years (assuming that the credit is made permanent and known to kick in during times of high unemployment), but there are few firms that will postpone expansions for years in hopes of gaining a tax credit.

The credit would be applied only to an individual's wages up to some cap (such as 30 percent of the first $14,700 of wages[10]), which would tend to provide an above-average subsidy of jobs for lower-skill and lower-wage workers. More specifically, under the tax credit, the credit to a firm will be equal to: 30 percent of the first $14,700 of wages paid to each additional employee over and above 102 percent of the baseline employment with no cap. Ideally, new firms will receive a smaller credit: the lesser of 15 percent of the above quantity.[11] Ideally, this would lower the costs of the credit, because there is a higher chance of windfalls with startups that were already planned by their owners.

The Targeted Job Creation Grant Program

The second approach, the Targeted Job Creation Grant Program, would be a refinement of the Minnesota Emergency Employment Development Act strategy. On a pilot basis, North Carolina policymakers would make a targeted discretionary grant program available to Tier 1 counties. (If successful, it could be expanded statewide.)

The state would offer private employers $6.75 per hour in wage subsidies and $1.75 per hour in benefits (these figures represent 2003 inflation-adjusted amounts of the original MEED figures) for a 26-week period to employ certified job applicants suffering severe economic distress. Local or regional Workforce Investment Boards would award subsidies, on a discretionary basis, to identified employers that hire selected individuals from disadvantaged groups. To be eligible, a worker must have been a state resident for at least one month, be unemployed, and be currently ineligible for unemployment insurance (or have exhausted his or her six-month UI payments), *or* be a currently UI-eligible individual who has been displaced by a mass layoff (as certified by the Worker Adjustment and Retraining Notification law) or a member of a household with no other source of income than UI benefits.[12] To reduce displacement of current workers, the subsidies would be available only for newly created jobs.

Preference would be given to firms that can provide good on-the-job training in both "soft" and "hard" skills and that are committed to "rolling over" these subsidized hires into permanent jobs with some prospect for advancement. Indeed, as an incentive for long-term placements, if an employee continues in the job for at least one year after the initial six-month subsidy, employers will pay no reimbursement to the state. However, for employees that are hired for fewer than 18 months, employers will be required to repay up to 70 percent of the subsidy (the actual amount will be prorated).

Since these are grants, not tax credits, these subsidies are ideal for new, young, and/or small firms. (They can be used immediately, not just when the firms have profits or when they file their taxes.) Moreover, there is little uncertainty about such a program: potentially participating businesses already exist in North Carolina; they do not have to be coaxed to come. They must only have expansion plans that require a little financial boost. The upfront grant nature of the subsidy also means that it could improve an enterprise's financial position for obtaining bank loans.

Like MEED, it also probably makes sense to provide these grants to nonprofits and local public agencies. Except for the requirements to create a permanent job and to pay back some of the subsidy, all the same rules would apply.

Furthermore, having this temporary public job alternative is important for a number of reasons. In many Tier 1 counties, government payrolls are one of the major sources of jobs, and recent economic distress is forcing some local and county governments to terminate some positions. Secondly, there are a number of community improvement projects that could be implemented and that would not significantly compete with the private sector.[13]

HOW MANY JOBS, AND WHAT WILL THEY COST?

What sort of impact might these two strategies have on the North Carolina economy? It is difficult to say. We can only make an educated projection (and a highly speculative one at that). Here is our reasoning and data work.

We estimate on a net basis that our Job Growth Tax Credit, after subtracting jobs that would have happened anyway, will generate 26,806 jobs per year.[14] The cost is roughly $14,800 per job.[15]

For the Targeted Job Creation Grant Program, we project costs and benefits for a program restricted to Tier 1 counties so as to keep costs down and help the most troubled places. If we further deal only with net jobs (employment that occurred because of the grant), we estimate that it would create about 2,291 net jobs annually in Tier 1. The cost is $16,370 per job. If one was citing gross jobs created, the quantity of jobs would be doubled and the cost would be roughly halved. Let's compare this net number to the data for the Lee Act as cited in the Luger and Stewart report.[16] In 2002, 7,702 jobs were created across the state. Of these, 465 were in Tier 1 counties (Luger and Stewart 2003). Thus, our figures are approximately 5 times greater than the Lee Act outcomes.

Now, to look at the full picture: Our two options create jobs at a blended cost of $15,527 per job. In the latest in-house assessment of the Lee Act, the author comes up with a range of job creation figures, from 87,000 to 147,000 (Luger 2003). A paltry 4 percent of these (i.e., 3,400 to 5,900) are estimated to have been induced by the Lee Act (Luger and Bae 2005). The cost is about $39,475 (Table 7.1).

Our employment numbers are much bigger than those attributed to the Lee Act, reflecting that these proposed programs are targeted to job creation and labor intensity and that they would apply to startups, business expansions, and new recruitment projects, not just the footloose facility waiting to land somewhere.[17]

Doesn't this proposal generate proportionately more low-wage jobs? Yes, it does. There are times when more jobs (any job) are needed. In addition, not all job seekers will have the time, the capacity, or the opportunity to get retrained and find a better job. The creation of more jobs pushes all wages up. The Job Growth Tax Credit is also meant to be a countercyclical tool. It is triggered when it is most needed—during a recession and the early recovery period. The availability of federal Trade Adjustment Assistance wage supplements mitigates the low-wage problem for jobless workers over 55 years old. If they have lost their jobs due to imports or trade-induced relocations and have landed new jobs that pay less than the old wage and less than $50,000, they may receive 50 percent of the difference between their old and new wages for up to two years.

DESIRABLE PROGRAM FEATURES

The fundamental virtue of these two alternatives is that a strong rationale could be made for them even if there was no incentive competition. The Job Growth Tax Credit is promoting economic activity during a recession and strengthening the early stage of the recovery. On the other hand, the Targeted Job Creation Grant is trying to encourage more private employment in economically disadvantaged and depressed counties.

Analogous employment programs have been run successfully both here and abroad. Research documents that wage subsidies for the job-

Table 7.1 Incentive Comparisons

Program	Subsidy type	Objectives	Mechanism	Number of jobs	Cost per job
Targeted Job Creation	Grant	• Foster job creation in poor tier 1 counties • Promote the expansion of small business	• Grant subsidy for 6 months to firms hiring unemployed job seekers • Up to $6.75 for wages/$1.75 for benefits • Penalty for jobs terminated before 18 months	2,291 jobs for tier 1 counties	$16,370
Job Growth Tax Credit	Tax credit	• Encourage job creation during recessions and early recoveries	• 30% tax credit per employee of first $14,700 of salary above 102% of baseline employment • Triggered by 5% unemployment	26,806 jobs statewide	$14,700
Lee Act Tax Credit	Tax credit	• Drive private investment into poor counties • Encourage job creation • Attract premier property • Foster R&D • Training credit	• For machinery and equipment 4–7% of investment above threshold • Job creation credit up to $12,500 per job	3,400 jobs statewide	$39,425

less or less-skilled workers are likely to be more effective when utilized in conjunction with labor market intermediaries that help provide some training, placement services, and job retention assistance.[18] The benefit/cost ratio can be increased, and the overall expenses can be limited by targeting the program to certain communities and potential workers. If the recession truly ends, the strategy can be easily converted into a welfare-to-work operation and even use welfare monies as a means of funding these wage subsidies.

This strategy is appealing because it does not fit conveniently into any one of the boxes typically used to describe comparable programs.[19] It is an economic development tool. It supports small businesses that will be the main users of the program. (Larger firms are eligible as well.) It is a temporary, countercyclical adjustment program for mainstream workers. And it balances the above with more of a focus on the harder-to-employ, disadvantaged worker.

This program would also help level the playing field for all communities. Many will never land a prime business attraction project, but all have indigenous firms that might expand with an injection of money. All can play and win in this game. Further, it focuses on aiding those workers who are suffering right now, unlike the approach of the Lee Act, which is structurally indifferent to who gets hired.

The two proposed programs also complement each other. The first is administratively less demanding and will be attractive to more established firms. The second will require more oversight but will be very attractive to small firms and startups; it targets those needing new employment. Moreover, the two have different funding advantages and disadvantages. The first option does not require any real out-of-pocket revenues from the state, while the second will entail a specific appropriation.

A further comparison with the Lee Act is especially telling. Given what's been happening to the state since it was enacted, a policymaker could come up with a new litmus test for new program development. For example,

1) Does the development reform or new option encourage investment in those communities that are being hardest hit by economic restructuring and dislocation?

2) Does it improve the reemployment prospects of displaced workers?

3) Does it help the state's businesses and sectors compete successfully on the basis of innovation, productivity, timeliness, flexibility, and quality in the new global economy?
4) Do development strategies help to ensure an adequate revenue base for financing essential public services?

The Lee Act only compares favorably with our proposals on the third item. But it does so at an unacceptable cost relative to benefits.[20]

Lastly, our two approaches can be linked with a statewide First Source hiring program.[21] Such agreements help local/state governments target more of the jobs resulting from new business projects to local residents, the unemployed and the economically disadvantaged. Such agreements require private companies that receive public monies to use the public sector or designated nonprofit contractor as the "first source" for new job hires. The state or local government (or a nonprofit broker and job training/placement "shop") acts as the "job developer" on behalf of the private firm, identifying and screening potential workers, arranging training services, and so forth. The private sector is under no obligation to hire these workers, but must interview them before seeking any other possible employees. Such programs have been run very successfully in Portland, Oregon; Berkeley, California; and Minneapolis, Minnesota. Berkeley's program, for example, has been used since 1986 to meet business and construction contractors' needs for workers, while giving special attention to filling entry-level and intermediate-level jobs with qualified local workers (particularly, unemployed and underemployed minorities, women, youth, and disabled persons).[22]

A BUFFALO HUNTER'S REBUTTAL?

Continuing the argument in the prologue, the proponent of using fewer performance-based incentives might argue as follows.

- You can put so many conditions and complexities on an incentive that it becomes a disincentive.
- The local developer can claim that she needs a more attractive incentive to do her job. (Of course, if the state government is footing the bill, she has nothing to lose and everything to gain.)

- Furthermore, the incentive proponent can argue that the Job Growth Tax Credit is not really equivalent to a conventional job creation or machine and equipment credit, because it is not available at all times. The grant program is mainly a small business subsidy, targeted at the most needy areas. So, it too is not helpful for attraction purposes.

Does this leave the author of this paper with no ammo for a counter-argument? Here is my response:

My critics are right: the alternatives proposed in this chapter are less attractive to business. This is inevitable, because the financial interest of the shareholders of the business prospect and the state government are not completely in sync. The shareholders want to maximize the incentive offer, get it in cash rather than in-kind, and have the least strings attached. The state (or local, if it's financing the incentive) government has a different bottom-line: it wants jobs and private investment on its terms, which includes, most importantly, a fiscal surplus generated by their incentive investment.

But there is a political dimension as well. If the citizenry understands and supports cost-effective incentives offered by fiscally responsible public officials that are targeted at priority economic development and employment challenges, then this chapter's proposals look stronger.

The Buffalo Hunter still has a final response. He points out that his way of working still possesses more political muscle and it is more widely understood. "Unilateral disarmament is not an option," he says. "I assure you, citizens, that I will never leave you undefended. I will court every opportunity for jobs."

He also has a constituency base that can be more easily mobilized. Local developers, chambers of commerce, and county officials, along with governors and secretaries of commerce want tools for deal making. At this time, they are rewarded for winning or losing this game. They are deeply interested and engaged in keeping incentives around while other constituencies, such as school teachers, unions, communities that will never land a plum plant, environmentalists, and advocates for the poor and progressive taxation are only marginally engaged in this fight.

Looking again at the North Carolina case surfaces another dimension that should be discussed. There *is* growing interest in reforming the Lee Act. Some, even in the mainstream economic development community, may be willing to let William S. Lee go. *But this is only acceptable if JDIG gets more resources.*

The state's relatively new JDIG has some good elements.[23] The committee that manages the JDIG funds has authored an excellent series of guidelines for making decisions and holding firms accountable for private investment and job creation. I especially like the required upfront fiscal impact analysis, the cap on the costs per job, the limit on number of projects per year, disclosure and reporting requirements, quality job and company standards, employment-triggered releases of funds, the contractual breach language, and the sanctions for noncompliance.[24]

The virtue of this program is its vice: it is very flexible, which means that it allows for highly tailored incentive packages. This customization, along with the size of the subsidy, makes it extremely attractive to prospects. But there's a downside: it also raises the specter of the "winner's curse"—in the heat of the state-to-state competition and in the absence of knowing what the firm's bottom line is or what other communities may be offering, you pay too much for the honor of hosting this firm.

This is why I argue that the upfront fiscal impact analysis is so important. These fiscal projections must be conservative and must not use inflated multipliers. They must count all the state and local incentives on the table and recognize that a certain number of jobs will go to nonnatives. They must use a reasonable discount rate over time, and they must factor in somehow and subtract the percentage of jobs that would have happened anyway.

Given the importance of the fiscal impact analysis in avoiding the winner's curse, its credibility and integrity might be increased if the analysis were conducted not by the Commerce Department, but instead by the Department of Revenue or Fiscal Research in the General Assembly. (There are no accusaitons here of wrongdoing; the change, however, could remove any potential doubts and concerns.)

The likelihood of a favorable ratio of benefits over costs is much more likely if the unemployed or the working poor get a shot at these jobs. This is why imposing a "First Source" hiring requirement on JDIG or any other subsidy is so important.

In my view, any expansion in dollars and numbers of projects annually must be contingent on these reforms of JDIG.

One further recommendation: I strongly suggest that any new incentives proposed to the General Assembly must have a fiscal note attached to them and must specify the management information system and outcome measures that must be in place before the incentive is open for business. This would greatly aid the General Assembly and commerce staff in monitoring and evaluating the incentive's results.

So, who won the argument? In some ways, it looks like the buffalo hunter once again had the last word, but hopefully not the last laugh. That's why it all comes down to innovative accountability reforms for the short-term and civic education, advocacy, and politics for the long haul.

CONCLUSION

Business incentives for attracting private capital are, at best, a necessary evil. Indeed, in giving away public resources, states are trying to influence *where* the jobs will be located, not *whether* the jobs are created. The offer typically is not: "If you can help us financially, then we can afford to take a risk to build a new line of profitable business." Rather, it is: "We have a new line of profitable business, so we're going to build a new plant. How much will you give us to build it near you." This whole "auction" is largely a waste of limited public resources.

To conclude, this is the current situation in North Carolina. CFED's two "models" are being translated into legislation by General Assembly staff. CFED was asked to testify before the Joint Select Committee on February 19, 2004. Some progress has been made in getting this Committee concerned about the recent rise in mortgage foreclosures. Plans are in the works to establish an ad hoc coalition for incentive reform and improved displaced worker services. The jury is still out regarding the substance and political viability of a more job creation–focused approach to business incentives.

Notes

1. Many of these ideas were developed in collaboration with a CFED colleague, Lillian "Beadsie" Woo. We also received a great deal of good advice from economists John Bishop, Tim Bartik, and Robert Haveman.
2. Between 1996 and 2001, the accumulated value of the tax credits generated was $1.16 billion, of which $208 million were claimed. "Generated" credits are ones in which a business has successfully applied for a credit. "Claimed" credits are ones where a business has actually invoked the credit and is paying fewer taxes. Some credits can actually expire over time if they are not claimed.
3. Sample projects included Boeing and Merck. These might be called ad hoc subsidies rather than "statutory-based" subsidies.
4. To date, North Carolina has funded six projects. Most were located in Tier 5 counties, the most affluent. They include General Dynamics Armament and Technical Products (headquarters and light manufacturing); Infineon Technologies North American Corporation (semiconductor company from Germany, with U.S. headquarters in California and operations across the United States); R.H. Donnelley Corporation (publishing company, headquarters relocating from Vermont); GE Nuclear Energy (headquarters moving to North Carolina); and Goodrich Corporation (expansion of existing facility, moving from Illinois and New Jersey).
5. For a much more detailed critique, see Schweke and Woo (2003a). We have also crafted a more incrementalist reform of the Lee Act.
6. For a thorough description and defense of these models, see Schweke and Woo (2003b).
7. This option was an adaptation of the federal New Jobs Tax Credit (1977–1978). The background literature on it is cited in Schweke and Woo (2003b).
8. The grant program is based on the successful Minnesota Emergency Employment Development Act in the 1980s.
9. In the interests of fairness and the potential to create a larger employment impact, when enacted, the tax credit should be limited to firms in those sectors that produce goods and services that are either exported to other states or countries or are substitutes for goods and services that would otherwise have to be imported. The Lee Act has some eligibility wording that could be used or adapted. Moreover, CFED has a list of those industries that should be eligible for the tax credit and will gladly make it available upon request.
10. The mathematical rationale is as follows: a firm that chooses to hire 10 people for a total cost of $250,000 in salaries gets a better tax deal than a firm that hires 5 people for $250,000. Firm 1 can take a credit of $44,100, while firm 2 only gets $22,050. The tax credit's structure, therefore, subsidizes a higher percentage of lower-waged employees' salaries. $14,700 is the figure for North Carolina's FUTA wages. This is for the unemployment insurance tax that firms pay.
11. There may be legality issues with having two rates, so this may not be possible.

12. The Targeted Job Creation Grant could be made administratively simpler by being available for hiring any unemployed North Carolinian, but we were trying to address those people in greatest need.
13. For more detail about public versus private job creation, see Johnson, Schweke, and Hull (1999).
14. We assume that 30 percent of the job growth is directly attributable to the tax credit. The typical time for the national economy to go from peak to trough is seven years. We can assume, then, that the tax credit would be operational for about half that time, or three years. That brings the total number of jobs created to 80,417.
15. This figure may be too high because some of the firms that might use the Job Growth Tax Credit will use the grant program. So, we may be counting the type of firm with potential to add some jobs twice. However, we qualify this possible overcounting worry by noting that the two options target different sized firms to some extent. The grant program is more attractive to small, new and young firms. The tax credit is more of a winner for large and established enterprises.
16. It should be noted here that the Institute for Economic Development at the University of North Carolina has authored two reports evaluating the Lee Act, one in 2001 and another in 2003, plus an interesting report on the North Carolina economic development system (see next footnote). In each report, different estimates are given for the Lee Act. Sometimes they are only statewide numbers. Other times they look at Lee tax credits, in particular, Tiers. Sometimes they are citing net jobs, other times they are gross jobs. The 2001 and 2003 Lee assessments used different numbers to derive net jobs. In 2001, the authors claimed that 50 percent of the jobs were due to the Lee Act. In 2003, the number was 4 percent. So, it is often difficult to get comparable benchmarks.
17. We think both options are wise and complementary, but if you can only do one, the Targeted Job Creation Grant is the most compelling, because it focuses on citizens most in need.
18. See Katz and Molina publications in Schweke and Woo (2003b). Also go to "Job Initiative" program of Anne E. Casey Foundation at http://www.aecf.org. There is an extensive list of relevant publications to consult for more research on the role of labor market intermediaries.
19. In short, the programs are synergistic. Their creators (Haveman, Bishop, Bartik, and others) sought to "think outside the box" when they were developed.
20. Some might argue that the 4 percent figure is too low. It might be, but Luger's (2003) calculation is the best number we have at this point. And it does underscore the danger and reality of inevitable windfalls in any subsidy program.
21. The administrative monies for implementing the direct grant program can also cover much of the expenses of upgrading county and regional job placement services.
22. Excellent discussions of First Source Agreements can be found in Molina (1998) and Lyall and Schweke (1996).
23. JDIG has been catching some heat because four of its first five deals have gone to Tier 5 (affluent) counties. In addition, there is still the inevitable problem that

eventually North Carolina competitor states will replicate JDIG or come up with another incentive "gizmo." The whole process starts again.
24. JDIG could still be strengthened in the areas of performance contracting and sanctions for noncompliance.

References

Arend, Mark. 2006. "Synchronicity." *Site Selection*, November. http://www.siteselection.com/issues/2006/nov/cover/ (accessed December 18, 2006).

Johnson, Cliff, William Schweke, and Matt Hull. 1999. *Creating Jobs: Public and Private Strategies for the Hard-to-Employ.* Washington, DC: Corporation for Enterprise Development/Center on Budget and Policy Priorities.

Luger, Michael I. 2003. "2003 Assessment of the William S. Lee Tax Act." Working paper. Chapel Hill, NC: Office of Economic Development, Kenan Institute of Private Enterprise, University of North Carolina–Chapel Hill.

Luger, Michael I., and Suho Bae. 2005. "The Effectiveness of State Business Tax Incentive Programs: The Case of North Carolina." *Economic Development Quarterly* 19(4): 327–345.

Luger, Michael I., and Leslie Stewart. 2003. *Improving North Carolina's Economic Development Delivery System: A Report to the North Carolina General Assembly.* March, pp. D1–D2. Chapel Hill, NC: Office of Economic Development, University of North Carolina.

Lyall, Victoria, and William Schweke. 1996. *Using Alliance-Based Development Strategies for Economic Empowerment.* Washington, DC: Corporation for Enterprise Development.

Molina, Frieda. 1998. "Making Connections: A Study of Employment Linkage Programs." Working paper. Washington, DC: Center for Community Change.

Schweke, William, and Lillian G. Woo. 2003a. *Is the Lee Act Working for North Carolina?* Report to the Corporation for Enterprise Development, Washington, DC.

———. 2003b. "There Are Job Creation Alternatives To Traditional Business Incentives: A New Direction for North Carolina." Working paper, December. Washington, DC: Corporation for Enterprise Development.

8
Nine Concrete Ways to Curtail the Economic War among the States

Greg LeRoy
Good Jobs First

More than 10 years ago I wrote a book titled *No More Candy Store: States and Cities Making Job Subsidies Accountable* (LeRoy 1994), which likened the choices that many companies faced between all of the "sweet" job subsidy deals offered by competing states and cities to a kid in a candy shop. Too often a mess resulted—very few jobs were created and/or the company went out of business or relocated. One could get very depressed thinking about how hard it will be to solve this crazy "candy store" mess. A lot of people with huge financial self-interests are tied to the status quo: footloose corporations, site location consultants, accounting firms and tax consultants, industrial real estate brokers, mayors, governors, and building contractors.

Given how deeply entrenched this wasteful system has become, only an *organizing approach* to the problem can undo it. By this I mean reforms that bring everyday taxpayers back into the process, that actively enable and encourage grassroots groups like community organizations, environmentalists and labor unions, as well as journalists and government watchdogs, to wade in. With all due respect to some who have proposed sweeping lawsuits or legislation that I would call "silver bullets," such ideas don't stand a chance against a problem so deeply embedded as this one.[1]

Reforms, of course, involve legislation. Some new laws are necessary, but they should be simple laws based on common sense that are strongly enforced—laws with clear intentions that courts cannot pervert. Don't forget, today's candy store mess is a dream for lawyers and accountants, since it consists of so many hundreds of convoluted laws and tax gimmicks.

SUNSHINE: THE BEST ANTISEPTIC

The first two necessary reforms involve disclosure. Taxpayers need to see how much money each company received in tax breaks and other subsidies—especially corporate income tax breaks that are usually undisclosed.

This disclosure is the cornerstone of reform. Think about other major reforms the United States has enacted in the past 40 years.

- When community groups alleged that banks were discriminating against minorities or those living in older neighborhoods by denying loans to worthy borrowers because of their race or their address, they demanded and won the Home Mortgage Disclosure Act. That law requires banks to disclose the number and dollar value of all their housing loans every year, by census tract. The data revealed blatant discrimination, and prompted Congress to pass the Community Reinvestment Act, which has enabled hundreds of community groups to win billions of dollars for neighborhood revitalization from many of the nation's largest banks.

- When community groups and labor unions alleged that chemical factories and other big polluters were endangering their health with toxic emissions, they demanded and won the Toxic Right to Know law, which requires companies to disclose the content and quantity of all emissions. Using that data, coalitions have won hundreds of agreements with companies to reduce hazardous emissions and otherwise improve local safety.

- During Watergate, when citizens become frustrated with reports of corruption, they demanded to know who was giving money—and how much—to politicians. The resulting disclosure produces data compiled by the Federal Elections Commission. And while many people call our campaign finance system "legalized corruption," at least we know who bankrolls whom. If we did not have that information, none of the more recent campaign finance laws, like McCain-Feingold, could have taken hold.

REFORM 1: STATE ECONOMIC DEVELOPMENT SUBSIDY DISCLOSURE

By disclosure, I mean annual, company-specific, public reporting of costs and benefits. How much did each company get? Which subsidy program did the money come from? What did the company do with the money? How many jobs did it create? How well do the jobs pay? Do they provide health care?

Seems pretty simple, doesn't it? Every state and city should be able to disclose such basic facts. But as we've seen in so many horror stories, most governors and mayors aren't watching the store. Some even pretend to perform cost-benefit analysis by adding up their own press releases.

Twelve states have already enacted some form of economic development subsidy disclosure (Connecticut, Illinois, Louisiana, Maine, Minnesota, Nebraska, North Carolina, North Dakota, Ohio, Texas, Washington State, and West Virginia). These states vary a lot in terms of the quality and completeness of their disclosure, but we certainly have enough experience now to talk about what works best. (You can see details about each state's disclosure law in Chapter 3 of our research manual, *No More Secret Candy Store*, at www.goodjobsfirst.org.)

Any state can be investigated, regardless of whether it's on the list. You can normally get quite a bit of information about deals in a state, especially if you are willing to wage a paper war under the state's Open Records Act or Freedom of Information Act. With a lot of time and persistence (and possibly some money for processing charges), you might be able to cobble together as much information as you could get quickly for free in a state with disclosure. But taxpayers shouldn't have to wage a costly paper war with bureaucrats; they should be able to quickly and easily find out where their economic development money is going and whether their taxpayer investments are paying off. That's what I mean by disclosure. Indeed, the information should be on the Web, just like it already is in some states.

Let's look at an example. Minnesota is one of my favorite disclosure states. Although the Gopher State's law does not cover corporate income tax breaks, it does cover lots of other subsidies—and the data are on the Web! Since its original law was passed in 1995 and improved twice later, hundreds of Minnesota deals have been disclosed every year. Figure 8.1 shows an example of one deal, in Caledonia, Minnesota.

So here we have a tax increment financing deal (box 11) worth $275,515 (box 16) to create one new job (box 17) at Dairy Queen (box 12) paying $4.50 an hour (box 18). Now, I don't know how many ice cream cones they sell in Caledonia in February, I mean, I really hope that's a full-year job. Health care? I doubt it. I suppose we should be grateful that the company is reporting an actual wage of $5.15 an hour, but then, that may be due to the federal minimum wage getting raised in the interim. But isn't that an awfully big subsidy for a poverty-wage job? Until the state enacted disclosure, Minnesotans didn't know there were deals like this happening.

Notice how unbureaucratic this disclosure system is. A city staff person fills in the top half of the form (based on its files from the original deal), then she calls the company and asks about jobs created and wages paid. Then she mails the form to the state Department of Employment and Economic Development (DEED) in St. Paul, and DEED scans the forms and posts them on its Web site.

Of course, I prefer a state's disclosure system to include corporate income tax breaks, and some already do. West Virginia has been reporting on every company that claims any major kind of corporate income tax credit for more than a dozen years. Maine has been disclosing three since it enacted disclosure in 1998. North Carolina enacted disclosure in 2002; you can see company-specific data at www.dor.state.nc.us/publications/williamslee.html.

More information on the disclosure form would be helpful. Will these jobs be accessible by public transportation? Does this deal involve a relocation? If so, from where and to where? Were the jobs accessible by public transportation before? Will they be accessible after the relocation? Otherwise, how do we know if the jobs are even available to low-income workers who cannot afford a car?

Nine Concrete Ways to Curtail the Economic War among the States 187

Figure 8.1 1998 Minnesota Business Assistance Form

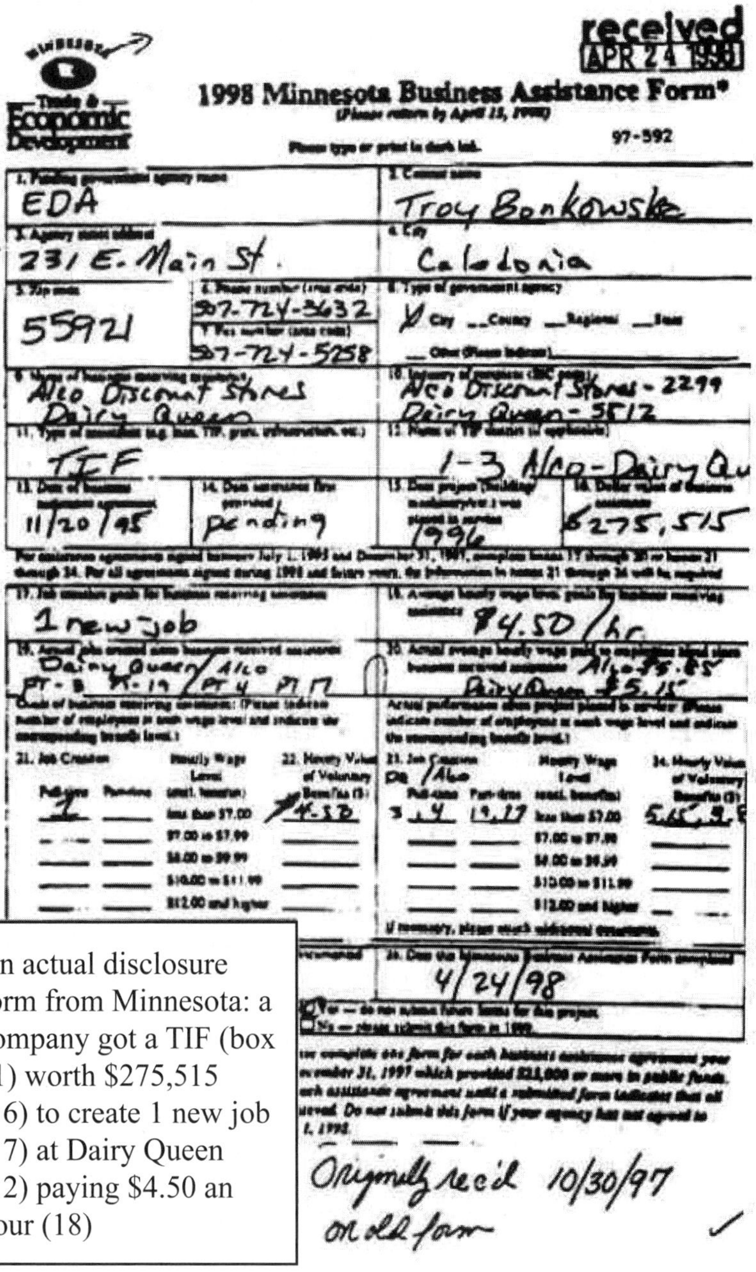

An actual disclosure form from Minnesota: a company got a TIF (box 11) worth $275,515 (16) to create 1 new job (17) at Dairy Queen (12) paying $4.50 an hour (18)

REFORM 2: DISCLOSURE TO CORPORATE SHAREHOLDERS OF STATE TAXES PAID

Publicly traded companies (those that are listed on stock exchanges) already disclose how much they pay in federal income tax each year, in their annual reports and Forms 10-K. They also already disclose how much they pay in all state and local taxes, but they are only required to disclose the total from all 50 states in one aggregate number. So, for instance, when looking at General Motors' Form 10-K, it is not possible to determine how much the company's taxes have gone up or down in Michigan the past dozen years.

The solution would be simple: require publicly traded companies to include a 50-state matrix in their Form 10-Ks showing how much tax they paid in each state. Breaking it down into three categories in each state would be best: income tax; property tax; and sales, utility, and excise taxes. This would surely produce data that would grab people's attention. We already know from accountability campaigns in states such as Connecticut and New Jersey that many big companies there pay tiny amounts of income tax—as little as $200 a year, far less than low-income families—thanks to gimmicks like the Delaware royalty loophole.

If taxpayers learned that large companies in their state were paying almost no income tax, they would demand to know why. Indeed, a 1986 revelation by Citizens for Tax Justice that many huge corporations were paying zero federal income tax was memorialized in the famous poster: "I pay more income tax than General Electric, W.R. Grace, General Dynamics, Boeing, Dow Chemical, and Lockheed All Put Together!"

The ensuing outrage prompted a major progressive reform, closing some corporate loopholes; the 1986 law is considered the best thing to happen to the federal tax code in decades. There is a large body of evidence from both state-specific and national studies that companies are gaming state income tax codes even harder than Uncle Sam's. For example, the Center on Budget and Policy Priorities points out that in the second half of the 1990s, when the U.S. economy was sizzling, federal corporate income tax revenues grew an average of 6 percent a year. But *state* corporate income tax collections rose at just half that rate. Same companies, same profits, same years, half the tax (Mazerov 2003, p. 3). Combined reporting would solve much of that.

REFORM 3: CLAWBACKS OR MONEY-BACK GUARANTEES

A clawback rule or contract simply says that a company must hold up its end of the bargain, otherwise taxpayers have some money-back protection. Eighteen states and dozens of cities already use clawbacks, which basically after a company gets a subsidy (say, two years later), it must create a certain number of jobs at a certain wage and benefit level. The clawback may also require other public benefits such as a certain number of dollars invested to modernize a facility. Then, if the company does not meet the targets, taxpayers get paid back. The rule can be prorated so that, for example, if the company falls 10 percent short, it has to pay back 10 percent of the subsidy; it can also be set for a steeper penalty, if the company falls far short.

I can hear the business lobbyists wailing again about poisoning the "business climate." But I think just the opposite is true. From the mid-1980s to the mid-1990s, there was a string of lawsuits in which cities tried to get subsidy money back from companies that were shutting plants (*Chicago v. Hasbro/Playskool; Norwood, Ohio v. General Motors; Duluth v. Triangle; Yonkers v. Otis Elevator; Ypsilanti Township v. General Motors*). The latter is best known: Ypsilanti Township alleged that statements made by GM in public hearings amounted to an oral contract obligating the company to stay in exchange for huge property tax breaks.

Now, given the prevailing business climate dogma, these lawsuits were huge events, with mayors risking their cities' reputations for being friendly to business. The lawsuits speak to incredible frustration and anger, even desperation. If the cities had negotiated clawbacks with the companies, it's unlikely that there would have been any lawsuits. The companies' obligations would have been spelled out in black and white—just like any private-sector contract—and there would likely never have been a dispute. Clear obligations on both sides of the table and no litigation: isn't *that* a good business climate?

REFORM 4: JOB QUALITY STANDARDS

Why give a company a subsidy and then allow it to pay a poverty wage? Subsidizing low-wage jobs only means taxpayers get stuck with even higher, hidden costs—in the form of Food Stamps, Medicaid, Earned Income Tax Credit, and housing assistance. Thanks to the living wage movement—and to good old common sense—this reform is already taking root. As of our last updated survey, at least 43 states, 41 cities, and 5 counties now attach wage and/or health care requirements to economic development incentives (Purinton 2003).

I hasten to add that while these numbers have risen sharply since I began surveying for them in 1989, we still have a long way to go. Most jurisdictions still only apply these rules to one program (we found a total of 165, including 107 state rules) but if the 50 states have an average of 30 or more subsidies each, or a total of at least 1,500, that means about 93 percent of state subsidies still allow companies to pay as little as that Dairy Queen in Caledonia, Minnesota.

REFORM 5: UNIFIED DEVELOPMENT BUDGETS

About 35 states publish what is called a tax expenditure budget. That is, they provide the legislature with a report that says the state lost X dollars in revenue to A, B, and C tax credits. But most of these reports are incomplete or unreliable. Incredibly, there is no standardized national set of accounting rules or guidelines for the states to track these expenses. (A group called the Government Finance Officers Association, which is the largest professional association of state and local treasurers and comptrollers, formed a committee to study the issue of subsidies in the late 1980s, but its work never went anywhere. The Government Accounting Standards Board, which sets guidelines for how governments should keep their books, has no firm rules telling states how to account for tax expenditures.)

This is a big issue because tax expenditures for economic development (i.e., companies claiming corporate income tax credits or sales or utility tax exemptions that remain undisclosed) often dwarf other forms of spending such as grants that do show up clearly in budgets because they require appropriations. It's no exaggeration to call appropriations the top of the iceberg and tax expenditures the bottom. So most state legislatures are flying in the dark when it comes to the big picture. They don't know how big the bottom of the iceberg is, much less what they are getting for it.

The solution is a unified development budget, as advocated for by groups in Texas, California, North Carolina, and Illinois. A unified development budget provides legislators with a comprehensive inventory of all forms of spending for economic development, including all the tax breaks as well as all the appropriations. Illinois enacted a unified development budget requirement as part of its disclosure law in 2003, but the first such budget issued by the state was very incomplete. In other states, research groups have cobbled together their own versions, a tedious exercise requiring a lot of budget sleuthing.

Although there is not yet much experience with this safeguard, the idea is sound. Give taxpayers and lawmakers a document that puts the whole iceberg on the table every year or two. A document that treats tax breaks no differently than appropriations, that portrays them both correctly as simply different forms of the same thing: state spending. And then let people decide if they have the right balance. Chances are, with an accurate mapping of the whole iceberg, more people will turn their attention to the previously hidden bottom part, the secretive tax breaks, where most of the money is. Especially in times of budget deficits and fiscal strain, there is a better chance that legislators will look at both the top and the bottom as they seek to balance their budgets.

REFORM 6: SCHOOL BOARD INPUT ON ABATEMENTS AND TIF

As Good Jobs First documented in 2003, only two states effectively shield school funding from revenue losses caused by property tax abatements and revenue diversions caused by tax increment financing (TIF). A few states give school boards limited input, but the great majority give school boards no say in the process (Good Jobs First 2003). It's a big issue for school finance; although local revenue sources for schools are less important than they used to be, as states play a greater role, property taxes remain the largest single source of funding for K-12, and in some states, they still account for more than half. But with 43 states allowing abatements and 48 using TIF, the threat to school funding is present in every state.

It's crazy public policy when you think about it: voters elect members of the school board and expect them to meet their obligation to educate the kids. But then along comes a city council or a county board doling out abatements or TIF, eating the school board's lunch. Call it an inter-governmental *free* lunch. Can you imagine the opposite happening: school boards unilaterally grabbing chunks of the budget for police and fire services?

Protecting education funding matters doubly for economic development. Good schools are a key amenity that help cities attract and retain good employers, especially those that require highly skilled (read: well-paid) workers. And with the baby boom generation approaching retirement, the growth rate of the U.S. labor force is plummeting, suggesting that we may face chronic skilled labor shortages. For both these reasons, the states and regions with good schools will be the economic development winners of the twenty-first century.

School boards should have a full voting seat on any board that abates or diverts property tax revenue away from schools. And school boards should have veto power over that portion of property tax that would be lost to the schools in each specific abatement or TIF deal.

REFORM 7: A FEDERAL "CARROT" AGAINST JOB PIRACY

The federal government often uses the power of its purse as a "carrot" to entice the states to reform their programs. A fraction of federal highway funding was held back from states until they raised their legal drinking age to 21. The No Child Left Behind Act uses federal funds to encourage school reform (though many doubt its effectiveness).

There is no reason the same idea could not apply to economic development. Ten percent of a state's money from the U.S. Departments of Commerce and Labor could be held back until a state adopted certain reforms. Just a few strategic ones would suffice: a certification by the governor that the state will not use taxpayer dollars to pirate jobs from another state, and adoption of disclosure and a unified development budget.

REFORM 8: PROPERLY DEFINE SITE LOCATION CONSULTANTS AS LOBBYISTS

Miriam Webster's Collegiate Dictionary defines lobbying as "to attempt or influence or sway (as a public official) towards a desired action." That sure sounds like the work of a site location consultant to me, since the deals they orchestrate routinely involve the passage of local ordinances for property tax abatements, industrial revenue bonds and/or zoning, and bigger deals sometimes involve state legislation as well.

Site location consultants work both sides of the street; that is, they work for companies looking for places and places looking for companies. It is an apparent conflict of interest that allows them to profit by controlling the key information about a deal. It's like a trial lawyer who represents children who got cancer from a nearby chemical plant also working for the chemical company. Or better yet, like a blackjack dealer who knows what your down card is.

Somehow, site location consultants have come to occupy a space where they defy norms about professional ethics and the proper representation of opposing parties. Let's be clear: there *are* opposing interests at play here. Companies want to pick the public pocket for every dime they can get, and public officials (or at least most of them) are trying to land the deal while spending as little as possible. But the bargaining table is sloped sharply because the site location consultant controls all of the information between the company and the sites competing for the deal. And in some cases, the site location consultant has a monetary self-interest in upping the ante of subsidies because he is working on commission of up to 30 percent of the value of those subsidies.

To help remedy this, states ought to legally classify site location consultants as lobbyists. In many states, that would require them to disclose at least a little about their activities. More importantly, it would block them from receiving success fees (read: commissions) and thereby remove their most outrageous incentive to fuel the candy-store arms race.

The long-term objective here is to split the profession into two. Site location consulting ought to consist of fish and fowl, i.e., consultants who work for companies and others who work for cities, counties, and states. There should be a robust, adversarial process in which the taxpayers benefit from a side of the profession that specializes in aggressive bargaining, professional cost-benefit analysis, and cold market judgments about corporate behavior.

REFORM 9: PROMOTE SMART GROWTH AND CURTAIL THE "ECONOMIC WAR AMONG THE SUBURBS"

In some respects, the "war among the states" alarm is misleading. Far more common than state versus state competitions for deals like the Boeing 7E7 are deals in which two or three jurisdictions within the same metro area compete for a deal. Indeed, when we looked at 29 subsidized corporate relocations in the Twin Cities metro area, only one company had even considered locating just across the state line in Wisconsin. Most relocating companies cannot afford to move to another state; they want to retain their workforces, and stay close to their customers and suppliers. They simply need more space or a better location within the same metro area.

The state versus state competitions tend to be more high-profile, such as those involving new auto assembly plants, so many people are unaware that intraregional competition is far more common. Only four states—Connecticut, Ohio, Minnesota, and Maine—collect information about subsidized relocations as part of their disclosure systems, and none has ever analyzed the data. To their credit, local development officials in some regions, by informal arrangements, seek to deter the use of subsidies to pay for relocations within their areas.

States should deny subsidies altogether to retail deals (except in truly depressed inner-city markets that are demonstrably underserved, such as those that lack basic retail items such as groceries, medications, and clothes). Retail is not economic development; it is what happens when people have disposable income. (It has lousy upstream ripple effects—all those goods from China—and paltry downstream ripple effects, since retail jobs are overwhelmingly part time, low wage, and without health care.) And big-box retail, which has become so expert at mongering subsidies, undermines existing retailers and is a primary cause of abandonment of urban core areas and the loss of open space at the suburban fringe.

States should also repeal point-of-sale sales tax collection rules. That is, they should not allow the city where a retail sale occurs to collect any share of the tax. Allowing one suburb to build a mall that pirates sales tax revenue from the core city and dozens of surrounding suburbs simply undermines the tax base of older areas. And it creates a perverse incentive for another suburb to build yet another mall further out, and so the leap-frog sprawl continues. For the same reason, those states that allow sales tax to be "TIFed" should repeal it; that just puts the perverse incentive on steroids. In today's sprawling metro areas, people live in one jurisdiction, work in another, and shop in a few others. Sales tax revenues ought to be shared statewide and regionally, reflecting that reality.

In metro areas, states should explicitly link economic development to public transportation, so that in order to get a subsidy, the project must be accessible by transit (i.e., within a quarter of a mile of a regularly served transit stop). That would reduce companies' abilities to whipsaw suburbs against each other (by taking exclusionary suburbs out of the race), steer more jobs onto the transit system, help low-income families gain access to more jobs, give more commuters a choice about how to get to work, and improve air quality. In a 50-state survey, we found that not a single state effectively coordinates any of its subsidy programs with public transit, even though the average state now has more than 30 subsidies. It is a huge wasted opportunity for transportation dollars to leverage smart growth, since states spend five times more on economic development than on public transportation (Khan 2003). In 2006, the Illinois legislature passed a "location efficient incentives" bill, which the governor signed into law. Illinois thus became the first state to intentionally make such a link, giving a slightly larger state tax credit to deals located close to transit and/or affordable housing.

Finally, states should deny development subsidies (as Maryland does under its Smart Growth Act) to any kind of deal that is not located in an area that already has infrastructure. Making developers bear the full infrastructure cost of sprawling fringe development helps tip the scales in favor of urban reinvestment. If land use policies bring jobs and tax bases back to older areas, the need for subsidies to revitalize those areas will diminish.

ACCOUNTABILITY AND THE "BUSINESS CLIMATE"

I can hear the business lobbyists howling already. "This is invasion of taxpayer privacy. This will threaten small businesses. This will poison the business climate," they're crying. Well, to them, I say three things.

First, there is no evidence that any of the 12 states cited here have harmed their business climates by having disclosure. (Nor, for that matter, is there evidence that any state has hurt its business climate with any other kind of reform I have cited, such as wage rules or money-back guarantee clawbacks.) As the person who has been out there publicizing these safeguards for 12 years, I think I would have been presented with such evidence if there was any, and I have not.

Second, nothing proposed here will invade anyone's privacy or harm any small businesses. By disclosure, I am not talking about public release of any companies' state income tax returns. I am not talking about seeing a company's profits or losses, nor am I talking about disclosure of how much most companies paid in state income tax. But I do think that as a taxpayer, I ought to have the right to see how much a company claimed on a tax credit. Because when a company claims a credit and pays less income tax, it is the same thing as if the government wrote a check to the company for some other economic development purpose, like a training grant. When a company claims an income tax credit, it means the company is paying less for public services and I have to pay more. I want to know how much more.

Third, lots of other kinds of tax breaks and subsidies are already public information. If a company gets a property tax abatement, I can see the details at the county tax assessor's office. If a company got a training grant, I can get that file at the Workforce Investment Board. If a company got a low-interest industrial revenue bond, I can go the county industrial development authority and get that information. Why should income tax credits be treated any differently? They were sold to us as "jobs, jobs, jobs," so we should be able to see how much those jobs are costing.

Notes

A more detailed version of the remedies discussed here was published in LeRoy (2005).

1. In May 2006, in *DaimlerChrysler v. Cuno*, the U.S. Supreme Court ruled that the plaintiffs lacked standing in federal court to contest a state investment tax credit that a lower court had ruled unconstitutional. In a separate ruling, the Supreme Court upheld a ruling by the same lower court that a property tax abatement was constitutional.

References

Good Jobs First. 2003. "Protecting Public Education from Tax Giveaways to Corporations: Property Tax Abatements, Tax Increment Financing, and Funding for Schools." National Education Association Working Paper, January. Washington, DC: National Education Association.

Khan, Mafruza. 2003. *Missing the Bus: How States Fail to Connect Economic Development with Public Transit.* Washington, DC: Good Jobs First. http://www.goodjobsfirst.org/pdf/bus.pdf (acessed December 18, 2006).

LeRoy, Greg. 2004. *No More Candy Store: States and Cities Making Subsidies Accountable.* Washington, DC: Good Jobs First.

———. 2005. *The Great American Jobs Scam: Corporate Tax Dodging and the Myth of Job Creation.* San Francisco: Berrett-Koehler Publishers.

Mazerov, Michael. 2003. *Closing Three Common Corporate Income Tax Loopholes Could Raise Additional Revenue for Many States.* Washington, DC: Center on Budget and Policy Priorities. http://www.cbpp.org/4-9-02sfp.htm (accessed December 18, 2006).

Purinton, Anna. 2003. *The Policy Shift to Good Jobs: States, Cities and Counties Attaching Job Quality Standards to Economic Development Subsidies.* Washington, DC: Good Jobs First. http://www.goodjobsfirst.org/pdf/jobquality.pdf (accessed December 18, 2006).

The Authors

Timothy J. Bartik is a senior economist at the W.E. Upjohn Institute for Employment Research.

Peter Fisher is a professor in the graduate program in urban and regional planning at the University of Iowa and research director at The Iowa Policy Project.

Greg LeRoy is the founder and director of Good Jobs First, a national resource center promoting corporate and government accountability in economic development and smart growth for working families.

Ann Markusen is a professor in the urban and regional planning graduate program and director of the Project on Regional and Industrial Economics, Humphrey Institute of Public Affairs, University of Minnesota.

Katherine Nesse is a PhD student in urban and regional planning at the University of Illinois at Urbana-Champaign.

William Schweke is vice president for learning and innovation at the Corporation for Enterprise Development, where he conducts research dedicated to reforming North Carolina's policies on economic development.

Adinda Sinnaeve is head of section at the European Commission, Directorate General for Trade.

Kenneth P. Thomas is an associate professor of political science and fellow at the Center for International Studies, University of Missouri–St. Louis.

Rachel Weber is an associate professor in the urban planning and policy program at the University of Illinois at Chicago.

Index

The italic letters *f, n,* and *t* following a page number indicate that the subject information of the heading is within a figure, note, or table, respectively, on that page.

10-K forms, 188

Accountability mechanisms, 150, 153, 154–155, 163
Ad hoc subsidies, 179*n*3
African Americans, 24, 164
Air Force Academy, intercity competition for, 5
Albuquerque, New Mexico, clawbacks in, 150
Anchor Hocking, 150
Arlington, Texas, intercity competition by, 49
Australia, 1, 5
Austria, EFTA and, 97
Auto industry
 regional competition for, 6, 43, 48–49
 subsidies under NAFTA to, 7–8
 See also specific companies in, e.g., General Motors (GM)

Backroom deals. *See* Transparency, lack of
Baltic states, EU, 100*n*4
Benefit-cost analyses, 51
 better, as alternative incentive reforms, 117, 118, 123, 124, 147
 medium-term calculations for, 32, 125, 126*t*–128*t*, 129–132
 problems when cost outweighs benefit, 111–113, 141–142
Berkeley, California, 120, 152, 175
Bidding wars, 11, 97
 end of, 5, 47
 principals in, 7, 9–10, 46
 racing to the bottom with, 18, 20, 161–162
Bismarck, North Dakota, negotiated hiring by, 148
Block exemptions, EC system of, 93–94

Block grants, Michigan, 132–133*n*2
Boeing, 30
 intercity competition for, 22, 111–112, 167, 179*n*3, 194
Bond rating agencies, 46–47
Brazil, rise of incentive competition in, 2, 6, 25
Brownfield properties, 109–110, 124, 132*n*1
Bulgaria, 7, 100*n*4
Bush administration, supply-side theory of, 79
Business climate rankings, 11, 167, 189, 196
Business growth
 incentives for, in Michigan, 132–133*n*2
 social benefits of, 119–120, 134*nn*12–13
Business incentive reform. *See* Economic development incentives, alternative incentive reforms for; Job creation, business incentive reform through
Business organizations
 approach to subnational governments by, 12, 49, 144
 cost reductions in, 2, 10
 in the EU, 89, 90, 99*n*1
 information asymmetries and, 43, 46, 145–146
 investment markets and, 45–47, 53*n*1
 longevity and retention of, 68–69, 116, 132–133*n*2, 134*n*10
 mobility of, 7, 25, 156
 rent-seeking activity of, 2, 11, 13, 18, 21–23
 siting factors for, 10, 18, 65, 142, 148, 155–156, 156–157*n*7
 spatial competition for, 16–17

201

202 Markusen

Caledonia, Minnesota, 186, 187*f*, 190
California, 5, 49, 191
   attractive qualities lessen concern over competition in, 152–153
   local hiring in, 120, 175
Cambodia, ineffective incentives in, 8
Cambridge, Massachusetts, competition concern in, 152–153
Canada, 1, 7–8, 45, 47
Capitalist systems, economic privacy under, 45, 196
Cataluña, devolution in, 13
CFED (Center for Enterprise Development), 166, 167, 178, 179*n*1
Chicago, Illinois, 189
   incentives to Boeing by, 22, 111–112
   TIF for retail development in, 151–152
Chicago v. Hasbro/Playskool, 189
Chile, devolution in, 13
China, 2, 6, 7, 194
Citizen taxpayers, 76*t*
   costs of business incentives to, 14–15, 17–18, 27, 142, 167, 190, 196
   participation of, and incentives, 44, 50–52, 123, 124
      grassroots coalitions in, 153, 154, 183, 184
   public services and, 14–15, 16–17, 23, 144, 156*n*2
Citizens for Tax Justice, 188
Class warfare, 79–80
Clawbacks
   alternative incentive reform as, 118–119, 120, 123, 196
   contractual safeguards as, 149, 150, 155, 189
   disclosure timing for, 156–157*n*7
Cleveland, Ohio, zero-sum bargaining in, 150–151
Colorado, intercity competition involving, 22
Commission, Siemens v., 92
Communications technology, 28, 179*n*4

cost reductions in, 2, 10, 45–46, 105–106, 106*f*
Community Reinvestment Act, 184
Competing for Capital (Thomas), 19
Competition between cities, 5, 7, 65, 161
   facilities siting and, 22, 48–49
   influences on, 14, 45
   reform of, and smart growth, 194–196
Competition between nation-states, 8–9, 18, 45
Competition for capital
   bargaining leverage and, 25, 141–157
   government negotiation with, 150–155, 157*n*8, 189
   interests in, 144–145, 150–151, 156*n*2, 193–194
   performance standards in, 147–148, 155–156, 156*n*6
   positive outcomes for the public sector, 146–150, 156*n*1, 156*nn*3–4
   power in, 145–146
   regulatory context for, 142–143
   fiscal consequences of, 2, 24–25, 57–82
      conclusions about, 78–81
      entitlements in, 65–71, 78, 80
      measurement of, 59–62, 67–68, 177
      package deals in, 62–65, 78, 80
      policy tools in, 57–59
      tax policy in, 71–78
   history of spatial, 3–4, 18
   investments and
      firms in, 4, 10, 53*n*1
      governments in, 5, 8, 14, 20–23, 43–47, 53*n*1
      regulation of, 16, 19
   role of, 78–81
   See also Incentive competition; Subsidy competition; Tax and subsidy competition
Competition for jobs, spatial, 12, 21–23
Competition reform, 32–33
   disclosure in, 184–189, 187*f*, 190–191, 196
   EU model system, 97–99

Competition reform *(continued)*
  guarantees in, 8, 52, 189–190
  job market and tax capacity in, 3, 16, 23
  methods of, among subnational states, 183–197
    clawbacks, 189; *see also main heading* Clawbacks
    disclosure of state subsidies, 185–186, 187*f*
    disclosure of state taxes paid, 188–189
    federal "carrots," 192–193
    job quality standards, 190
    promotion of smart growth, 194–196
    registration of *de facto* lobbyists, 193–194
    stakeholder input, 191–192, 194–196
    unified development budgets, 3, 31, 190–191
  policy challenges of, 31–33, 47, 52–53
Connecticut, 188
  eminent domain ruling concerning, 51, 54*n*5
  subsidies and, 147–148, 156*n*6, 185, 194
Conservative approaches
  contractual safeguards and, 154–155
  investment markets and, 80, 81
  supply-side theory in, 25, 79, 80, 81, 82*n*6
Corporate income tax, 184
  decline of, 71–72, 73*ff*, 74, 74*f*, 78
  federal rates, 72, 82*n*4
  public disclosure of amounts paid, 188–189
  rates before and after incentives, 70, 71*f*
  state and local rates, 106
    business location effect of, 107–108, 133*n*3, 134*n*7
    maintain tradition despite reform, 113–114
  state apportionment of, 71–72, 81–82*n*3
Corporate Location (magazine), 12
Cost-benefit analyses. *See* Benefit-cost analyses
Council of State Governments, tax break classification by, 48
Courts
  EC, 91, 93
  Michigan, 51, 54*n*5
  U.S., 51, 53, 54*n*5, 197*n*1
  West Virginia, 150
Coventry Healthcare, 148
Croatia, EU and, 100*n*4
Cuno v. Daimler-Chrysler, 53, 197*n*1
Cyprus, EU, 100*n*4
Czech Republic, EU, 100*n*4

Daimler-Chrysler, Cuno v., 53, 197*n*1
Dairy Queen, 186, 187*f*, 190
Dallas, Texas, intercity competition by, 22, 49, 52*n*2
Debarment, nonperformance provision as, 149
DEED. *See* Department of Employment and Economic Development
Defense industry, plant locations in, 11
Deindustrialization, 4
Delaware, tax loopholes in, 74, 188
Deloitte & Touche, 11
DeLorean, John, 7
Denver, Colorado, intercity competition by, 22
Department of Employment and Economic Development (DEED), Minnesota, 186
Detroit, Michigan, 144, 153
Devolution
  governmental, and rise of incentive competition, 2, 6–7, 10, 13–14, 33
  state-level, to local governments, 16–17, 143
Disclosure
  competition reform via, 5, 163, 184–189, 187*f*, 190–191, 194, 196
  timing for clawbacks, 156–157*n*7

Disclosure *(continued)*
　See also Transparency
Discretionary incentives, 156*n*1
　benefit-cost calculation for, 125,
　　126*t*–128*t*, 129–132
　as policy tool, 57–58, 116
Disintegration, vertical, 2, 10
Division of labor, 2, 10, 29
Downtown redevelopment, TIF and,
　50–52
Duluth v. Triangle, 189

Earned Income Tax Credit, 190
Eastern Europe, 7, 100*n*4
EC. *See* European Commission
Economic base theory. *See* Export base
　theory
Economic development
　citizen participation in, 44, 52
　issues of concern in, 17, 21, 24, 52,
　　152–153
　public officials and, 15, 156*nn*3–4
　responsibility for, 2, 4, 7, 142–143
　retail development as, 49, 151–152
　theories for growth in, 28–31
　unified budget for, as competition
　　reform, 3, 31, 190–191
Economic development incentives
　alternative incentive reforms for,
　　113–123; *see also* Job creation,
　　business incentive reform through
　as beneficial, 103–104, 124, 132*n*1,
　　161–162, 176–178
　federal policy in reform of, 121–123
　forces leading to, 104–113,
　　132–133*n*2
　medium-term benefits and costs
　　calculations for, 32, 125, 126*t*–
　　128*t*, 129–132
　tax expenditures for, 190–191
　as wasteful, 67, 103, 111–112, 123,
　　141, 161–162, 175–176, 178, 183
Economic effectiveness, 8, 65, 174,
　180*n*18
Economic efficiency
　inefficiency *vs.,* 13–14, 17, 48, 94–95

　mobile capital and, 2, 15–17, 31
　prisoner's dilemma and, 23, 24
Economic growth
　legislative committee for, 167, 178
　regional markets and, 28–29, 30–31
　supply-side theory and, 25, 79, 80
EFTA. *See* European Free Trade
　Association
Eminent domain, 44, 51, 54*n*5
Employment cushions, 153
Employment subsidy, definition, 168
Empowerment Zones, 122–123, 124,
　132–133*n*2
Endogenous theory, export *vs.,* 28–29
Enterprise Community funding,
　Michigan, 132–133*n*2
Enterprise Zones, 62, 64, 68, 69, 81*n*2
Entitlement incentives, 58
　benefit-cost calculation for, 125,
　　126*t*–128*t*, 129–132
　fiscal consequences of competition
　　for capital, 65–71, 78
　See also Tax cuts; Tax incentives
Environmental consequences
　as policy challenge, 31, 44, 48
　trade-offs in competition with, 23, 24,
　　184
　See also Regulatory environments
Estonia, EU, 100*n*4
EU. *See* European Union
Europe, growth machines in, 14
　See also specific countries in, e.g.,
　　Germany
European Commission (EC)
　communication by, 91–92, 96, 100*n*3
　powers of, 89–91, 100*n*2
　procedural operations of, 93–96, 99
　treaty of, 87–88, 90; *see also* Treaty
　　of Rome (1957)
European Free Trade Association
　(EFTA), Surveillance Authority,
　97
European Union (EU), 17
　membership rules for states in, 6, 7,
　　53, 97, 100*n*4

European Union (EU) *(continued)*
 regulatory environments for abuse control in, 1, 31, 33
 state aid control in, 87–100; *see also main heading* State aid control
  as model system, 43–44, 97–99, 162
  rationale for, 87–91
  system strengths of, 91–93
  weaknesses of, 93–96
 WTO and, 9, 92, 96
Export base theory, 27–31
 Tiebout's endogenous theory *vs.*, 28–29

Fantus Corporation, 11
Federal systems, 143
 competition reform under, 97
 "carrots" in, 192–193
 income taxes in, 188–189
 Eastern hemisphere countries with, 6–7
 economic development incentives under, 132–133n2, 168, 179n7
 intervention as reform of, 121–123, 124, 134n15, 141
 Western hemisphere countries with, 6, 13
Finland, EFTA and, 97
Firms. *See* Business organizations
First Source programs, as alternative incentive reform, 120, 134n14, 175, 177, 180nn21–22
Food stamps, 190
Form 10-K, 188
Francis Howell School District, 49
Free trade, 7–8, 97
Freedom of Information Act, state-level, 185

Game theory, 47
 incentive competition and, 1, 48
 information asymmetries and, 14, 22
 prisoner's dilemma and, 2, 18–19, 52n2
 zero-sum bargaining in, 150–151, 163

GE Nuclear Energy, 179n4
General Dynamics, 179n4
General Motors (GM), 48–49, 144, 188, 189
Germany, 13, 30, 179n4
Goldsmith, Mayor Stephen, 154–155
Good Jobs First, 33, 117, 153, 185
Goodrich, 179n4
Government Accounting Standards Board, 190
Government Finance Officers Association, 190
Governmental roles
 actions as
  attracting firms with different methods, 16–17, 19, 20–23, 64, 122–123
  bargaining for local economic development, 31, 62, 141–157, 156nn1–4
  bidding and racing to the bottom, 18, 20, 144
  blunting and regulating competition as, 1, 43–44, 183
  collecting and spending revenue, 77–78, 149, 188–189
  negotiating good deals, 150–155, 157n8, 189
  using power of its purse, 192–193
 devolution of, 2, 10, 16–17, 143
 investment imperative in, 43–47, 53n1
 as "laboratories of democracy," 124
Grassroots coalitions, 154
 reform and, 153, 183, 184
Growth machines, local political influence of, 14

Hasbro/Playskool, Chicago v., 189
Hazelwood, Missouri, TIF in, 52
Hiring subsidy, definition, 168
Hispanics, unemployment rate, 164
Home Mortgage Disclosure Act, 184
Hungary, EU, 100n4
Hysteresis, 48

Iceland, EFTA and, 97
Illinois, 72, 179n4
　progressive measures in, 185, 191, 195
　See also Chicago, Illinois
IMF. See International Monetary Fund
In-migration, 60, 61, 67, 119
Incentive competition
　analytical approaches to, 2–3, 15–25
　　market for jobs and tax capacity model, 20–23
　　normative issues in, 24–25, 31
　　prisoner's dilemma model, 17–20, 24, 44, 47
　　Tiebout-type model, 13, 16–17, 23, 24, 143
　geographic prevalence of, 3–9, 194–196
　institutional sources of, 2, 9–14, 23, 43–52, 193–194
　outcomes of, 3, 25, 26–27
　policy responses to, 31–33, 194–196
　political sources of, 2, 14–15, 176
　rise of, 1–2
　routes to jobs and, 27–31
　See also Economic development incentives
India, 2, 6–7, 14, 25
Indiana, 150
　Indianapolis, 65, 154–155
Industrial development, 4, 5, 29
　See also Manufacturing firms
Infineon Technologies, 179n4
Information asymmetries, 9
　governmental disadvantage and, 43, 46, 145–146
　opportunistic behavior and, 19, 22, 31, 43
　race to the bottom and, 18, 20
　as rent-producing devices, 2, 13
　site location consultants and, 14, 47, 193
Infrastructure development
　alternative incentive reform as, 121, 124
　costs of, 141, 144, 145, 147

economic development incentives in Michigan, 132–133n2
Institute for Justice, Web site, 53n5
International development, 29, 33
International Monetary Fund (IMF), 8, 13
Interstate commerce, 25, 192
Investment markets
　conservative think tanks and, 80, 81
　governments and firms in, 45–47, 53n1, 118, 141
　large project opportunities in U.S., 43, 46
Iowa, 65, 74
Ireland, bidding wars and, 7

Japan, economic growth of, 29–30
JDIG. See Job Development Investment Grant
Job creation, 1, 15, 147
　business commitments to, 21, 65
　business incentive reform through, 161–178
　　case study (see under North Carolina)
　　desirable program features, 172–175, 173t, 180nn21–22
　　job quantity and cost, 171–172, 180n14
　　new models of, 168–171, 174, 180n19
　　rebuttal to, 175–178
　costs per job for, 6, 62–63, 70, 107–108, 134nn5–6, 142, 171–172, 173t, 180n15, 186, 187f, 196
　　annual cap on, 167
　incentive competition in, 27–31
　labor supply for, 60–61, 108
　public service, at a tax price, 16–17, 67
　tax revenue and, 66–67, 81n1, 106–107, 133–134n4, 147
Job Development Investment Grant (JDIG), 166–167, 177, 180–181n23, 181n24
Job displacement, job creation and, 60, 61, 170

Index 207

Job growth, 108–111, 168–169, 179*n*7, 179*nn*9–11
Job Growth Tax Credit, as incentive reform model, 168–169, 171, 172, 173*t*, 179*n*7, 179*nn*9–11
Job quality
 minimum standards of, 117–118, 153
 retail development and, 49–50, 52–53*n*3, 194–195
Job training, 144
 customized, as alternative incentive reform, 121, 124
 EU system and, 90, 92, 93
 labor market intermediaries and, 174, 180*n*18
 subnational states and, 132–133*n*2, 170
JobNet program, Oregon, 120
Jobs market, 12, 15
 layoffs in, 153, 170
 reform of, 32–33
 tax capacity and, 2, 20–23

Kansas City, Missouri, metropolitan region, 44, 51, 149
Kelo v. New London, 51, 54*n*5
Kentucky, unified development budget in, 31
Keystone Opportunity Zones, Pennsylvania, 62
Kucinich, Mayor Dennis, 150–151

Labor market intermediaries, effectiveness of, 174, 180*n*18
Labor supply, 24, 192
local hiring of, as alternative incentive reform, 120, 124, 134*n*14
 mobility of, 30, 134*n*8
 new jobs filled by, 60–61, 68–69, 108, 119
 relocation of, 111–112
Labor unions, disclosure and, 145, 183
Lao PDR, ineffective incentives in, 8
Latin America, 14, 29
 See also specific countries in, e.g., Brazil
Latvia, EU, 100*n*4

Lee Act, 32, 165–166, 177, 179*n*5
 compared to reform models, 171–172, 173*t*, 174–175, 180*n*20
 controversy about, 166–167
 evaluation of, 171–172, 180*n*16
 reform models, 168–171, 179*n*6, 180*n*17
 job growth tax credit, 168–169, 171, 172, 173*t,* 179*n*7, 179*nn*9–11
 targeted job creation grant program, 168, 170–171, 172, 173*t,* 179*n*8, 180*n*17, 180*nn*12–13
Legislation, 183
 federal, 184, 188, 192
 state, 185
 Illinois, 195
 Maryland, 195
 Minnesota, 44, 52, 146–147, 156*n*5, 170, 171
 North Carolina, 32, 165–166
Liechtenstein, EFTA and, 97
Limited liability companies (LLCs), 72, 74
Lithuania, EU, 100*n*4
Living wage movement, 190
Loans, 147–148, 150, 156*n*6, 184
Lobbyists, 189, 193–194
Los Angeles, California, 152, 153
Louisiana, subsidy disclosure system in, 185

Maine, subsidies and, 185, 186, 194
Malta, EU, 100*n*4
Manufacturing firms, 70, 71*f,* 132–133*n*2, 179*n*4
Market for investment. *See* Investment markets
Market for jobs. *See* Jobs market
Maryland, 61, 195
Massachusetts, 72, 152–153
Mastercard International, facilities, 48–49, 52*n*2
McCain-Feingold reforms, 184
Medicaid, 190
MEGA program, Michigan, 116, 132–133*n*2, 134*n*10

Merck, 167, 179*n*3
Metropolitan regions, 117, 123, 124
   See also specific core cities, e.g., St. Louis, Missouri, metropolitan region
Mexico, NAFTA and, 7–8
Michigan
   economic development incentives in, 62, 104, 116, 132–133*n*2
   eminent domain in, 51, 54*n*5
   intercity competition involving, 49, 144
   MEGA program in, 116, 132–133*n*2, 134*n*10
Michigan Supreme Court, 51, 54*n*5
Military bases, intercity competition for, 5
Milwaukee, Wisconsin, public officials in, 153
Minnesota, 175, 189
   legislation in
      Minnesota Emergency Employment Development (MEED) Act, 170, 171, 179*n*8
      transparency model, 44, 52, 146–147, 156*n*5
   relocation subsidies in, 53, 194
   subsidy disclosure as competition reform in, 185–186, 187*f*
Minorities, 153, 164, 184
Missouri
   Kansas City and suburbs in, 44, 51, 149
   St. Louis city and suburbs in, 44, 49–52, 65, 153
   sunshine law as needed reform, 52, 184
   TIF in, 49–52, 53*n*4
Mobile capital, 114
   efficiency of community outcomes and, 2, 13–14, 15–17, 17, 31, 48
   export-oriented and retail, 1, 4, 27–31
   rise of competition for, 4–9, 25, 43
   as source of competition, 43, 44, 45–46
Montgomery County, Maryland, economic development in, 61
Mountain Association for Community Economic Development, unified development budget plan by, 31
Murdoch, Rupert, 5
NAFTA (North American Free Trade Agreement), auto industry subsidies under, 7–8
National Bureau of Economic Research, 63
National Governors' Association, 17
Nebraska, 65, 185
Netherlands, EU state aid in, 90
New Jersey, 153, 179*n*4, 188
New Jobs Tax Credits, federal program for, 168, 179*n*7
New London, Kelo v., 51, 54*n*5
New Markets Initiative, federal dollars for, 122–123, 124
New York (city), 48, 153
New York (state), competition concerns in, 152–153
Nicaragua, devolution in, 13
No Child Left Behind Act, 192
No More Candy Store (LeRoy), 183, 185
No-raid agreements, capitalistic systems and, 47
Nonperformance provisions, spending public funds and, 149
North America, 7–8, 48–49
   See also specific countries in, i.e., Canada; Mexico; United States
North Carolina, 121, 170, 191
   CFED work in, 166, 167, 178
   governmental entities in
      Department of Commerce, 166–167
      General Assembly, 166, 177, 178
      Joint Select Committee on Economic Growth and Development, 167, 178
   job creation and business incentives in, 25, 164–167; *see also* Lee Act
      controversy over incentives, 32, 166–167, 179*n*3
      cost and impact of, 171–172, 173*t,*

North Carolina *(continued)*
  job creation and business incentives *(continued)*
    cost and impact of *(continued)*
      179*n*2, 179*n*4
    models of job creation in, 168–175, 173*t*
    subsidy disclosure system in, 185, 186
North Dakota, 148, 185
Northern Ireland, bidding wars and, 7
Norway, EFTA and, 97
Norwood, Ohio v. General Motors, 189

O'Fallon, Missouri, 49, 50–51, 50–52
Ohio, 21, 53, 185, 189, 194
  enterprise zone tax abatement in, 69, 81*n*2
  site-selection industry interaction with, 22–23
  zero-sum bargaining in, 150–151
Omaha, Nebraska, 65
Open Records Act, state-level, 185
Oregon, local hiring in, 120, 175
Organisation for Economic Co-operation and Development (OECD), incentive competition in countries of, 2
Otis Elevator, Yonkers v., 189

Passive investment companies, tax avoidance by, 74
Peckham Guyton Albers and Viets, 50–51
Penalties, nonperformance and, 149
Pennsylvania, 29, 62, 72
Performance standards
  bargaining leverage in competition for capital, 155–156
  benefit-cost analysis and, 117–118
  clawbacks upon failure to meet, 119, 123
  less use argument for, 171–172
  as way to effect good deals, 147–148, 156, 156*n*6, 163

PGAV. See Peckham Guyton Albers and Viets
Philadelphia, Pennsylvania, endogenous regional growth around, 29
Philips Semiconductor, 150
Poland, 7, 100*n*4
Politics, 31, 45
  as incentive competition source, 2, 10, 14–15, 20
  influences on, 14, 153, 163, 176, 184
Portland, Oregon, local hiring in, 120, 175
Portugal, EU state aid in, 90
Prisoner's dilemma model, 52*n*2
  as analytical model of incentive competition, 2, 17–20
  economic efficiency in, 23, 24
  one- *vs.* two-sided, 44, 47
Public officials, 32, 144
  economic development and, 15, 150–151, 154–155, 156*nn*3–4
  influence on, 153, 162, 184
  validity claims of supply-side theory and, 81, 82*n*6
Public purpose doctrine, 143, 147
Public sector
  good deals for, 146, 155, 156*nn*3–4
  ways to effect good deals for
    enforcement mechanisms, 148–150, 156–157*n*7
    ex ante decision analysis, 146–147, 156*n*5
    performance standards, 147–148, 156, 156*n*6
Public services
  business taxes that fund, 113–114
  costs of, 61, 144
  positive outcomes for, 146–150, 156*nn*3–4
  subsidy competition and, 17–20, 26, 32
  tax base *vs.,* 20–23, 152
  tax price for, 14–15, 16–17, 23, 24, 80, 190–191
Puerto Rico, bidding wars and, 7

Quality of life issues
  equity, 24, 25, 31, 33, 48
  living wage, 190
Queensland, Australia, bidding wars
  and, 5

R&D. See Research and development
Reagan administration, tax cuts and,
  78–79
Recalibrations, nonperformance
  provision as, 149
Recisions, nonperformance provision
  as, 149
Reforming wasteful systems. See
  Competition reform; Economic
  development incentives,
  alternative reforms for; Job
  creation, business incentive reform
  through
Regional development, EC and, 89, 90
Regional governments, 44
  economic development responsibility
    of, 2, 4, 7, 10, 14, 16
  investment competition between, 5, 8,
    14, 45
  policies abandoned by, 13, 141
  preoccupation of, 20–23
Regional markets, 1, 2
  economic growth of, 28–29, 30–31
Regulatory environments, 90
  federal intervention in incentive
    policy in, 122, 141
  firms and antipollution laws, 46, 184;
    see also Environmental
    consequences
  governmental control of investment
    competition as, 1, 6, 16, 19, 31, 44,
    192–193; see also State aid control
  local government and bargaining
    leverage in, 141, 142–145
Renaissance Zones, Michigan, 62,
  132–133n2
Rents
  economic, as alternative incentive
    reform, 114–115

firms extraction of, 2, 11, 13, 18,
  21–23
Republican party, taxes and, 25, 78–79
Research and development (R&D)
  American development programs for,
    105, 132–133n2
  EU aid to, 90, 91, 92
Residential development, 61, 63–64
Restraint on trade, 25
Retail development, 43
  job quality in, 49–50, 52–53n3,
    194–195
  mobile capital and, 1, 4, 27–31
  TIF for, 49–52, 53n4, 151
Retention incentives, 48
  benefit-cost calculation for, 125,
    126t–128t, 129–132
R.H. Donnelly, 179n4
Risks, economic development and, 152,
  155
R.J. Reynolds, 76, 167
Rochester, New York, fiscal challenges
  in, 153
Romania, EU and, 100n4

S corporations, 72
St. Charles County, Missouri, TIF
  subsidies in, 50
St. Louis, Missouri, metropolitan region,
  65, 153
  facilities consolidation in, 48–49,
    52n2
  tax and subsidy abuse in, 44, 49–52
San Francisco, California, economic
  development risks in, 152
School funding, business incentives and,
  49, 191–192
Scoreboard project, Europe, 96, 100n3
Siemens v. Commission, 92
Site location consultants, 15
  definitions of, and competition
    reform, 193–194
  game skills development by, 14, 19,
    43
  influence of, 44, 46–47

Site location consultants *(continued)*
  rise of incentive competition and, 2, 10–13, 21–23, 32
Site Selection (magazine)
  interregional siting factors in, 155–156, 156–157*n*7
  trade publication for site brokers, 12, 22–23, 63, 167
Skills development, 14, 19, 43, 154
Slovakia, EU, 100*n*4
Slovenia, EU, 100*n*4
Slow growth objectives, 152
Smart growth, suburbs and, 194–196
Smart Growth Act, Maryland, 195
SME (Small and medium-sized enterprises)
  European experience with, 90, 92, 93
  tax advantages, 89, 99*n*1
  U.S. economic development programs for, 105, 170
South Korea, devolution in, 13
Southeast Asia, incentive policy initiatives in, 8
Starve-the-beast strategy, tax base erosion and, 79–81
State aid control
  definition, 88–89
  EU rationale for, 87–88
  procedures of, 90–91
  rules of, 44, 52–53, 89–90
  See also under European Union (EU)
Statutory incentives, eligibility requirements for, 156*n*1
Steel industry, 65, 92
Stockman, David, 79, 80
Subnational governments. *See* Regional governments
Subsidies
  American experience with, 149
  community benefits and, 63, 144, 153
  consequences of business expansion, 61–62, 151
  federal intervention in incentive policy, 122, 124
  European experience with, 96
  EU synonym for, 87, 88–89
  tax advantages of, 89, 99*n*1
  types of, 7–8, 47–48, 49, 53, 57–58, 64, 166, 168, 179*n*3
Subsidy competition, 33
  economic development and, 30–31
  equity and, 25, 44
  EU management of, 6, 43–44; *see also* State aid control, 87–100
  public good from, 17–20, 26, 62
  drawbacks as well as, 23, 24, 31, 38
  job creation and, 162–164, 168–175, 178
  reform of, 162, 185–187
  sources and processes of, 43–52, 148–149
Sunshine laws, 52, 184
Supply-side theory, 25, 79, 80, 81, 82*n*6
Sweden, EFTA and, 97

Taiwan, exports role in, 29
Targeted Job Creation Grant Program, as incentive reform model, 168, 170–171, 172, 173*t*, 179*n*8, 180*nn*12–13
Tariffs, economic growth and, 29
Tax abatements. *See under* Tax cuts and incentives
Tax and subsidy competition, 43–52
  capital mobility as source of, 43, 44
  governmental investment imperative as source of, 43–47, 53*n*1
  international organizations and, 8–9
  location incentives used and abused in, 44, 47–52, 189
  policy recommendations for, 52–53
  See also Subsidy competition
Tax capacity
  incentive competition and, 20–23, 25
  tax base as, 1, 12, 152
Tax credits, 53, 58, 156*n*1
  court rulings on, 53, 197*n*1
  federal program for, 168, 179*n*7, 190
  job growth and, 168–169, 179*n*7, 179*nn*9–11, 180*n*14

MEGA program in Michigan, 116,
132–133*n*2, 134*n*10
North Carolina and, 165, 166, 179*n*2
Tax cuts
   for business in supply-side theory, 25,
80
   as discretionary policy tool, 58, 115
   fiscal responsibility and, 24, 66, 81,
82*n*6
   Republicans and, 78–79
Tax cuts and incentives, 167
   abatement agreements as, 49,
132–133*n*2, 191–192
   discretionary policy tools, 58, 69,
Tax cuts and incentives (continued)
   abatement agreements as (continued)
     discretionary policy tools
(continued) 81*n*2, 155, 191–192,
197*n*1
   benefit-cost calculation for, 125,
126*t*–128*t*, 129–132
   as entitlements, 65–70, 71*f*
   public good from, 17–20
   See also separately Tax cuts; Tax
incentives
Tax incentives
   business investment and, 4, 10, 48, 65
   EU and, 89, 99*n*1
   tax rates, 70, 71*f*, 115
   TIF as, 49–52, 53*n*4, 58, 132–133*n*2,
151–152, 186, 187*f*, 191–192
Tax increment financing (TIF)
   as discretionary policy tool, 58, 195
   in Michigan, 132–133*n*2
   public disclosure of, 186, 187*f*
   retail development and, 49–52, 53*n*4,
151–152
   school funding and, 191–192
Tax loopholes, 74, 188
Taxes, 122
   erosion of, 23, 24, 25, 70–74
   exemption from, 47, 143
   loss of, 69–70
   payment of, 16–17, 23, 81*n*1,
188–189
   progressivity of, 75–76, 79–80

regressivity of, 25, 75–77, 76*t*, 78
   types of
     business, 75, 113–114
     capital gains, 25, 80
     excise, 75, 76
     income, 25, 58, 70–77
     inheritance, 80
     payroll, 75
     personal, 62
     property, 58, 64, 69, 152
     sales, 43, 49, 76, 77, 195
Texas, 22, 49, 52*n*2, 185, 191
Tiebout, Charles
   endogenous theory of, *vs.* export-base
theory, 28–29
   incentive competition argument of,
13, 16–17, 23, 24, 143
TIF. *See* Tax increment financing
Tobacco tax, as regressive, 76
Toxic Right to Know law, 184
Toyota, interregional siting factors for,
156–157*n*7
Trade magazines, titles for site brokers,
12
Trade-offs, 23, 24
Transparency, 116, 154
   lack of, in location incentives, 44, 50
   Minnesota legislation for, 44, 52,
146–147, 156*n*5
   See also Disclosure
Transportation technology, 28
   access to, 65, 195
   cost reductions in, 2, 10, 45–46,
105–106, 106*f*
Treaty of Rome (1957), 6, 43–44
   See also European Commission (EC),
treaty of
Triangle, Duluth v., 189
Turkey, EU and, 100*n*4
Twin Cities area, Minnesota, TIF in, 53,
194

Unemployed workforce, incentives for
new jobs filled by, 119–120,
123–124, 169, 170
Unemployment rates, 153, 164, 165

Unified development budgets,
   competition reform and, 3, 31,
   190–191
Union Pacific Railroad (UP), 65
United Airlines, 65, 150
United Kingdom, economic growth of,
   30
United States, 184
   capitalistic system of, 45, 47
   before and after NAFTA in, 7–8
   mobile capital and rise of
      competition in, 4–5, 25, 43, 80
   economic growth of, 29–30
   federal system model in, 13, 14, 168,
      179n7, 192–193
   regulatory environments for abuse
      control in, 1, 143, 192–193
U.S. Center on Budget and Policy
   Priorities, 188
U.S. Congress, 122, 141, 163, 184, 192
U.S. Federal Election Commission, 184
U.S. Space Command, intercity
   competition for, 5
U.S. Supreme Court
   eminent domain ruling by, 51, 54n5
   tax rulings and, 53, 197n1
University of North Carolina, Lee Act
   evaluation by, 180n16
Up-front incentives, 150
   alternative incentive reform as, 118,
      119
   benefit-cost calculation for, 125,
      126t–128t, 129–132
UP. *See* Union Pacific Railroad

Vermont, jobs moved from, 179n4
Vietnam, ineffective incentives in, 8

Wages
   benchmarks for, 147, 148
   contractual safeguards and, 154–155
   public disclosure of, 186, 187f
   subsidies for, 63, 168, 172, 190
   zero-sum bargaining on, 150–151
Wal-Mart, TIF and, 49–50, 195
Wales, devolution in, 13

Washington (state), subsidy disclosure
   system in, 185
Welfare implications, incentive
   competition and, 18, 19–20,
   26–27, 190
West Virginia, 150, 185, 186
Westchester County, New York
   competition concerns in, 152–153
William S. Lee Quality Jobs and
   Business Expansion Act, North
   Carolina. *See* Lee Act
Winner's curse, 17–20, 162, 177
Wisconsin, public officials in, 153
Worker Adjustment and Retraining
   Notification law, layoff
   certification under, 170
Workforce Investment Board, 170, 196
World Association of Investment
   Promotion Agencies, 12
World Bank, 8, 13
World Trade Organization (WTO), 8–9,
   162
   rules of, 92, 96

Yaseen, Leonard, 11
Yonkers v. Otis Elevator, 189
Ypsilanti, Michigan, intercity
   competition by, 49
Ypsilanti Township v. General Motors,
   189

About the Institute

The W.E. Upjohn Institute for Employment Research is a nonprofit research organization devoted to finding and promoting solutions to employment-related problems at the national, state, and local levels. It is an activity of the W.E. Upjohn Unemployment Trustee Corporation, which was established in 1932 to administer a fund set aside by Dr. W.E. Upjohn, founder of The Upjohn Company, to seek ways to counteract the loss of employment income during economic downturns.

The Institute is funded largely by income from the W.E. Upjohn Unemployment Trust, supplemented by outside grants, contracts, and sales of publications. Activities of the Institute comprise the following elements: 1) a research program conducted by a resident staff of professional social scientists; 2) a competitive grant program, which expands and complements the internal research program by providing financial support to researchers outside the Institute; 3) a publications program, which provides the major vehicle for disseminating the research of staff and grantees, as well as other selected works in the field; and 4) an Employment Management Services division, which manages most of the publicly funded employment and training programs in the local area.

The broad objectives of the Institute's research, grant, and publication programs are to 1) promote scholarship and experimentation on issues of public and private employment and unemployment policy, and 2) make knowledge and scholarship relevant and useful to policymakers in their pursuit of solutions to employment and unemployment problems.

Current areas of concentration for these programs include causes, consequences, and measures to alleviate unemployment; social insurance and income maintenance programs; compensation; workforce quality; work arrangements; family labor issues; labor-management relations; and regional economic development and local labor markets.